Digital Technologies for Agriculture

NIPA GENX ELECTRONIC RESOURCES & SOLUTIONS P. LTD.
New Delhi-110 034

About the Authors

Dr Narendra Singh Rathore is having basic qualification in the field of Agricultural Engineering and he has completed M.Tech. in Energy Studies from IIT Delhi and Ph.D. in Farm Machinery and Power Engineering. Dr Rathore is having total 40 years' experience in different capacity i.e. worked as Dy. Director General (Education) & Dy. Director General (Engineering) in ICAR New Delhi, Vice Chairman in National Education Accreditation Board, National Director in World Bank Sponsored NAHEP, Founder Vice Chancellor SKNAU, Jobner, Rajasthan, Dean College of Dairy and Food Technology, Dean (Student Welfare), Dean College of Technology and Engineering, HOD in Renewable Energy, PI- AICRP on Renewable Energy and Project Coordinator TBU-IC and RBTC etc.

Presently Dr Rathore is working as Vice Chancellor, Maharana Pratap University of Agriculture and Technology, Udaipur, Rajasthan, India. In addition he also worked as Vice Chancellor of Mohan Lal Sukhadia University, Udaipur and Guru Govind Tribal University Banswara, Rajasthan.

Dr Rathore has attended many advanced international training including Food and Agriculture Business Management from Cornell University USA, Tree establishment and Agro Forestry from University of Arizona USA, Bio Energy from University of Oxford and Waste Recycling from University of Murdoch, Western Australia. He is having 38 Awards & fellowship including Young Scientist award, Outstanding book award, Outstanding Services award, Commendation and Team award, Hindi Research Paper award, World Bank IDM award, Best Teacher award, Energy Conservation award, National Technology Day award, Global Dairy Innovation award etc to his credit.

Dr Sunil Joshi is presently working as Professor and Head of Department of Electronics & Communication Engineering, Maharana Pratap University of Agriculture and Technology, Udaipur, Rajasthan, India. He is also working as Chairman of Digital Technology Cell of the University. Dr Joshi has also served in Indian Space Research Organization (ISRO) as Scientist. He has received his B.E. and M.E. in Electronics and Communication Engineering, from M.B.M. Engineering College, JNV University, Jodhpur. Dr Joshi received his Ph.D from Malviya National Institute of Technology, Jaipur.

Dr Joshi is having more than 29 years of research and teaching experience and published one patent and more than 85 research papers and articles in international and national journals and conferences. He has delivered a number of invited talks at national and international forums and visited U.K., Germany, Singapore for academic and research presentations. Dr Joshi has so far guided eight Ph.D and more than twenty five M. Tech. thesis. His main research areas are Wireless MIMO systems, Massive MIMO, Millimeter Waves, Optical Communication

Systems, WSN & IoT. As Principal Investigator, he has successfully undertaken a number of R & D Projects sponsored by Ministry of Electronics & Information Technology, AICTE and DST.

Dr. Naveen Choudhary is Professor and Head of Department of Computer Science and Engineering at College of Technology and Engineering, Maharana Pratap University of Agriculture and Technology, Udaipur, Rajasthan, India.

He is B.E. in Computer Science and Engineering from Dayananda Sagar College of Engineering, Bangalore University and further received his degree of Master's of Technology in Computer Science and Engineering from Indian Institute of Technology (IIT) Guwahati. He earned his Ph.D from Department of Computer Engineering, Malaviya National Institute of Technology (M NIT) Jaipur. His research has been published in reputed journals and conferences. Dr. Choudhary has published more than 85 scientific papers and is also the author of the book Principles of On-Chip Interconnection Networks (Himanshu publication, 2013). He is also the editor of the book Essentials of IT - Rajasthan state – Certification Information Technology (RS-CIT, VMOU, 2018). His teaching and research interest includes Network-on-Chip, Distributed Systems, Object Oriented Analysis and Design and Machine Learning.

Digital Technologies for Agriculture

Narendra Singh Rathore
Vice Chancellor
Maharana Pratap University of Agriculture and Technology
Udaipur, Rajasthan, India

Sunil Joshi
Professor and Head
Department of Electronics and Communication Engineering
Maharana Pratap University of Agriculture and Technology
Udaipur, Rajasthan, India

Naveen Choudhary
Professor and Head
Department of Computer Sciences and Engineering
Maharana Pratap University of Agriculture and Technology
Udaipur, Rajasthan, India

NIPA GENX ELECTRONIC RESOURCES & SOLUTIONS P. LTD.
New Delhi-110 034

NIPA GENX ELECTRONIC RESOURCES & SOLUTIONS P. LTD.

101,103, Vikas Surya Plaza, CU Block
L.S.C.Market, Pitam Pura, New Delhi-110 034
Ph : +91 11 27341616, 27341717, 27341718
E-mail:newindiapublishingagency@gmail.com
www: www.nipabooks.com

For customer assistance, please contact
Phone: + 91-11-27 34 17 17 Fax: + 91-11- 27 34 16 16
E-Mail: feedbacks@nipabooks.com

ISBN: 978-93-90591-91-6

Composed and Designed by NIPA.

Preface

Digital Technology in present context has emerged as one of the disruptive technologies that can supplement the traditional agricultural production techniques for increasing production, productivity and profitability of agriculture sector and is considered as one of the most promising applications for sustainable agriculture development.

During corona period, world has changed forever and adoption of emerging technologies was only solution for survival. As far as agriculture education field is concerned, quick learning coupled with forced entrepreneurship is the only solution for making this sector as more profitable. All government and non government organisations are effectively working for self sufficient economics based on agriculture sector. Interestingly, agriculture got new opportunities for increasing productivity and marketing through improved technologies including digital technologies.

The GDP share of agriculture has significantly increased from 14% to 19.9% in present year. It is because of changing scenario in agriculture practices & management including good agriculture practices, food safety, integrated farming system, agriculture processing and value addition and agriculture marketing etc. Further, digital technologies can effectively work in above mentioned subsectors for increasing efficiency and minimization of cost of cultivation. New agricultural applications in smart farming and precision farming through digital technologies will enable the sector to increase operational efficiency, lower costs, reduce waste, and improve the quality of their yield and finally helps in increasing income of farmers manifold.

Digital technologies available are most promising for changing present scenario of agriculture including production, productivity, profitability, quality, remunerative farming, climate resilience agriculture and extension tools for technology transfer for federating farmers into business group. In this book efforts have been made to discuss these different emerging digital technologies and for deciding strategies for effective implementation of these practices in this sectors specially for monitoring and prediction of crop yield on real time basis. The agriculture industry and automation agencies are exploring new opportunities for using digital solutions for crop monitoring, improving yields, profitability, and farming practices.

The salient features of different digital technologies for making agriculture as a profitable profession are compiled with the aim to understand these technologies in modern agriculture for more farm income.

This book aims to give an introduction of pertinent digital technologies specifically for people working in agriculture domain and aims to develop basic understanding and acquaintance about the digital technologies and its applications in precision agriculture for increasing production, productivity and profitability.

It is hoped that this book will be useful as reference book for scientists and students pursuing course in agricultural sciences and engineering studies. This will also give new dimensions to research scientists for their critical thinking and dissemination of different digital technologies in agriculture field.

Authors

Contents

1

Introduction

The term digital is derived from the word digit or digitus, a Latin word for finger, as fingers are often used for discrete counting. A variable is discrete when it is countable in a finite time and its instantaneous value at any timing/instant belongs to a set of finite values. The physical existence of digit is in the form of a stored positive and non-positive (negative) value of charge in a semiconductor storage device called memory. Positive is generally expressed or represented by the number '1' and negative by the number '0'. A string of digits '1' and '0' are called data and individual digit is termed as a bit. A string of eight bits is called a byte. The electronic technology that deals with generation, processing, analysis, computation, storage, transmission and reception of data for a specific purpose or task is termed as Digital Technology. The high-speed processors, graphical processing units (GPU), specific algorithms, software tools, telecommunication network, electronic gadgets, internet, smart phones, tablets etc are the major constituents of digital technologies used for various applications. A hybrid of different digital technologies enables immense amount of information and data to be compressed on small storage devices that can be easily preserved, processed and transported.

One of the important goals of agricultural production is to achieve good quality and maximum crop yield at a minimum cost. An early detection and timely management of the factors responsible for poor crop productivity and low crop yield is an effective way of addressing farming economics. Infestation by different pathogens and pests, poor weed management, degradation of soil due to excessive use of pesticides, fertilizers, and emerging pesticide resistance are some of the major reasons for low exploitable yield. Further, under natural uncontrolled conditions, crops are exposed to a combination of biotic and abiotic stresses that adversely affect host metabolism, and lead to large yield losses. Infections of crops with various diseases alter thermal and/or spectral characteristics of leaves, canopies in spectral regions due to necrotic or chlorotic lesions, canopy dryness, and premature senescence or browning. It is therefore, important to ensure crop protection by disease forecasting and management for maintaining the crop productivity and quality.

Hyper spectral Imaging System (HIS), also known as imaging spectroscopy or 3D spectroscopy, combines imaging and spectroscopy into a single system. A multi-spectral, multi- temporal, and multi-resolution observation capability of such technique can provide an alternative to conventional methods for facilitating sustainable agriculture by mapping, and monitoring the crop, retrieval of biophysical parameter, and site specific management/ decision support for agricultural development. Besides, optimum utilization of water and fertilizer resources through sensor based monitoring and control of soil parameters can substantially reduce crop investment as well as its quality. Presently, satellite borne hyper spectral imaging known as Remote Sensing and Global Positioning System (GPS) imagery are commonly used to assess spatial variability in crop yield, but such type of imagery has less accuracy on account of limited spatial resolution captured by long distant satellites, presence of clouds, sand and dust storms, fog, snow etc. Recently, aerial imagery is widely suggested for crop surveillance and yield prediction. The images in the form of sensor data can provide high spatial cloud free information of the crop's spectral characteristics. Healthy crops are characterized by strong absorption of red energy and strong reflectance of Near-Infrared (NIR) energy. The strong contrast between absorption and scattering of red energy and near infrared bands can be combined in to different quantitative indices expressed as vegetation indices. The vegetation indices are used as important parameters to predict the crop yield. A close sight at plant leaf temperature by thermal sensor, and chlorophyll and other pigments of plant leaves through periodic hyper spectral sensor mapping helps in an early detection of plant diseases or insect attacks and to timely control through crop management and decision support. Concurrently, a real time sensing of soil parameters like moisture, pH, humidity, pressure, and macronutrients at different stages of crop growth is carried out. The soil sensor data and hyper spectral imagery data of open field crop during complete period from sowing through harvesting can be collected and sent to the cloud server. It may facilitate development of prognostic tools for disseminating prescriptions and advisories to the end users (farmers) through ICT tools including mobile apps, social media, digital media for crop management and hence to enhance the farming economics in terms of increased crop productivity and the yield.

The agriculture industry in India, involving conventional methods and age old work fundamentals, beliefs and practices, is emerging as more vulnerable section among all the productive professions. In Agriculture sector we can plan best of its modernization strategies to stand viable in spite of possibility of appearances of challenges. The digital technologies are the modern format of

Information and Communication Technologies (ICT) that offer many important works in agriculture, called digital farming for increasing its productivity and profitability. In present context, Indian agriculture sector is facing number of problems such as low productivity with poor quality production and inadequate marketing for better profitability. The Climate- Resilience Agriculture (CRA) approach is therefore, required to achieve long- term higher productivity and farm incomes under climate variability. It is expected that existing data in agriculture field should be quickly collected and analyzed with appropriate techniques for getting proper inference. The ICT is a broad domain and it refers to any device that can store, retrieve, alter, transmit, or receive data in a digital format, such as personal computers, smart phones, digital television, email, or robots. There are number of digital technologies based on ICT, which has got good potential in agriculture field, some of them are summarized as below:

i. Artificial Intelligence (AI), Machine Learning (ML) and Deep Learning (DL) for crop monitoring and forecasting based on image, voice and speech recognition for increasing production and productivity.

ii. Robotics for mechanization and efficiency enhancement in farm operations. It may be autonomous and automatic for making different on-farm application which are simpler, convenient and efficient as compared to the conventional techniques.

iii. Geospatial technologies i.e. GIS, GPS for precise weather forecasting, crop monitoring and yield prediction for different on-the-farm applications.

iv. Sensing technologies for soil parameters, water quality, environmental temperature, humidity, pH, pressure measurement etc. These technologies are useful for deciding schedule of different on-the-farm applications to achieve higher efficiency.

v. Imaging technology i.e. image processing for Post-Harvest Measurement, Augmented Reality (AR), Virtual Reality (VR), Extended Reality (ER) and Mixed Reality (MR) for Education and Extension for dissemination of emerging technologies.

vi. Internet of Things (IoT) for predicting planting, irrigation, fertilization herbicides, pesticides spraying to achieve higher efficiency.

vii. Block Chain Technology for checking piracy, traceability, making digital payment, content aggression of different unit operations etc.

viii. Communication protocols such as Barcodes, QR codes, RFID, NFC, Bluetooth etc.

ix. Big Data Analytics for predicting, diagnostic and prognostic analytics.

x. Cloud and Cloud Computing for sharing, exchange and processing of data and information globally.

The integrated solutions using fusion of technologies such as Sensors, Internet of Things (IoT), Artificial Intelligence (AI), Machine Learning (ML), Deep Learning (DL), Drones etc find extensive scope of application in precision agriculture. The application of these technologies in precision agriculture can lead to precise and effective crop surveillance and predictions, soil health monitoring, glass green houses, hydroponic farming, aeroponics, vertical farming, etc. The digital technology driven agriculture, i.e. Agriculture 4.0 or Digital Farming or Smart Farming has become a relevant concept and efficient means of modern agriculture.

In present technological context, AI has become a major domain of engineering and mathematical sciences that deals with creation of intelligent systems, machines, or computers. It is applicable in multiple disciplines, including mathematical and engineering sciences, agricultural sciences, economics, biological sciences and a variety of other fields. While Artificial Intelligence (AI) has a wide range of practical applications across industries, it can have a revolutionizing impact on improvisation of agriculture and farming practices. One of its important imperatives is to adopt the modern technical solutions to make farming more efficient. A hybrid of digital technologies with AI-enabled cognitive solutions can critically change the future of farming and agriculture sector. The AI and ML powered solutions can help farmers to increase crop production and its quality with minimal inputs and also can help to speed up time to market. In fact, AI can easily be an efficient answer for proper agricultural management and as a result, an efficient tool for smart marketing of agriculture products.

The deployment of sensors on crop field and the management of sensor data with the help of Cloud based Artificial Intelligence algorithms and Big Data Analytics help accelerating the growth of Smart Farming, since data has become a major component in assisting farmers with critical decision- making. The set of these new practices like Vertical farming, Hydroponics, Aeroponics and Green House Farming will facilitate the farmers to perform their work partially from home, as well as from the farm with physical distancing, and will increase the crop productivity and its quality with optimum resource utilization, thus reducing overall expenditures and increasing the income of the farmers. The concept of Agriculture 4.0 implies the farmers to follow the principles of Precision Agriculture equipped with unmanned operations, using robot, and autonomous decision support systems using AI.

The adoption of modern agricultural practices may attract the technology friendly young generations of the country to opt agriculture as a preferred profession, distracting them to migrate towards urban belts lest a huge problem of returning migration should happen again. There is a tremendous scope of improvisation in training and education methodologies of the farmers by incorporating AI and ML approaches in extension education. Besides, information sharing and quick accurate decision making capability would support the implementation of sustainable smart farming technologies. The Augmented Reality (AR) can act as a powerful and effective tool to develop extension modules with 3-D animations for dissemination of modern agricultural practices to the farmers and rural people in their local language. This may be useful for assessment of technologies, including modification, perfection of farming techniques for proper demonstration of different applications and capacity building.

The digital transformation of agricultural industry can capacitate the stakeholders obtaining production target based on a technology enabled farmer centric model leading to Smart Farmer philosophy. Smart Farming is a new concept which includes managing farms and its allied activities using digital technologies to increase quantity and quality of products while optimization of human labour required for adequate crop production. The role of a Smart Farmer is not confined only to manual operations and intuitive decisions on crop fields, but it extends much beyond to the level which includes technology enabled decision making from stage of sowing to the harvesting and subsequently replacing and reducing intermediates in the food supply chain. The technology driven crop fields embedded with surveillance, predictions, and control mechanism; digitalized supply chain of agricultural produces backed up with smart warehouses; Smart agro-processing industry for value addition, etc are the inherent components of modern-day smart agriculture. Therefore, it is essential to plan then prepare and proceed positively and finally pursuing different on farm activities persistently.

The deployment of On-farm sensors and IoT network can provide relevant parameters pertaining to soil health, crop growth, and maturity status of the crop for harvesting. The IoT network interconnects all the sensors, devices and other farm appliances, for necessary control of various farm operations. The emergence of the cutting edge technologies like Artificial Intelligence (AI), Machine and Deep Learning, Cloud Computing, Satellite, Imagery and Big Data Analytics are creating an ecosystem for smart farming. Fusion of all such technologies enables the farmers achieve higher average yield and better price control. Besides, the emerging farming techniques like vertical farming, hydroponics, green house farming etc. can be very effective as natural partners of the conventional farming.

In present context, there is a need for efficient utilization of agriculture input to reduce cost of production and to articulate modern agriculture practices and mechanization for increasing quantity and quality of production. Further, it is important to propagate processing and value addiction techniques and proper marketing of produce either online or offline mode. Besides, there is requirement of diverting agriculture towards specific production, which can be easily be measurable at initial inception and addressable in real position, realistic and in time bound manner. In this case, digital technologies offer number of promising options.

2

Sensor Technology

2.1 Introduction

Sensor is a physical device used to detect manifestations or variations in a process value and collect data in real time assessment mode for measuring and predicting system/device performance and finally analyzing it to attain a specific task or application. Sensor technology is now-a-days used for interdisciplinary applications for data collection, system analysis and monitoring. In agricultural practices, there are number of factors influencing the crop production such as soil, water, seed, fertilizer, machines, climate and farmer himself. The data related to these segments are useful for predicting the yield and avoiding unforeseen circumstances. Sensors are omnipresent in all living biological entities including human, animals, birds, insects, plants, seeds, soil and water etc. As an integral part, the natural sensors play important role in the existence, self-defense, survival and to maintain the life cycle of these living entities. On the other hands, in physical systems, sensor is a man-made physical element or device which detects the presence and variation of any physical or ecological process information and data and converts it into some form of energy (electric, magnetic, acoustic, etc) which is measurable and can be further processed to achieve a specific application and pre-decided objectives. The conversion processes may be electrochemical, biochemical, optical, electromagnetic, electromechanical, piezoelectric etc. to some convenient form of energy. The input to the sensor is derived from physical environment and may be heat or temperature, moisture, pressure, force, vibration, light, motion, volume, density and humidity etc, and the output may be in the form of electric, magnetic, mechanical, acoustic energy etc. In theory, a sensor is a device that responds to a change in a physical phenomenon, such as temperature, force, pressure, or volume. A transducer, on the other hand, is a device that converts one form of energy into another form of energy that can easily be processed for numerous applications. The terms transducer and sensor are frequently used interchangeably. It signifies that a sensor is a form of transducer that converts energy from the physical environment into electrical energy that may then be sent into an engineering environment and computing system, or controller to attain the desired end result.

2.2 Importance of Sensor Technology

The sensors play a critical role in establishing a link between the physical and digital worlds through collection and capturing of real world processes and phenomena, and convert it into a form that can easily be engineered, processed, stored, and acted upon for better efficiency or to attain a certain task. When embedded into a variety of systems, devices, machines, and environments, sensors can play a high impact role in socio-economical and anthropological benefits for the mankind and society as whole. In present condition, for improving any system, reliable and accurate data are required. These can help provide early warning to protect agricultural crops from biotic and abiotic stresses and damage. It also help in avoiding possible failure of catastrophic infrastructure, conserve precious natural resources, improve productivity, enhance security, and enable new applications such as context-aware systems and smart home technologies that are simple, convenient, and cost-effective. The widespread use of distributed sensor systems is aided by amazing developments in technologies such as Very Large Scale Integration (VLSI), Micro-electromechanical Systems (MEMS), and Wireless Communications (WLC). Furthermore, new generation semiconductor technologies continue to generate latest generation processors and memories with increased processing capacity and improved efficiency while shrinking in size for easier storage, installation, and transportation. The shrinkage of size in computer and sensing technologies allows for the development of small, low-power, and low-cost sensors, actuators, and controllers for accurate and reliable data and information collecting. Sensor-based technologies are increasingly being used for crop surveillance and monitoring in order to predict yield, as well as for monitoring and protecting civil infrastructure such as bridges, highways, and tunnels, as well as the national power grid for power generation and pipeline infrastructure for distribution. In order to monitor large geographic area, hundreds of sensor nodes are required. Also sensor nodes are used for modeling and forecasting environmental pollution and flooding for resilience systems, collecting structural health information on bridges using vibration sensors, and controlling water usage for irrigation.

In present situation, many countries have placed milestones in agriculture production and its cost. It is observed that the lowest cost rice is produced by Vietnam. New Zealand is producing low-cost milk, China's cotton is having lowest cost of production in the world and cost of production of grain in Australia is the lowest one. Therefore, it is essential to monitor and analyze the agriculture statistical data of these countries data in real time assessment and finally articulating it in Indian condition to improve the agriculture sector. Also, sensor technology can play important role by deployment of appropriate number of sensors and nodes on the farm and collecting sensor data for further analysis using advanced computing algorithms. The sensor data analytics can help to identify the parameters to reduce the production cost.

2.3 Sensor Data Acquisition

The output signal of a sensing device or transducer in its raw form is very weak in power and also exposed to a number of internal and external process noise (system generated unwanted and undesirable signal) which is not easy to examine. Such a weak sensor output signal corrupted with noise cannot be directly used to drive output devices like displays, controllers, relays, switches, etc for further operation. It is therefore, essential to filter the sensor output signal to separate out the noise signals and also to increase the power level of the sensor output signal with suitable amplifiers and impedance matching circuits. A Data Acquisition System is a front end circuit hardware also called Signal Conditioning unit which is always connected immediately after the sensor device as shown in Figure 2.1.

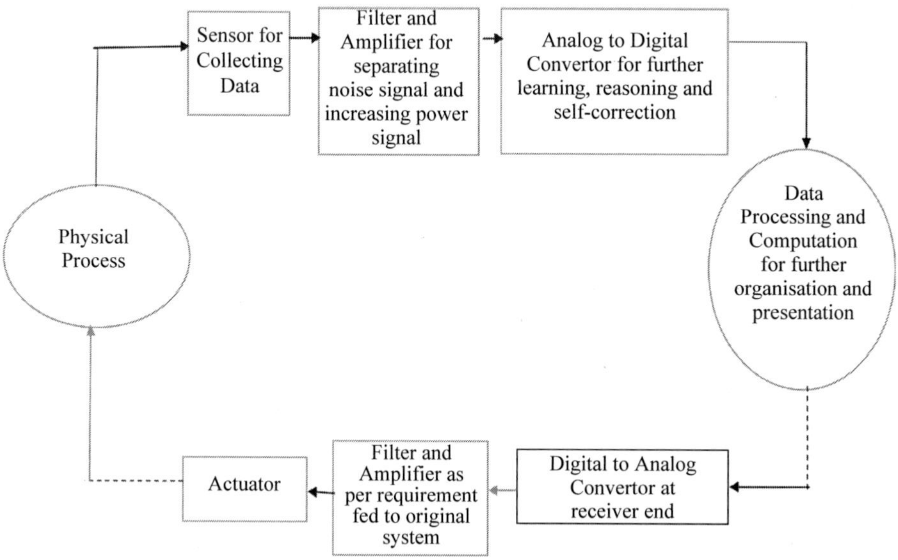

Fig. 2.1: Sensor Data Acquisition Block Diagram

The sensor output signal is passed through a signal conditioning stage comprising appropriately designed filters and amplifiers to prepare the sensor output signal for further use and analysis. Signals often require amplification (or attenuation) to change the signal magnitude to better match the following circuits. Furthermore, signal conditioning frequently employs filters to reduce undesirable noise within specific frequency ranges (e.g., high pass filters can be used to remove 50 or 60 Hz noise picked up by surrounding power lines).

The output of the transducer is conditioned through appropriately designed filters and amplifiers followed by conversion of analog signal to a digital signal format using an analog-to-digital converter (ADC). The signal has finally been converted to digital form and is ready for further processing, storage, computation, or display in the original system, as well as its final prediction outputs.

2.4 Classification of Sensors

The type and specifications of a sensor is an important step while selecting it for a specific application. The characteristics, screening, accuracy, precision, dynamic range, stability, sensitivity etc are some of the important specifications which should be carefully examined from sensor data sheet while picking it for operation and improvement. It depends on the physical property to be monitored and objectives of final prediction, for example, such properties include temperature, pressure, light, volume or humidity. Sensor can be classified on following pattern:

1. Based on power supply (Active and passive sensor)
2. Based on physical properties
3. Based on conversion of physical properties into electrical signals
4. Based on conversion phenomenon

The active sensors are self-excited devices or elements that produce electrical output consequent upon a direct reaction to applied stimulation or a measurement input. These sensors don't need an external voltage source to generate an output electrical signal proportional to variation in a physical phenomenon or process. Photo voltaic cells or solar cells, piezoelectric materials, thermocouples etc are some of the examples of such sensors.

Passive sensors, on the other hand, respond to an applied stimulus by changing some passive electrical quantity, such as capacitance, resistance, or inductance. As a result, in order to convert passive electrical quantities such as capacitance, resistance, or inductance into electrical output, a passive sensor requires an external ac or dc voltage source. Photo diodes, thermometers, strain gauges, and other such sensors, require an external power source (bias) to operate.

The sensors can also be classified depending on the applied methods and electrical phenomena used to convert physical properties into electrical signals. Resistive sensors rely on physical characteristics such as temperature, pressure, and volume to modify the electrical resistivity of a conductor. The conversion phenomena, i.e. the input and output, can also be used to classify sensors. Few examples of typical conversion phenomenon are Photoelectric, thermoelectric, electrochemical, and electromagnetic. Table 2.1 lists the numerous types of sensors and their classifications based on the physical parameter to be sensed.

Table 2.1: Classification and examples of Sensors based on Physical Properties

S.N.	Physical Property	Type of sensor
1	Temperature	Thermistors, thermocouples, RTD's
2	Pressure	Pressure gauges, barometers, ionization gauges, transducers
3	Optical	Photodiodes, phototransistors, infrared sensors, CCD sensors
4	Acoustic	Piezoelectric resonators, microphones and acoustic sensors
5	Mechanical	Strain gauges, tactile sensors, capacitive diaphragms
6	Motion, Vibration	Accelerometers, gyroscopes, photo sensors, kineticmeter
7	Flow	Anemometers, mass air flow sensors, venture mounted electric gates
8	Position	GPS, Ultrasound-based sensors, infrared-based sensors
9	Electromagnetic	Hall-effect sensors, magnetometers, EMF detector
10	Chemical	pH sensors, Electrochemical sensors, Infrared gas sensors, EC sensors
11	Humidity	Capacitive and resistive sensors, hygrometers, MEMS-based humidity sensors
12	Radiation	Ionization detectors, Geiger-Mueller counter, Resistance Radiation detector

(i) Temperature Sensor: For many reasons, temperature is one of the most regularly monitored environmental variables. By checking temperature of a system, device or ecosystem one can easily predict its likely changes and its future expansion. Figure 2.2 shows typical temperature sensors: LM35 and NTC thermistor. The thermocouple, thermistors, semiconductor temperature sensors, resistance temperature detectors (RTDs), and other temperature sensors are commonly used for sensing temperature. Different types of sensors can be used for temperature measurement in various applications depending on the requirements.

LM35-Temperature Sensor IC 10K Ω NTC Thermistor

Fig. 2.2: Temperature Sensor (*Courtesy*: Texas Instruments)

The changes in the temperature corresponds to a change in its electrical property like resistance/conductance and a corresponding change in current and voltage that is calibrated to accurately measure temperature.

(ii) Proximity Sensors: As shown in Figure 2.3, a proximity sensor is a non-contact type sensor that detects the presence of an object in order to predict its related properties. This type of sensor determines the existence of objects as well as the object's attribute. There are numerous varieties of proximity sensors, including: Photoelectric sensors, Capacitive sensors, Inductive sensors.

Proximity sensors can be implemented using different techniques like Optical (like Infrared or Laser), Ultrasonic, Hall Effect, Capacitive, etc. It is used to detect electromagnetic field and its associated electromagnetic radiation and looks for its changes to predict functioning of main system.

Fig. 2.3: Inductive Proximity Sensor (*Courtesy*: Texas Instruments)

Some of the applications of Proximity Sensors are Mobile Phones, Cars (Parking Sensors), Industries (object alignment), Ground Proximity in Aircrafts, Recycling plants, Self-driving cars, Assembly lines etc.

(iii) Infrared Sensor (IR Sensor): The infrared (IR) sensor is an optical detector device used in applications such as proximity and object detection. Nearly all mobile phones and aircrafts use infrared sensors as proximity sensors. IR sensors are miniature photo chips that contain a photocell and are used to emit and detect infrared light. The light emitting diode (LED) and the receiver are the two pieces of an infrared sensor. Infrared sensors are commonly utilized in remote control technology, security alarm, and automatic lighting applications. The IR sensors can be used to identify obstructions in the robotic vehicle's path and hence control the robotic vehicle's course. IR sensors can be used in agriculture fields to detect barriers in land preparation in self-driving tractors and power tillers in agro industries, as well as to monitor temperature and pressure for getting higher efficiency.

These can also be used to plan irrigation and make the most efficient use of water. Sensors for detecting infrared lights come in a variety of shapes and sizes.

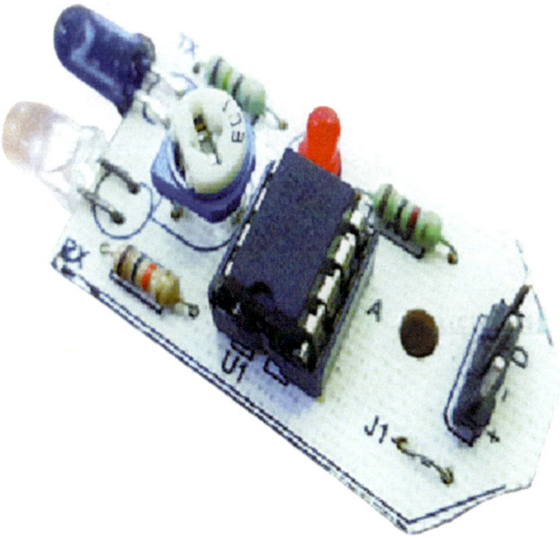

Fig. 2.4: Reflective Type Infrared Sensor (*Courtesy*: Vishay Semiconductor)

There are two types of infrared (IR) sensors i.e. emission type or transmission type IR sensor and detection type or reflection type IR sensors. A light emitting diode (LED) and LASER device emitting the IR light are example of IR emitter or transmitter. On the other hands, the photo diode, PIN diode, avalanche photodiode (APD) are examples of IR detector or receiver. Both sensors are positioned facing each other, so that when an object passes between them, the light interruption causes a change in photocurrent, which detects the object. The reflective type IR Sensor, as shown in Figure 2.4, is the other type of IR Sensor. In this configuration the transmitter and detector are placed next to each other, facing the object. When an object passes in front of the sensor, it is detected by the sensor. Mobile phones, robots, industrial assembly, and other applications use infrared sensors. Infrared sensors are often employed in the design of television remote controls. It's a basic IR sensor-based electronics project for remotely driving a robotic vehicle with a standard TV remote or an IR remote. In robotics, a robot user uses an IR sensor-based TV remote to deliver orders to the robotic vehicle from a distance. The IR receiver interfaced to the microcontroller at the receiver end receives the commands. The microcontroller generates the required signals to drive the motors, allowing the robotic vehicle to move forward, backward, left, or right.

(iv) Ultrasonic Sensor: The waves having frequency greater than sound waves are termed as ultrasonic waves. An ultrasonic sensor, as shown in Figure 2.5, is a non-contact device which makes use of ultrasonic waves for its operation. It can be used to measure distance and velocity of an object. The ultrasonic sensor receives the high-frequency sound waves emitted by active ultrasonic sensors in order to evaluate the reflected waves or echo. As a result, the distance to an object is calculated using the time delay between transmitting and receiving the echo. Passive ultrasonic sensors, on the other hand, are only used to detect ultrasonic noise that exists under specified conditions.

Ultrasonic Sensor

Fig. 2.5: Ultrasonic Sensor (*Courtesy*: Kuongshun Electronic)

An Ultrasonic Sensor can determine the distance of an item by measuring the time of travel of the sound wave (similar to SONAR). The Doppler Shift feature of a sound wave is used to determine an object's velocity. These sensors can be utilized for insect trapping and determining the maturity indices of fruits and vegetables in the agricultural area.

(v) Touch Sensor: Touch sensors are switches that are actuated when the user's touch a screen or a key. When the key is touched a resistive or capacitive circuit is completed and a corresponding amount of electrical signal is generated in the switching circuit. Based on the type of touch, the sensor can work as capacitance touch switch, resistance touch switch, and piezo touch switch.

(vi) Chemical Sensor: These sensors detect the presence of any chemical behavior/process of a system and respond by producing corresponding electrical signal. Such types of sensors are used in a variety of industries to assess the performance of particular company based on changes in liquid or chemical level. The primary goal of these sensors is to detect any changes in the liquid or chemical fluctuations in the air. These are crucially deployed in larger towns and cities since it is critical to keep an eye on changes and ensure the safety of population. Chemical sensors are used in commercial atmospheric observation and process management, which can include chemicals that have been purposely or accidentally evolved, harmful or radioactive exposure, reusable operations in space stations, the pharmaceutical industry and many more. Electrochemical gas type, Chemical FET, Chemi-resistor, Non-dispersive IR, pH glass electrode type, Zinc oxide Nano-rod, Fluorescent chloride types are the most often used chemical sensors for industrial purpose.

(vii) Gas Sensor: The presence and quantitative changes in gaseous composition of air or of any other environment can be detected with the help of gas sensors. These sensors are similar to chemical sensors, but are exclusively used to observe changes in air quality and to detect the presence of different types of gases. These are used for air quality monitoring, recognition of poisonous or flammable gas, dangerous gas supervision in coal industries, oil and gas enterprises, chemical laboratory investigations, engineering, paint, plastics, rubber, medicinal and petrochemical, and others, similar to chemical sensors. Hydrogen, Ozone, Hygrometer, Carbon-dioxide, Electrochemical gaseous, Catalytic bead, Air pollution, Carbon monoxide, and other gas sensors are among the most widely used. The carbon dioxide, ethylene etc are some of the important gases which need to be monitored in many agricultural applications including green houses, poly houses, artificial ripening units, cold storage units and other food processing systems. The gas sensors are very effective in controlling CO_2 and ethylene for preserving and ripening of fruits in artificial ripening units and also in many agro industry operations.

(viii) Humidity Sensors: Humidity is a term that refers to the amount of water vapour or suspended water molecules present in the atmosphere or present in other gaseous substances. The sensors that measures presence and percentage of humidity are called humidity sensors. In green house and poly houses, a controlled humid environment is important to create a crop conducive environment. Hence humidity sensors find extensive applications in agriculture and meteorological applications. The humidity sensors are typically used in conjunction with temperature sensors, and therefore, embedded electronic hardware is manufactured to determine both parameters in a single integrated hardware unit to simultaneously sense and measure humidity and temperature. With humidity measurement, one can ensure that the entire procedure runs smoothly, and if there is an abrupt change, it may take fast action because these sensors detect the variations more rapidly. Humidity sensors are also used to increase effectiveness of a drying chamber, as measurement of humidity along with temperature & flow rate are important parameters in drying process.

These humidity sensors are used in a variety of domains, including residential and commercial, for heating, ventilation, and cooling purpose. These sensors can also be found in a variety of different industries, including painting, hospitals, pharmaceuticals, meteorology, automobiles, greenhouses, and coatings. Humidity sensors are used in agriculture for thermal comfort in animal shelters, speeding up the drying process and adding value to food commodities, and energy conservation in agro-industrial setups.

(ix) Acceleration Sensor: The angular and acceleration values are calculated using this type of sensor. The basic purpose of an accelerometer is to calculate acceleration. On an accelerometer, there are two types of forces that show the impact i.e. static force and dynamic force.

Static Force: This is the frictional force that exists between any two objects. The tilting value of the robot can be calculated using gravitational force calculations. This computation is useful for robotic balancing and determining whether the robot is driving uphill or flat.

Dynamic Force: The amount of acceleration required for an object to move is measured in this unit. The velocity or speed rates at which the robot is moving are defined by the calculation of dynamic force using an accelerometer.

These accelerometer sensors come in a variety of forms. The type of selection is determined by the need of industry. The bandwidth, type of output (digital or analog), total number of axes, and sensitivity are only a few of the criteria that should be checked before choosing a sensor. These sensors are utilized in a variety of farm machinery to make processes more simple, convenient, and efficient.

(x) Sound Sensor: These sensors are typically microphone devices that detect sound and deliver the appropriate voltage level based on the observed level. With the addition of a sound sensor, a small robot may be built that can travel based on the volume of sound received. The design process for sound sensors is more sophisticated than that of light sensors. This is due to the fact that sound sensors produce a very small voltage difference, which must be amplified in order to produce a noticeable voltage change.

(xi) Tactile Sensors: This is a sensor that indicates the contact between the sensor and the object. Tactile sensors are likely to be used in common situations, such as in lamps that lower or increase brightness when touched, and in lift buttons.

(xii) Force Sensor: This is used to measure the force values of numerous robot- operated actions, such as machine unloading and loading, material hauling, and others. This sensor is also commonly used in the assembly technique to troubleshoot problems. There are a variety of methodologies used in this sensor, including joint sensing and tactile array sensing.

(xiii) Bio Sensors: A biosensor is a transducer device to detect the presence of a chemical substance, that combines a biological component with physiochemical detection process and transform it in the form of a signal. This signal is easily processed and displayed on electronic devices. The biological sensing component of such sensors is a biologically derived material or bio mimetic component e.g. a tissue, cell, antibodies, microorganisms, cell receptors, enzymes, antibodies, nucleic acids, etc. The transducer or the detector element, which transforms one signal into another one, works on the basis of physicochemical process e.g. optical, piezoelectric, electrochemical, electro-chemical-luminescence etc., resulting from the interaction of the analyte with the biological element. This simplifies the measurement and quantification. The biosensor device connects with the associated electronics or signal processors that are primarily responsible for the display of the results in a user-friendly way. The readers are usually custom-designed and manufactured to suit the different working principles of biosensors.

2.5 Wireless Sensor Networks

A sensor or group of sensors embedded with limited memory, on-board computation, and communication capabilities, is called a sensor node. A tether less network of multiple sensor nodes of same types or different types is called a Wireless Sensor Network (WSN). The WSN is a collection of sensor nodes that are connected wirelessly not only to each other but also to a central base station over a standard radio frequency. A wireless sensor network is formed when several sensors work together to monitor huge physical areas. In a WSN, a Sensor Node is made up of four basic components. As indicated in Figure 2.6, these components are; Power Supply, Sensor, Processing Unit, and Communication System. This is critical because many network applications necessitate hundreds or thousands sensor nodes, which are frequently deployed in inaccessible locations. As a result, a sensor in a WSN has not just sensing capabilities, but also on-board processing, communication, and storage.

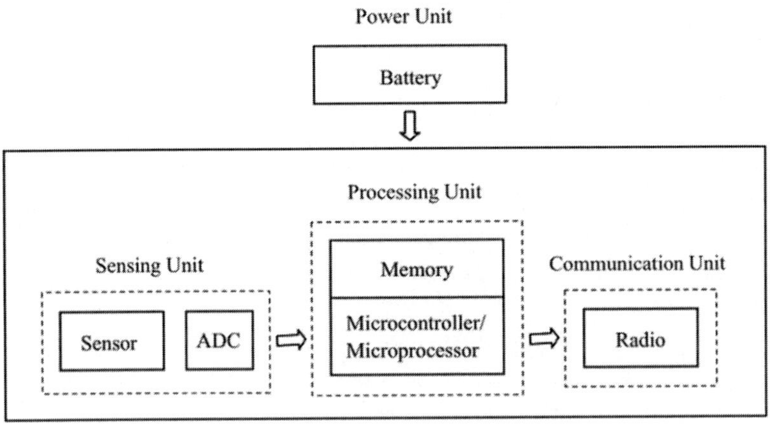

Fig. 2.6: Block diagram of a Sensor Node

With these improvements, a sensor node is often in charge of not just data collection but also in-network analysis, correlation, and fusion of its own sensor data and data from other sensor nodes. Sensor nodes use wireless radios to connect not only with each other but also with a base station allowing them to send sensor data to remote processing, visualization, analysis, and storage systems. Sensor nodes in a WSN can have a wide range of capabilities; for example, simple sensor nodes may monitor a single physical occurrence, whereas more complicated devices may combine many sensing approaches (e.g., acoustic, optical, magnetic). They can also have different communication capabilities, such as employing ultrasonic, infrared, or radio frequency technologies with different data rates and latencies.

The sensor gathers analog data from the physical world, which is then converted to digital data by an ADC. The main processing unit, which is commonly a microprocessor or a microcontroller, processes and manipulates data intelligently. A communication system consists of a radio system for data transmission and reception, which is commonly a short-range radio. Because all of the components are low-power devices, the complete system is powered by a small battery. Using all of these features, components and advancements, a sensor node is responsible for physical world data collection network analysis, data correlation, and fusion of data from other sensors with its own data.

2.5.1 WSN Architecture

When a large number of similar or dissimilar sensor nodes are deployed to attain a specific application task, a central network node called Base Station is usually provided to control and coordinate the data transmission and reception among external environment and the sensor nodes as shown in Figure 2.7. The networking of these sensor nodes is equally important when a large number of sensor nodes are deployed in a large region to cooperatively monitor a physical environment. Different type of communication technologies and protocols are used to establish wireless communication among sensor nodes and base station, depending on the size of application areas, number of sensor nodes and the range of communication. The details of communication technologies are explained in chapter-6.

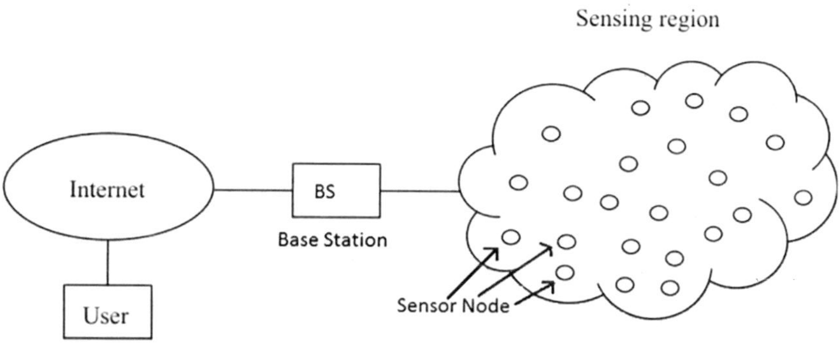

Fig. 2.7: Wireless Sensor Network

The base station sends commands to the sensor nodes, and the sensor nodes collaborate to complete the task. The sensor nodes deliver the data back to the base station after gathering the required information. A base station can also connect to other networks via the internet. A base station receives data from sensor nodes and does minimal data processing before sending the updated information to the user through the internet.

2.5.2 Classification of Wireless Sensor Networks

Wireless Sensor Networks are highly application-specific and are deployed in accordance with the application's requirements. As a result, the features of one WSN will differ from those of another. Wireless Sensor Networks can be divided into the following categories, regardless of the application.

a) Static and Mobile WSN
b) Deterministic and Nondeterministic WSN
c) Single Base Station and Multi Base Station WSN
d) Static Base Station and Mobile Base Station WSN
e) Single-hop and Multi-hop WSN
f) Self – Reconfigurable and Non – Self – Configurable WSN
g) Homogeneous and Heterogeneous WSN

a. **Static and Mobile WSN:** In many applications, all the sensor nodes are fixed without movement and these are static networks. Some applications, especially in biological systems, require mobile sensor nodes. These are known as mobile networks. An example of mobile network is animal monitoring.

b. **Deterministic and Nondeterministic WSN: In a deterministic WSN, t**he position of a sensor node is pre-determined and fixed. Only a small number of applications allows for sensor node deployment in a deterministic manner. Due to a variety of circumstances such as the harsh environment or hostile operation conditions, the WSN is sight specific and nondeterministic in nature. Because, in many applications, establishing the position of sensor nodes is not practicable and therefore, such networks are nondeterministic. In such applications, the WSNs necessitate a properly designed control system to be used.

c. **Single Base Station and Multi Base Station WSN:** In a single base station WSN, just one base station is employed, and it is located near the sensor node region and connects all the nearby sensor nodes. In case of a multi-base station WSN, numerous base stations are used depending upon the size of application area, and a sensor node can send data to the nearest base station.

d. **Static Base Station and Mobile Base Station WSN:** The Base stations, like sensor nodes, can be either stationary or mobile. A static base station is located near the sensing region and has a permanent position. A mobile base station moves around the sensing area, balancing the demand on the sensor nodes.

e. **Single-hop and Multi-hop WSN:** When sensor nodes are directly connected to base station, it is called a single-hop WSN. In a multi-hop WSN, peer nodes and cluster heads are used to relay data, which reduces energy consumption.

f. **Self – Reconfigurable and Non – Self – Configurable WSN:** Sensor networks in a non-self-configurable WSN cannot organize themselves in a network and must rely on a control unit to collect data. Sensor nodes in most WSNs are capable of organizing and maintaining connections, as well as collaborating with other sensor nodes to complete tasks.

g. **Homogeneous and Heterogeneous WSN:** When all the sensor nodes have equal energy consumption, computational power and storage capabilities, it is called a homogeneous WSN. Whereas in heterogeneous WSN, some sensor nodes have higher computational power and energy requirements than other and the processing and communication tasks are divided accordingly.

2.6 Sensors for Agricultural Applications

In Precision Agriculture, farming practices can be made more efficient and productive by deploying on-farm sensors. The sensors provide useful data of crop, soil, and environment/climate. The sensing technologies developed for agricultural applications can help farmers in monitoring of crop health, optimum irrigation and fertilization and soil health monitoring. In crop management, it is essential to know when to sow seeds, how to sow, when to irrigate, how much to irrigate, when and how to remove unwanted plants from main crop, when to harvest and how to store produce. These all details can be examined by sensing various parameters of plant leaves, soil, water etc. Even these data may be useful to predict when insect and pests will attack the crop.

Soil Sensors: The characteristic of soil is determined by its parameters like soil moisture, temperature, electric conductance, salinity, pH, carbon, micronutrients and macronutrients. There are sensors that can precisely measure real time values of all relevant soil parameters, except the sensing of micronutrients. The commonly used commercially used sensors for precision agricultural applications are tabulated in Table-2.2. The real time sensing of soil health parameters can provide accurate values of soil parameters. Based on sensor data, corrective measures can be taken for effective soil and crop management. The information about soil moisture can help the farmers for efficient irrigation system. Similarly, the Nitrogen (N), Phosphorous (P), Potassium (K) values determine the correct status of fertilizers in the soil, and hence can efficiently control the amount of fertilizers required for the crop.

Table 2.2: Common type of Wireless sensor nodes for Precision Agriculture

S.N.	Sensor node	Parameters
1	ECH2O Soil moisture sensor	Soil Temperature, Soil Moisture, Conductivity
2	Hydra probe II Soil sensor	Soil Temperature, Salinity level, Soil Moisture, conductivity
3	EC Sensor (EC250)	Soil Temperature, Salinity level, Soil Moisture, Conductivity.
4	BetaTherm 100K6A1B Thermistor	Plant Temperature
5	237 Leaf Wetness sensor	Plant Moisture, Plant Wetness, Plant temperature
6	Sense H2 Hydrogen sensor	Hydrogen, Plant Wetness, CO2, Plant temperature
7	Field scout CM1000TM	Temperature, Photosynthesis
8	YSI 6025 Chlorophyll sensor	Temperature, Photosynthesis
9	LW100, Leaf wetness sensor	Plant Moisture, Plant Wetness, Plant temperature
10	TT4 multi-sensor Thermocouple	Plant Moisture, Plant Temperature
11	LW100, Leaf wetness sensor	Plant Moisture, Plant Wetness, Plant temperature
12	TPS-2 portable Photosynthesis	Photo synthesis, Plant Moisture, CO2, temperature

S.N.	Sensor node	Parameters
13	PTM-48A Photosynthesis monitor	Photosynthesis, Plant Moisture, Plant Wetness, CO2, temperature
14	Cl-340 Hand-held photosynthesis	Photosynthesis, Plant Moisture, Plant Wetness, CO2, temperature, Hydrogen level in plant
15	CM-100 Compact Weather Sensor	Air Pressure, Temperature, Air Humidity, Wind Speed,

Optical sensors: In agriculture, a wide range of optical sensors for measuring agricultural crop reflectance are used for precision farming. The platform of such sensors determines how these sensors are categorized as follows:

i. Satellites onboard sensors: The satellite borne sensors make use of cameras, IR sensors, and Microwave sensors onboard to collect images of crop fields from space. Such satellites are called remote sensing satellite.

ii. Aerial sensors: Airplane and unmanned aerial vehicles (UAV) or drones make use of cameras, IR sensors, Near-Infrared sensors, thermal sensors onboard to collect images of crop field from long distances.

iii. Ground-based sensors: collect reflectance data from short distances and can store it in a text file.

The type of optical source or light emitter determines whether the ground sensors are of active or passive type. For the purpose of gathering images, active sensors have their own source of energy that is a light source. This source can be of a broad-spectrum light or light with a specific range of wavelength. On the other hands, the passive sensors, require an external source of light, such as the sun, and are unable to operate at night and perform poorly during wet and overcast seasons. When there are clouds or shadows, these may potentially suggest various, erroneous readings. In order to collect crop reflectance, passive sensors must be positioned at a precise distance from the plant. Another limiting issue is dew which can alter reflectance in both visible and near infrared wavelength. In other words, it raises reflectivity while reducing visiblelight.

Optical crop sensors use specific wavelengths to assess various crop conditions, ranging from monochromatic to multi-spectral (< 10 wave bands) and hyper spectral (>10 wave bands). Sensors can monitor the type and intensity of light wavelengths reflected from crop leaves back to the sensors by beaming light of certain wavelengths at them. Optical sensors are used to analyze crop conditions related to nitrogen by measuring crop reflectance. It can calculate LAI (Leaf Area Index), leaf chlorophyll content, soil cover, dry matter, water content, yield, nitrogen content, and a variety of other crop metrics. An optical sensor coupled to a GPS may build maps from reflectance readings using geographical coordinates. This map can be used to detect the areas of the field that are under increased stress, reducing the need for inputs.

Imaging sensors: The intermittent mapping of crop with imaging sensors is an accurate method of real time crop management. The biotic and abiotic stresses, infestations, pests, insects, etc can be accurately determined with the help of multispectral and hyper spectral imaging sensors. Further, the maturity indices of the crop can also be determined with such sensors to determine the accurate time of crop harvesting. The multispectral imaging sensors take images of the crop at broadly spaced discrete 5-6 spectral bands. On the other hand, hyper spectral imaging sensors captures images at few nanometer bands spacing across the spectrum and provides thousands of images with high degree of spatial and spectral resolutions. The details of imaging sensors are covered in chapter-8.

Water Potential sensors: The sensors which measure crop water potential, i.e. the relative changes in the leaf's turgor pressure are called water potential sensors. Figure 2.8 (a) illustrates working principle of a water potential sensor in which the leaf is placed between two magnets which measures the difference between plant turgor and magnetic pressure. The Figure 2.8 (b) shows actual deployment of water potential sensor on a lemon tree. The Low plant turgor will increase magnetic pressure, thus indicating that the plant lacks sufficient water, making, and irrigation necessary. Such sensors can measure changes in leaf turgor pressure in realtime.

Fig. 2.8: Water Potential Sensor **(a)** Working principle **(b)** Sensor implanted on Plant Leaf

Biomass Sensor: A biomass is plant material used as fuel to produce energy, either in the form of heat or electricity. It can also be used to produce fibers and industrial chemicals. The tree wood energy, crops and waste from forests, yards, or farms twigs bushes and dry leaves are some of the examples of biomass. Crop biomass sensors, which use an optical sensor, can be used for crop biomass density measurements. A pendulum system is generally used in the sensor that sweeps over the crop at a specific angle, detecting changes within the crop. The sensor is useful for measuring crop biomass because it limits nitrogen inputs over specified areas and ensures optimal plant protection.

Acoustic sensor: In acoustic sensing ultra sound waves are transmitted towards the plant to be sensed. The sensor emits the signal as a repeated sweep under a certain frequency, usually 50-100 kHz. The amplitude and phase of the reflected echo carries information about the geometric structure of the plant, i.e. the structure of the foliage. The geometric features derived from the echo signal gives physical structure of the foliage like size, shape, orientation, and overall positioning of the leaves. The acoustic sensors are used in agricultural applications is Acoustic sensors. Such sensors have miscellaneous applications in farm management. Some of the target applications are:

(i) Soil cultivation to detect the rows of plants from the soil

(ii) Weeding to detect the plants from the weeds

(iii) Herbicide application to detect the plants from the weeds and herbs

(iv) Fruit harvesting to find the fruit inside the tree canopy and to determine maturity indices.

(v) Grain and forage harvesting to detect the harvested area, thus avoiding overlapping and other losses.

The working principle of the acoustic sensor includes number of steps such as echoes reflected from the plant leaves and subsequently measuring the plant height. Besides, the leaf structure has a significant impact on the amount of reflected ultrasonic sound. The bigger the number of leaves on a plant and the larger the leaves, the more ultrasonic sound will be reflected by the sensor. It collects multiple echoes reflected from the plant leaves, and subsequently measures the plant height.

3

Artificial Intelligence

3.1 Introduction

Artificial Intelligence (AI) is technology which can store, retrieve, manipulate, manufacture, transmit or receive, analyze any digital information and can apply machine vision for increasing efficiency and workability of the system. The AI permits systematically scope of '3S' i.e. Safety, Security and Surveillance, which is also known as manmade intelligence. In fact, it needs more reliable and accurate data or information for processing and correction for predicting performance of any system and devices.

The Artificial Intelligence (AI) was first introduced in 1956 by John McCarthy, an American computer and cognitive scientist at Dartmouth, New Hampshire. The AI, formally became a field of study by John McCarthy along with Marvin Minsky, Nathaniel Rochester, and Claude Shannon, who started working on simulating human intelligence with machines.

An instinctive ability of human to think and analyze cognitively, to sense and respond, to act and react, to perceive and infer, may be termed as human intelligence. The Central Nervous System (CNS) of human body is a biological neural network comprising brain, neurons, spinal cord, peripheral nerves etc, and the intelligence is one of the trillion dimensions of CNS. The replication of a biologically intelligent system like CNS, with the help of physical and computational sciences leads to creation of Artificial Neural Network (ANN) that exhibits cognitive ability to think like human, termed as Artificial Intelligence (AI). The artificial intelligence may be considered as an ability of a physical system (Machines, Computers) to think and perform tasks and operations like human. The AI, also called machine intelligence, is the intelligence demonstrated by machines, in contrast to the natural intelligence exhibited by humans. The artificial intelligence in a machine or computer is achieved through powerful mathematical algorithms and its implementation with programming tools. The AI Systems often incorporate artificial intelligence, machine learning, and deep learning to create a sophisticated intelligent machine that performs given human functions.

In present technological context, AI has become a major domain of engineering and mathematical sciences that deals with creation of intelligent systems, machines, or computers. It can be applied in a wide range of disciplines, including computational sciences, engineering, agriculture, epidemiological sciences and a variety of other fields. While artificial intelligence and machine learning has a wide range of practical applications across industries, it has the potential to be used in agriculture sector to improve crop production and its quality. In this context, one of the most important imperatives is to adopt the modern AI and ML solutions to make farming more efficient. The integration of digital technologies with AI-enabled cognitive solutions is critical to the future of farming. AI and ML-powered solutions can help farmers to increase crop production with minimal inputs, but also enhance crop quality and speed up time to market. AI has three main processes i.e. learning (supervised and unsupervised system), reasoning (analysis and self- correction) and finally vision for more productivity and efficiency. In this chapter, we discuss about artificial neural network, sub domains of AI, applications and scope of AI in agricultural practices.

3.2 Artificial Neural Network

An artificial neural network (ANN) is a type of machine learning model that reveals an equivalent physical model of the human brain. It consists of an interconnected network of nodes known as artificial neurons, which take input, change their internal state (activation) in response to that input, and produce output based on the input and activation. As shown in Figure 3.1, an artificial neural network's design consists of an Input layer, a Hidden layer, and an Output layer. Each link can carry a signal from one artificial neuron to another, just like synapses in a human brain. When an artificial neuron receives a signal, it can process it and send it to other artificial neurons. An artificial neuron is a model of a biological neuron that mimics the functioning of a biophysical neuron with inputs and outputs, but it is not a biological neuron. With the advanced method of interpretation and decision making, one can get outcome based on output desired from ANN. Further, this outcome can be used to evaluate its future impact of any new technology or treatment.

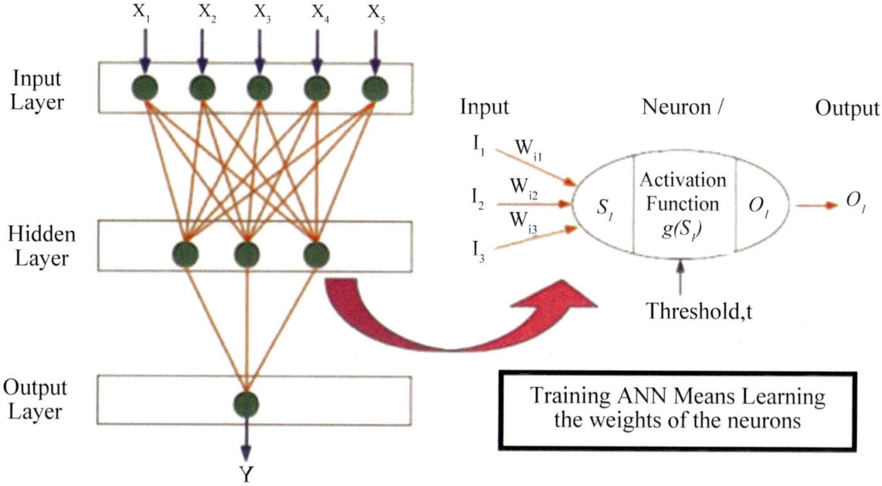

Fig. 3.1: Artificial Neural Network Architecture

The artificial neurons are normally grouped into layers, in which different layers may execute various modifications on its input. Signals move from the first layer (the input layer) to the last layer (the output layer), after multiple traversals of the layer. The neural network receives a pattern from the input layer. The input layer interacts with the outside world. On receiving a pattern, at the input layer, the output layer generates a new pattern. It also reveals the situation for which the neural network is being trained. The neural network's output layer is responsible for presenting a pattern to the outside world. The network is built by linking the output of specific neurons to the input of other neurons, establishing a directed, weighted graph. The output neurons are directly connected to the type of work that is to be performed by the neural network.

A process termed as *learning*, which is regulated by a learning rule, can change the weights as well as the functions that compute the activation. The neural network's Hidden layer is a layer that exists between the Input and Output layers. If a hidden layer is available, the activation function is used. The hidden layer is made up of hidden nodes. The neurons that are neither in the input layer nor the output layer is known as hidden nodes or hidden neurons. Programming computers for certain features such as knowledge, reasoning, and problem solving, perception, learning, planning, and the ability to operate and move objects are at the heart of artificial intelligence. AI research includes knowledge engineering as a key component. AI includes machine learning (ML) as well. Learning without supervision necessitates the ability to recognize patterns in streams of data, whereas learning with proper supervision necessitates categorization and numerical regressions. Some of the operational activities to be performed by machines designed with artificial intelligence are: Speech recognition; Learning; Planning; and Problem solving.

As demonstrated in Figure 3.2, all three components are increasingly becoming independent parts of the AI System's intelligence puzzle. Deep learning (DL) is a subfield of machine learning and DL and ML both are sub fields of artificial intelligence. The AI, ML and DL are frequently used in AI systems to develop a sophisticated intelligent machine that performs certain human duties with greater efficiency and productivity.

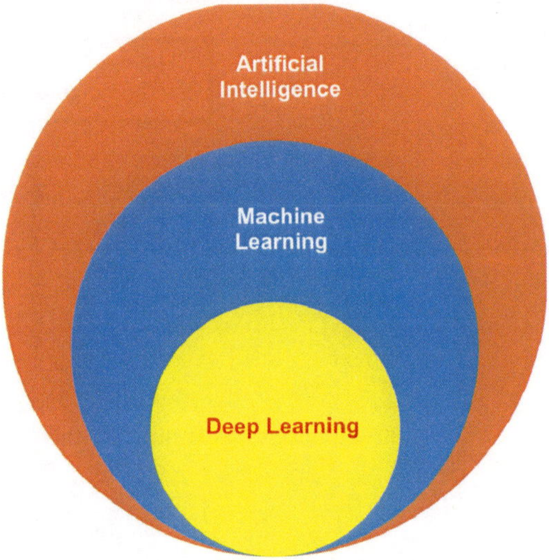

Fig. 3.2: Relationship of Artificial Intelligence, Machine Learning and Deep Learning

3.3 Machine Learning

The term machine learning (ML) was first explained in 1959, by Arthur Samuel, an American pioneer in the field of computer gaming and artificial intelligence. It states that "Machine learning is a field of study that gives the ability to the computer to self-learn without being explicitly programmed, that is, imbuing knowledge to machines without having to go through hard- coding and exhaustive programming." It's a type of artificial intelligence that allows the AI system to learn from its surroundings and apply that knowledge to make better judgments.

Artificial intelligence has a subfield called machine learning. Its goal is to allow machine or computers to learn and solve problems on their own. Without having explicit pre-programmed rules and models, a machine learning algorithm may discover patterns in observed data, develop models that explain the system, and generate relevant predictions, inferences, and decisions. Figure 3.3 depicts a diagram that explains the difference between traditional computer programming and machine learning.

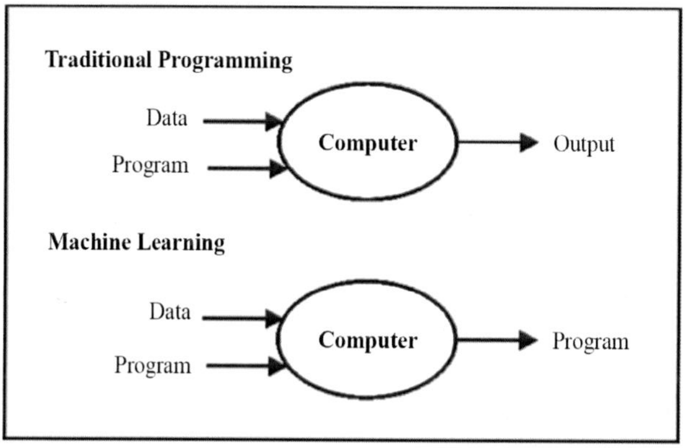

Fig. 3.3: Programming versus Machine learning

The machine learning is the process of programming systems to search through data for patterns and adapt actions accordingly. The majority of the current artificially intelligent systems are based on some form of supervised machine learning. For example, systems that automatically detect spam emails are trained to do so by extracting spams from millions of e-mails. With additional information, the algorithm will be able to comprehend and learn what constitutes an email. Machine learning differs from fully-AI systems it is not aware about the original object programme. In other words, if a new form of email arrives, it will be unable to tackle it. The ML applies a range of algorithms to iteratively learn, explain, and improve data in order to anticipate better results and predictions. These algorithms employ statistical approaches to identify trends and then act on them. The Machine learning can be divided into three main categories. These are: *Supervised Learning; Unsupervised Learning; and Reinforcement Learning.*

3.3.1 Supervised Learning

The supervised learning is elementary form of machine learning, in which a set of labeled data are used to train the algorithms. The supervised learning algorithms are trained on marked data with known inputs and outputs. There is a data set and predetermined output, with the assumption that the input and output have a relationship. The goal of supervised machine learning is to come up with a mapping function that best describes the input data set (X) in order to predict the output data set (Y). The input and output data may be known to us, but we need to find out the mapping function, that will give a specific degree of performance. The mapping function can then be used to new data to achieve similar results. To identify the function that makes Y = f(X), training data is used.

The data is entered into the learning algorithm as a collection of inputs called Features, represented by X, and the associated outputs, denoted by Y, and the system learns by comparing its actual outputs to correct outputs to discover errors. It then makes the necessary changes to the model. There are two portions to the raw data. The first section is used to train the algorithm, while the second is used to test the trained algorithm. The data patterns are used in supervised learning to predict the values of new data for the labels. The Supervised Learning is of two types i.e. Regression type and Classification type supervised learning.

(A) Regression Type Supervised Learning: The regression is a type of supervised learning in which labeled data is used to produce continuous flow of predictions. The regression reveals modeling of goal prediction values based on independent variables. It is mostly utilized in forecasting and determining the link between variables. Continuous values can be estimated/predicted using regression (Real valued output). For example, given a picture of face of a person, then the age of the person must be estimated from its face image. Similarly, an image of a crop field can be used to determine its ripeness and harvesting state or to determine any infestations on the plant leaves. The link between a dependent variable [*Outputs*] and an independent variable [*Inputs*] is investigated using theory of regression, a type of predictive modeling technique. This technique is used in weather forecasting, time series modeling, and process optimization. House Price Prediction is an example of the regression technique, in which the price of a house is predicted based on inputs such as the number of rooms, location, ease of transportation, age of the house, and size of the home. In machine learning approach, there are a variety of regression methods that can be utilized for various regression applications. The following are some of the most common regression algorithms:

Simple Linear Regression- In simple linear regression algorithm, the scores are predicted on one variable from ratings on a second variable using simple linear regression. The criterion variable, often known as Y, is the variable we are forecasting. The predictor variable, abbreviated as X, is the variable on which predictions are made.

Multiple Linear Regression- One of the most commonly used linear regression techniques is the multiple linear regressions. It is popular form of linear regression analysis technique and one of the algorithms of regression technology. It is a predictive approach that is used to explain the relationship between one dependent variable and two or more independent variables. The independent variables can be categorical or continuous.

Polynomial Regression- When the independent variable's maximum power is greater than one. It is called polynomial regression. The best fit line in such type of regression technique is shaped like a curve rather than a straight line.

Support Vector Regression- The Support Vector Regression technique can be used to solve not only regression problems, but it can also be used to solve classification challenge. It has all of the characteristics of a maximum margin algorithm. A non-linear function is leaned into a high-dimensional kernel-induced feature space using linear learning machine mapping.

Ridge Regression- Ridge Regression is a regression approach based on a method for assessing multiple regression data with numerous collinearities. The standard errors are reduced by adding a degree of bias to the regression calculations. It gives more accurate computations and predictions.

Lasso Regression- The Lasso regression is a type of shrinkage-based linear regression. In this approach the data values shrink towards a central point, such as the mean, in shrinkage. Simple, sparse models are encouraged by the Lasso approach (i.e. models with fewer parameters). This type of regression is suitable for models with excessive multi-collinearity or when it is intended to automate elements of the model selection process, such as variable selection and parameter removal.

Elastic Net Regression- Elastic net regression is a penalized generalized linear regression model that combines L1 (LASSO) and L2 (ridge regression) norms into a penalized model with sparsity (L1) and robustness (L2).

Bayesian Regression- Bayesian regression, which is a fairly natural method, can be used to overcome insufficient or poorly scattered data. It will allow the prior and noise to be combined with coefficients, allowing the priors to take over in the absence of data. More importantly, one can ask Bayesian regression which portions of its data fit it is confident in (if any) and which parts are highly doubtful.

Decision Tree Regression- A decision tree creates a tree-like structure using regression models. It phases the development of an associated decision tree while breaking down the data into smaller sections. As a result, a tree has been built with decision nodes and leaf nodes.

Random Forest Regression- Random Forest is a machine learning method that gives output even without hyper-parameter adjustment, and it is one of the algorithms used in regression techniques. Also, due to its simplicity and the fact that it can be used for both regressions and classification problems, this technique is commonly employed. The forest it creates is made up of a collection of Decision Trees, most of which are trained using the "bagging" method.

(B) Classification Type of Supervised Learning: This a type of supervised learning in which labeled data is utilized to produce non-continuous predictions. The input- output graph is non-linear, and the information output is not always continuous. The algorithm in the classification process learns from the data input and then applies what it has learned to classify new observations. It's possible that this data collection is only bi-class, or that it's also multi-class. Checking whether an email is spam or not spam by training an algorithm for different spam terms or emails is an example of a classification problem. In machine learning, there are a variety of classification algorithms that are utilized for various classification applications. The following are some of the most common classification algorithms: -

Logistic Regression/Classification- Logistic regression is a type of supervised learning that uses a logistic/sigmoid function. It estimates the probabilities to quantify the connection between a categorical dependent variable and one or more independent variables. It can be used when the dependent variable is discrete one which is binary or dichotomous. It signifies that, dependent variable can only have two possible values, such as either "Yes or No," and "Living or Dead."

K-Nearest Neighbours- The K-Nearest Neighbours (KNN) method is a simple classification algorithm and is also one of the most common type of learning algorithms. The purpose of an object is allocated to the class which is most prevalent among its 'k' nearest neighbors based on a majority vote of its neighbors. It can also be used for regression, with the output being the object's value, predicts continuous values. This number is the average or median of its 'k' closest neighbors' benefits.

Support Vector Machines- A Support Vector Machine is a type of Classifier that is formally described as a discriminative classifier by separating a hyper plane. The method creates an optimal hyper plane for categorizing fresh data. This hyper plane is a line in two-dimensional space that divides a plane into two halves, with each class on either side.

Kernel Support Vector Machines (KVSM)- The kernel-SVM algorithm is one of the classification techniques that use a set of mathematical functions known as the kernel. The core job is to take data and turn it into the appropriate format. Different types of kernel functions are used by different SVM algorithms. There are various types of functions that can be used. Linear and nonlinear functions, polynomial functions, radial basis functions, and sigmoid functions are only a fewexamples.

Naive Bayes- The Naive Bayes classification technique is based on Bayes' Theorem and assumes that the predictors are independent. In simple terms, a Naive Bayes classifier assumes that the presence of one feature in a class has no bearing on the presence of any other function. The Naive Bayes model is easy to build and works well with large datasets.

Decision Tree Classification- A decision tree is a type of classification model that takes the shape of a tree. At the same time, an accompanying decision tree is constructed sequentially, breaking down a vast data set into smaller portions. A tree with decision nodes and leaf nodes is the end result. There are two or more branches on a decision node. A classification or conclusion is represented by a leaf node. The root node is the initial decision node in a tree that corresponds to the best predictor. Both category and numerical data can be handled by decision trees.

Random Forest Classification- Random Forest is a supervised learning technique that uses a large number of decision trees to learn. It generates forest and makes it casual. The wood it constructs is an ensemble of Decision Trees, which in most cases increases the overall outcome by training the decision tree algorithm with the "bagging" method, which is a mixture of learning models.

3.3.2 Unsupervised Learning

The Unsupervised Learning is the second type of machine learning, in which the algorithm is trained on un-labeled data, i.e. data that hasn't been previously labeled. The objective is to look into the data and see whether there exists any structure or not. The data in unsupervised learning is unlabeled, and raw data is fed straight into the algorithm without any pre-processing or knowledge of the data's outcome. The data cannot be divided into train or test data and the program analyzes the data and creates clusters of data with new labels based on the data segments. This strategy performs effectively on transactional data. These methods are also employed in the segmentation of text subjects, the recommendation of items, and the detection of data outliers. The unsupervised learning is of two types i.e. *Clustering and Dimensionality Reduction.*

(A) Clustering: The Clustering is a type of unsupervised learning that includes grouping related items together before using the grouped data to form clusters. The goal of this unsupervised machine learning technique is to find similarities in data points and group them together, as well as to Figure out which cluster fresh data should be assigned to. There are a variety of clustering methods used in machine learning for diverse clustering applications. Some of the most common clustering algorithms are as follows:

K-Means Clustering- K-Means clustering is a Clustering method that groups together related data in a cluster. The K-means algorithm is a clustering technique that iterates to find local maxima in each iteration. The first letter is K, which stands for the number of groups you want to see. Place k centroids in different places of your space at random. Using the Euclidean distance method, calculate the distance between data points and centroids, then assign each data point to the cluster that is closest to it. Recalculate the cluster centers as the average of the data points to which they are linked. Repeat until no more changes are seen.

Hierarchical Clustering- Clustering strategy in which related data is clustered together in a cluster is known as hierarchical clustering. It's a clustering algorithm that generates a cluster hierarchy. The first step in this approach is to allocate each data point to its own group. The nearest two groupings are then united into a single cluster. This operation comes to an end when there is just one cluster left. To begin, sort each data point into the relevant group. Determine the group's nearest pair and merge them into a single cluster using Euclidean distance. Then combine the distances between the two closest clusters until all of the items are in one cluster.

(B) Dimensionality Reduction Technique: Dimensionality Reduction is a type of unsupervised learning in which the dimensions of the data are reduced to remove unwanted data from the input. This strategy is used to remove negative qualities from the data. It's the process of converting a set of data with many dimensions into data with the same number of dimensions but smaller. These methods are used to obtain better features in order to solve machine learning problems.

Dimensionality Reduction Algorithms are used for a range of dimensionality reduction applications in machine learning. Some of the most common dimensionality reduction techniques are as follows:

Principal Component Analysis (PCA)- This type of reduction technique converts old variables, which are a linear mixture of real variables, into a new set of variables. A new set of variables is referred to as "primary components." As a result of the transformation, the first primary component has the most potential variance, and each following element has the greatest potential difference if it is orthogonal to the above ingredients. By maintaining only the first m n components while retaining the majority of the data information, the data dimensionality is decreased.

Linear Discriminant Analysis (LDA)- This type of reduction technique creates linear combinations of original characteristics. It is one of the algorithms used in Dimensionality Reduction. However, unlike PCA, LDA does not aim to maximize explained variance. The LDA can increase the prediction performance of the extracted features and also, it offers customizations to solve specific obstacles.

Kernel Principal Component Analysis (KPCA)- This is a nonlinear version of PCA algorithms, and the variables that are transformed into variables of the new set, are a nonlinear combination of original variables. The transformed variables are referred to as Kernel Principal Component Analysis (KPCA) variables. It can extract more information from the original dataset by capturing a fraction of the high-order statistics.

3.3.3 Reinforcement Learning

Reinforcement Learning is another type of machine learning in which no raw data is provided as input and the algorithm must Figure out the situation independently. Figure 3.4 shows elements of reinforcement learning technique. The system uses reinforcement learning to determine which activities result in the most substantial rewards through trial and error. The agent, also known as the learner or decision maker, the environment, which describes everything the agent interacts with, and the actions, which indicates what the agent may do, are the three key components of this type of training. The reinforcement learning is commonly utilized in robotics, gaming, and navigation.

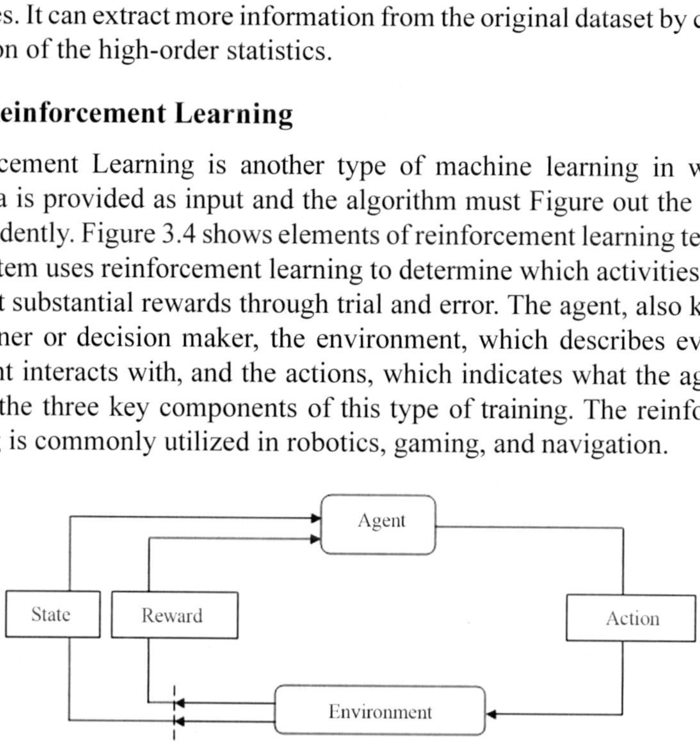

Fig. 3.4: Reinforcement Learning

The aim of the agent is to execute activities that maximize the predicted reward over certain time duration. The agent will get to the target much faster by following a sound policy. Consequent upon that, the goal of reinforcement learning is to discover the best available strategy. In machine learning, there are many Reinforcement Learning algorithms that can be used for various reinforcement learning applications. The following are some of the most important reinforcement algorithms-

Q-Learning- Q-learning is a type of reinforcement learning in which an agent tries to Figure out the best strategy based on its past interactions with the environment. An agent's record is made up of a series of state-action-rewards. As long as the number of times an action is tried in each state is not limited, Q-learning learns an optimal policy regardless of the method the agent is utilizing. It's regarded as an off-policy method since it learns the best policy regardless of the strategy.

State Action Reward State Action (SARSA)- This is a Reinforcement Learning algorithm that determines how frequently the action values are updated. Although the difference in SARSA and Q-learning implementations is little, it has a major influence. Action 2, which is the action executed by the agent in the second state, is another parameter in the SARSA approach. It allows the agent to calculate the future reward amount directly. After that, instead of expecting the best action to be made and the most significant reward to be earned, expect the opposite.

Deep Q-Network-Although Q-learning is a robust method, it suffers from a basic flaw: it lacks generality. The Deep Q-Network is a Reinforcement Learning *algorithm*. If you conceive about Q-learning as renewing numbers in a two-dimensional array (Action Space * State Space), it's similar to dynamic programming. It means that when the Q-learning agent encounters states that it hasn't seen before, it has no notion what to do. A Q-learning agent, to put it another way, can't estimate value for states that aren't visible. DQN solves this challenge by replacing the two-dimensional array with a neural network.

Markov Decision Processes- A mathematical representation of complex decision making process is the Markov Decision Process. It is a Reinforcement Learning technique that provides a mathematical model of decision making when the outcomes are partly random and partly under the control of decision maker. It incorporates a set of potential world states and by simply describing the task of learning through interaction, the Markov Decision Process is used to achieve a goal. The environment responded to the agent's actions, and the agent and the environment interacted regularly, supplying the agent with new conditions.

Deep Deterministic Policy Gradient (DDPG)- The Deep Deterministic Policy Gradient is a Reinforcement Learning method that combines both Q-learning and Policy gradients. It employs the actor-critic design model, consisting of two models 'actor' and 'critic'. The actor is a policy network and it takes the state as input and its output is the exact continuous action, instead of a probability distribution over actions. The critic is a Q-value network that takes in state and action as input and outputs the Q-value.

3.4 Deep Learning

The deep learning refers to a class of machine learning techniques that employ numerous layers to extract higher-level features from raw data. It's the next generation of Machine Learning, and it's also considered a subset of it. Lower layers in image processing; for example, may recognize edges, whereas higher layers may identify human-relevant notions like numerals, letters, or faces. The majority of recent deep learning models are based on artificial neural networks, notably Convolutional Neural Networks (CNN), while deep generative models such as the nodes in Deep Boltzmann machines and deep belief network can also include propositional formulas or latent variables structured layer-wise. Each level of deep learning learns to turn the data it receives into a little more abstract and composite representation. The raw input in an image recognition application could be a matrix of pixels; the first representational layer could abstract the pixels and encode edges; the second layer could compose and encode edge arrangements; the third layer could encode a nose and eyes; and the fourth layer could recognize that the image contains a face. Importantly, a deep learning algorithm can Figure out, which features belong to which level on its own. Deep Learning models are capable of making predictions without the assistance of humans. In many circumstances, human assistance is required to achieve the best result, whereas Deep Learning models employ artificial neural networks that function independently. The biological neural network of the human brain inspired the design of this network. It uses a logical structure to analyze data, similar to how a human would derive conclusions. Learning from the environment and then applying that learning to make judgments are the foundations of both machine and deep learning. There are different types of machine learning algorithms that can help you achieve this efficiently.

3.5 Applications of AI in Agriculture

The Artificial Intelligence (AI) and Machine Learning (ML) techniques have tremendous scope in agricultural applications and therefore, are rapidly being adopted in agriculture, both in handling agricultural goods, in modern precision farming, and also in agribusiness. The Cognitive computing, in particular, is emerging as the most disruptive technology in agriculture services, since it has the ability to understand, learn, and adapt to a variety of scenarios (based on learning) in order to boost efficiency and production. Artificial intelligence (AI) has the potential to play a significant role in Smart Agriculture decision-making, yield projections, and crop surveillance. As a result, farmers will no longer have to rely solely on intuition when it comes to agriculture and crop production; instead, AI technology will assist them in increasing their incomes and improving the way they cultivate and sell their crops. AI decision can readily answer any questions such as what, how, when, and where. Farmers can use the cloud-based AI and Machine Learning tools and software to suggest sowing dates, field preparation, soil test-based fertilization, farm yard manure application, seed treatment, and optimum sowing depth. To determine the plant or flower kind, AI, Deep learning, and other advanced approaches are utilized. This will assist farmers in providing a favorable environment for the plant's long-term growth. Eventually, the creation of more personalized fruits and plants will rise, resulting in a greater variety of products and manufacturing methods. Artificial intelligence techniques are rapidly evolving, and computer networks can be used to identify plant illness or any undesired weed on the farm. Greenhouse farming can give plants with a specific habitat, but it is not possible without human intervention. Here, wireless technology and the Internet of Things (IoT) come into play, and we may use the newest communication protocols and sensors to implement weather monitoring and control without the need for human intervention on the farm. Robots that are specialized in operating around the clock for speedy harvesting can also be used to collect fruits and crops at the appropriate stage. Focusing on AI-based methods has the significant advantage of addressing each problem individually, rather than generalizing, and providing personalized answers to a specific situation. AI is playing a positive role in improving overall agricultural output and can be used for the applications listed below:

(i) Smart Farming Using AI

The artificial intelligence (AI) plays an important role to enhance the total agricultural output, such as crop productivity and profitability etc. For a long time, farmers have relied on conventional farming methods including manual inspection and intuition for crop yield and the quality of crop. But now the modern technologies like AI can be used for precision farming and also for effective marketing of agro products. This allows farmers to increase their farm efficiency, revenues and improve the way they raise and sell food.

Fig. 3.5: Smart Farming Using AI

The major components of smart farming using AI techniques are sensors and Internet of Things (IoT) network connected to the cloud as depicted in Figure 3.5. In modern precision farming various farming activities may be planned, monitored, and controlled remotely in a real-time environment using smart sensors and data analytics. Modern cloud computing techniques can also be used to develop digital agriculture technologies that will improve the entire farm management operations. To enhance predictability and provide inputs to farmers on ideal sowing time, AI technology can be utilized to identify optimal sowing period, past climatic data, real-time Moisture Adequacy data (MAI) from daily rainfall, and soil moisture. It can also detect and estimate the risk of pest attack so that it can warn you ahead of time. Pest attacks are classified as High, Medium, or Low depending on the weather and crop growth stage. Farmers can also utilize AI to develop seasonal forecasting models in order to improve agricultural precision, productivity, and ultimately production. These models can predict upcoming weather patterns months in advance, which can help farmers, make better decisions. This could lead to approximately 30% increase in average agricultural yield per acre.

In present context, SMART farming means designing specific crop to grow, its measurement at the time of maturity in real time assessment method in time bound duration. Hence AI has got number of promising options to decide life cycle of a particular crop as per anticipated yield in its maturity period.

(ii) Predictive and Recommendation Analytics

The predictive and recommendation analytics techniques based on AI and ML can help farmers to be benefitted Farmers through advisories about crop sowing dates for various crops based on weather conditions. The Cropping patterns can also be tweaked using machine learning algorithms to increase the crop yields. ML can anticipate the amount of seed that should be planted to meet the growing needs using historical production data, weather forecasts, seed information, and demand and supply information.

(iii) Identifying Plant Diseases

An early detection of crop infestation and plant diseases can be very helpful to protect the crop and to take remedial measures in time. In such type of applications, regular images of the crops are captured. The crop images/photos are split into categories such as background, healthy part, and diseased part with the help of computer vision technologies. The adversely affected areas are then photographed and transferred for further analysis and validation. To detect plant diseases, algorithms based on Convolutional Neural Network (CNN) model and Deep CNN are developed to process the images and to generate concrete diagnostic observations. Similarly, pre- processing leaf photos aid early detection of pest infestations, allowing farmers to act fast and reduce losses. This identification of plant diseases is helpful for early diagnosis and implementation of timely action for its prevention and therby cost of cultivation can be minimized.

(iv) Livestock Management

In this application, radio frequency identification (RFID) tags are used which tracks animals using overhead cameras that identify numbers attached on their bodies, using machine vision technology. These advanced sensors can also monitor the health and behavior of animals. The sensors continue to monitor the running distances, duration, and speed of the animals at the farm and make charts and reports to indicate their health status. It can easily identify and convey any variations in body temperature, movements etc of the animal, so that proper remedial measures or medications if required, can be given to the animals. This is also one of the preventative strategies that can guide the farmers to detect the sick animals before they become fatal or spread to other animals.

(v) AI based Drones for Agriculture

Drones, or Unmanned Aerial Vehicles (UAV), have been in use for many applications since last three decades. Drone applications are currently expanding more rapidly in diversified areas. Agriculture is one of the most promising fields, where applications of drones can be very effective and also can solve many problems of farming to increase overall efficiency of the farming process. The drone technology can be a game changer in agriculture by virtue of its surveillance capability for efficient crop monitoring and management. It can help in vertical field capture and crop monitoring. Drones using artificial intelligence (AI) are utilized in agriculture for soil and field analysis, planting, crop spraying, crop monitoring, irrigation and fertilizer application, health evaluation, and yield prediction. Drone-based agricultural solutions have a lot of potential in terms of dealing with bad weather, increasing production, precision farming, and yield prediction and management. For the agricultural scientists, the drone applications in crop management is a potential area for developing AI and ML based prognostic tools to increase the crop production and thus more profitability.

(vi) Soil and Field Analysis

A hybrid of digital technologies with drone and AI is very useful in real time soil analysis and fertility evaluation. The soil analysis to determine its macro nutrients, micro nutrients and fertility are some of the the crucial health parameters in determining the crop type and production. The use of drones or unmanned aerial vehicles (UAVs) can help with accurate soil mapping prior to crop sowing. The sensor-equipped drone creates exact 3-D maps for early soil research and planning for seed planting pattern. It also provides a 3-D field map of detailed terrain, drainage, soil viability, and irrigation prior to the crop cycle. Drone solutions can also be used to manage nitrogen levels. Figure 3.6 depict a drone equipped with a multispectral sensor for monitoring soil health. Drones can be used to make exact 3-D maps for early soil analysis, seed planting plan, and gather data for regulating irrigation and nitrogen levels in soil and field analysis. Drone-assisted soil analysis gives data for irrigation and nitrogen management after planting. Drone-planting technologies can drastically reduce the cost of planting. It is a step ahead in maximizing the use of agricultural inputs, and it dramatically lowers the cost of farming.

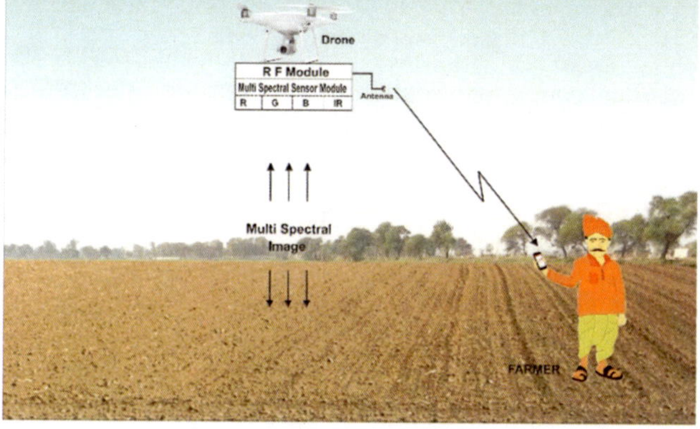

Fig. 3.6: Drone with Multispectral Sensor for Soil Health Monitoring

(vii) Crop Spraying

Aerial spraying of pesticides at appropriate and desired location of the crop area is an important aspect for its optimum utilization. Further, aerial spraying of pods containing seeds and plant fertilizers into the soil can be an effective means of precision farming, avoid excessive use of fertilizers and pesticides. It can lead to an efficient farm management with optimum resource utilization. Figure 3.7 depicts an aerial spraying drone that flies at a low altitude, approximately 3-5 meters above the ground, shooting pods containing seeds and fertilizers into the soil, delivering all the nutrients required for growing crops. The drone imaging sensors can scan the ground for crop spraying and spray in real time for a uniform coverage. The spraying conducted by drones are five times faster than traditional machinery for aerial spraying. Besides, drones can be programmed to spray liquids by varying the distance between them and the ground based on the topography. It can be utilized for personalized fertilization and can help to prevent the overuse of chemical fertilizer.

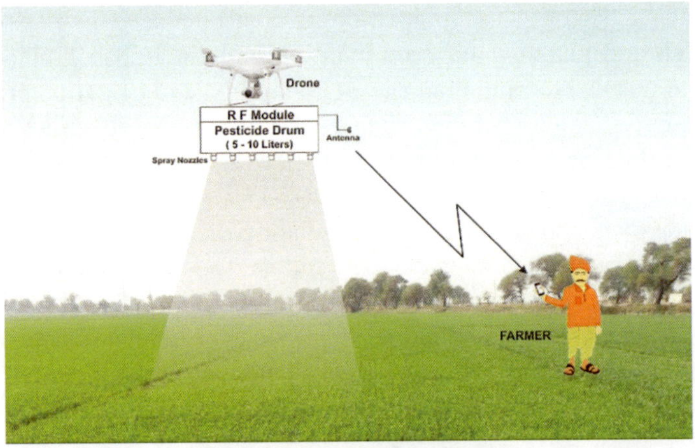

Fig. 3.7: Aerial Spraying Drone

The altitude of the drone can be altered with remote operation as per sight specific needs that are as per the change in topography and geography avoiding collisions. This is possible by using distance-measuring devices like ultrasonic echoes and lasers devices as used in the Light Detection and Ranging (LIDAR) approach. As a result, drones can scan the ground and spray the appropriate amount of liquid, regulating distance from the ground and spraying in real time to ensure even coverage. As a result, efficiency is improved and the amount of chemicals that enter groundwater is reduced. In fact, drones can perform aerial spraying up to five times faster than traditional technology and it is more effective in coverage.

(viii) Crop Surveillance and Monitoring

By using drone-based solutions combined with artificial intelligence and computer vision technologies, it is possible to make crop monitoring and health assessment solutions extremely accurate and effective. Figure 3.8 depicts a drone used to monitor crop yields. Sensor drones can identify which areas of a field are dry or in need of improvement in agriculture irrigation or fertilization. It can even predict which parts of the crop will begin to dry up and accordingly decide irrigation schedule.

The multispectral and hyper spectral images captured by drone cameras can be converted in to false color composites. The images can also be obtained by the remote sensing satellites. The satellite imagery although provides the most advanced type of crop surveillance and monitoring, however, the images must be ordered ahead of time and can only be taken once per day, are less exact, and have lower resolution. Furthermore, such imaging services are expensive, and the quality of the images is also compromised at times due to poor weather conditions. Drone imaging, therefore, is relatively inexpensive and produces high-resolution imaging, allowing real time and more accurate and precise analysis of the crop. This helps in crop monitoring periodically and forecasting its yield.

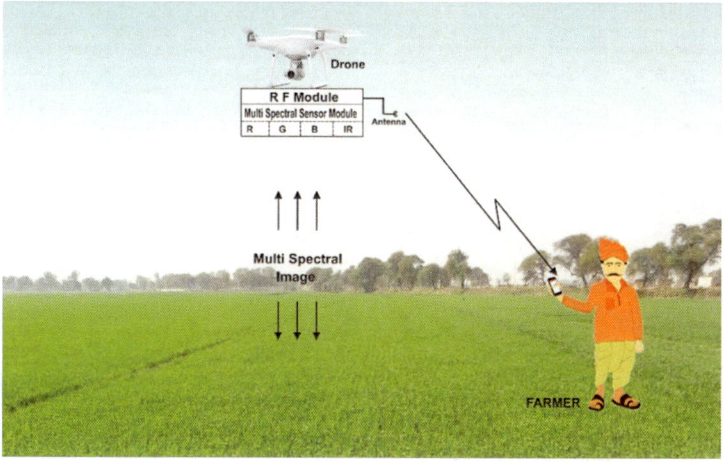

Fig. 3.8: Drone for Crop yield Monitoring using Multispectral Imaging

In crop surveillance and health assessment, the drones used are generally equipped with multi spectral sensors, scans the entire crop field in a short duration. It is quite cost effective and efficient method of real time continuous monitoring of crop. The multi spectral sensors captures the images and generates data in the visible and near-infrared bands, exposing changes in plants, indicating their health, and alerting farmers to disease or insect attack. To identify regions with weeds, pests, and crop counting, high-resolution precision field photos are put via a convolution neural network image processing method. It also warns about locations with useful crops in need of water, as well as the plant stress level at mid-growth stage. In the case of sick plants, multispectral images can be generated utilizing drone devices by scanning crops in both RGB and near-infrared light. This allows quick identification of plants which have been adversely affected as well as their position in a large field so that corrective measures can be applied immediately. The spatial information system for acres of land is defined by multi spectral images, which integrate hyper spectral photos with 3D scanning techniques. Drone photos of pest identification and crop counting are shown in Figure 3.9. The temporal component provides direction for the plant's full lifecycle. Drones, when used in conjunction with soil sensors, can provide a 3D GPS accurate representation of the field and data that the human eye cannot see. Drone surveillance is substantially faster when the typical farm size is in the hundreds of acres. The drones can cover a substantial portion of ground in a shorter amount of time than its manual counterparts, allowing big farms to be regularly and effectively inspected. The aerial imaging of crops with high precision provide a far better perspective of the crop for pest monitoring, water leak detection, and crop counting to estimate the yield.

Fig. 3.9: Drone images showing Pest Detection and Crop Counting [Courtesy: J.G.A Barbedo]

Further, the drones equipped with hyper spectral, multispectral, and thermal sensors can detect areas of a crop field that are dry or in need of improvement through irrigation and other remedial measures. Drones also enable for the calculation of the vegetation index, which describes the relative density and health of the crop, as well as the display of the heat signature, which is the amount of energy or heat emitted by the crop.

4

Internet of Things

4.1 Introduction

Internet of Things (IoT) is networking of physical objects, devices, machines, systems etc to interconnect each other for exchanging data through standard internet protocols. The IoT is also termed as Machine-to-Machine (M-to-M) communication. The term 'Things' in IoT includes objects embedded with sensors, actuators, mobile phones, routers, hubs, computers, wearable's and smart devices etc. The definition of IoT changes with its evolution and according to the IEEE, IoT is defined in two ways (i) definition for small-scale framework and (ii) definition for large-scale framework. In case of small-scale framework, IoT is defined as a technology forming a network by which uniquely identifiable 'Things' could connect to the Internet. These 'Things' may vary from sensing devices to potential programs with capabilities like sensing, collecting, screening, storing, transmitting, receiving, altering, modification, and perfecting of data. Under this definition, the received information in the form of data about the 'Things' will be stored and the present state and working of the 'Things' can be altered from anywhere, anytime and by any means." In case of large-scale framework, IoT is defined as a self-conFigured, adaptive, complex network that connects 'Things' to the Internet. These interlinked objects/things have physical as well as virtual depiction in the digital network with sensing capability, programmable attributes and are unique in identity. These are depicted in the form of information such as thing's/device's identity, location, current status, or other relevant information.

The IoT is growing day by day with the increment in number of machines globally and also due to technical advancement in the hardware as well as software technologies. It is estimated that by the year 2025, there would be 75 billion interconnected devices through IoT network for worldwide specific tasks and applications. The IoT technology brings innovation that will develop interaction among smart devices and humans, attaining the goal of smart cities introducing advanced infrastructure, smart agriculture, smart health care, improving the quality of life and supports better use of available resources.

The IOT technology can warn you about future through predictions. It can be used for monitoring and evaluation of system, device, operation and function as per required farming tasks.

4.2 History

In 1926, Nikola Tesla envisaged the idea of "Connected World" in an interview for the Colliers Magazine. After the invention of Internet in 1983, the communication among the devices increased at an enormous speed which attracted many scientists and researchers to connect the various devices with each other via internet for data analysis and knowledge extraction. Kevin Ashton in 1999 introduced the term "Internet of Things" (IoT) during a RFID (Radio-Frequency Identification) presentation and quoted "if we develop this system having computers and devices to connect through internet then it's easy to manage, track, repair and replace services more efficiently without the consent of manual power which can reduce waste, cost and loss". Also in 1999, Gershenfeld in his work explained a phrase "When Things start to Think" i.e. Things can access Internet without manual command (Hassan 2018)

A simple example of IoT is ATM (Automated Teller Machine) introduced in 1967, later it became the first one to access the Internet in 1974 by itself. Another example is vending machine generally used in stores. In 1990, John Romkey developed the first smart toaster that was connected to Internet and presented his work in Interop conference. Since then, IoT has started evolving, applicable in different domains such as industries, health sector, transportation, defense, agriculture, education, automation, homes and so on. In the year 2000, LG proposed a plan for wifi compatible refrigerator, this would be one of the first smart-home objects. Later in the year 2003, many renowned companies started using term "IoT" in place of "M2M" (Machine to Machine) communication as in; IoT sim cards in place of M2M sim cards. In 2008, IPSO (Internet Protocol for Smart Objects) was formed for implementing new innovative ideas in the field of IoT. "IPv6 (Internet Protocol version 6)", the latest version of internet is released in the year 2011 after IPv4, this became the turning point in the era of IoT.

Just after that, in 2013/2014 sensors were implemented in IoT network for home automation to control thermal state, lighting, garage doors, etc. by using mobile phones. After that a revolution in the field of IoT has started and humans are going towards achieving smart cities and smart industries goals through IoT (An example of first IoT city is Dublin). Therefore, future of IoT is huge and a lot of things are yet to be achieved as it is in growing stage.

4.3 Wireless Sensor Network (WSN)

A collection of sensors or sensor nodes interconnected wirelessly not only to each other but also to a central base station through a standard radio frequency is called Wireless Sensor Network (WSN). A wireless sensor network is formed when several sensors work together to monitor huge physical areas or ecosystem. The WSNs are capable of monitoring physical parameters such as humidity, temperature, pressure, pollutants, noise, flow-rate or motion etc. There is no need of any special infrastructure for Wireless Sensor Networks and it is a network with feature like self-configuration. Fig. 4.1 depicts Basic Wireless Sensor Network architecture. It collects the physical parameters from an open environment and send it first to the sink node or router (generally known as "base station") where data is aggregated and analyzed. This sink acts as a gateway for user to access the sensor network data. If end-user got some query then, it is resolved by sending commands and inputs through the personal computer via sink to the sensor field. The communication between base station/sink and user may be direct, or by using the Internet, satellite, or other wireless medium.

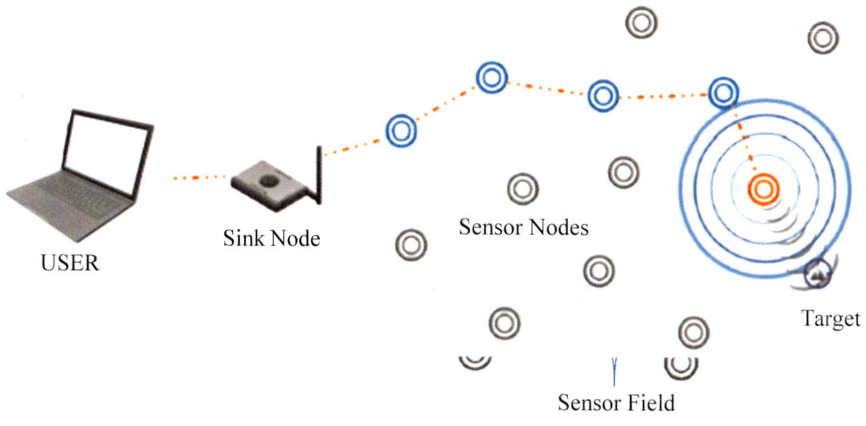

Fig. 4.1: Elements of Wireless Sensor

In any Wireless Sensor Network, there may be more than one end user and also more than one base station. Any typical WSN system consists of numerous sensor nodes (most probably in hundreds and thousands) connected to sink that may or may not be connected to Internet. These sensing devices have inbuilt battery supply, microcontroller, transceiver, and memory which are then connected to a processing unit. But these sensor nodes are resource constrained because of limited memory, battery life, speed and channel bandwidth. These nodes send radio signals to each other for intra communication. As we know this network is self-conFigured, so after deploying them in a wireless medium they organize themselves and communicate with multi-hop technique most of the times.

IoT versus WSN

In a Wireless Sensor Network, sensors are not directly connected to the Internet. Although they can connect with the Internet through a base station/sink node/ router. User can access the data by communicating with the router (central node). Also, WSN technology may or may not have Internet connection all the time. The internet is an integral part of IoT systems. It means to be an IoT system it must be connected to Internet all the time. As a result, all 'things' directly share the information with the cloud. For example, when a temperature sensor collects the data of any physical body it immediately uploads the same information to the internet for further data analysis after which the data is processed by the server for further user interface. The things consist of sensors, personal computers, mobile phones, humans, etc.

WSN acts as a subset of IoT which may collect, reiterate and process data as per predetermined and pre-decided terms and conditions. As shown in Figure 4.2, it can be seen that WSN is a subset of IoT. WSN is said to be a part of IoT system because it is a network of sensors in a sensor field collecting the data and sending it to a router which is connected directly to the Internet in an IoT System.

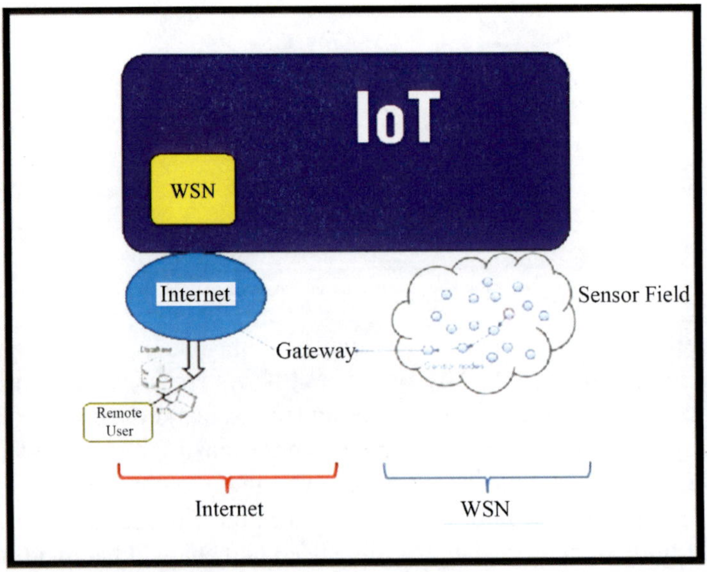

Fig. 4.2: Relationship between Internet of Things and Wireless Sensor Network

The term "Wireless Sensor Network" which clearly indicates that it only includes wireless devices or sensors to form a network, if there is any wired device in the network it is no more "Wireless Network". But in IoT, necessarily not all devices have to be wireless, in fact anything or any device that can directly connect to Internet is considered as IoT device whether it is wired or wireless. It can be explained with few more examples: If a refrigerator is connected directly to the internet for sending its temperature reading on a real time basis, then we can say it is an IoT device despite of being a wired object, but not considered as WSN device. One more example i.e. Number of humidity sensors form a network to collect the soil humidity on a regular basis for a large land area is considered as a "Wireless Sensor Network". Whole network of sensors is wireless but not necessarily connected to the Internet, therefore, it is not considered as an IoT system.

4.4 Building Blocks of Internet of Things

Basic building blocks of an elementary IoT system are: Sensors and Actuators, Processor, IoT Gateways, and Application area as shown in Figure 4.3.

(i) Sensors and Actuators: The sensors and actuators interact with the outside environment and sense the physical parameters like temperature, humidity, light intensity, force, density etc. and convert into corresponding digital values to be sent to microcontroller/processor. The controller/processor collects the information and transmits it to the cloud or server through network gateway. The cloud analyzes the information and stores it or sometimes when necessary it gives feedback to actuators for improved operations.

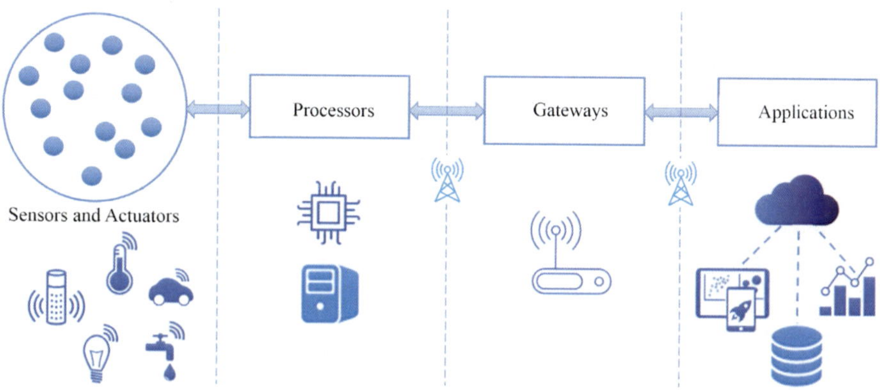

Fig. 4.3: Basic Building Blocks of IoT system

(ii) Processor: The Processor unit is the heart of the IoT system whichconsists of microcontroller, memory, Arithmetic Logic Unit, Peripheral devices, etc. to

perform some set of predefined operations through the command of instruction sets. All logical and mathematical operations, read/write operations and data transmission is controlled and performed by processing unit.

(iii) Gateways: The Gateways are used to connect IoT devices with other devices and server. The Protocol transformation is also performed by IoT gateways. If any device transmits and receive data through Zigbee Technology, then it will use Zigbee protocol to communicate. Other protocol used for network communication is TCP-IP. In some cases, where both protocols are used then there is need of a gateway which can transform the information transmitted from the device using Zigbee protocol to the information in TCP-IP protocol used by another IoT device or server, also information received from cloud/ server having TCP-IP protocol is changed into Zigbee protocol used by the IoT device. These type of gateways are known as two-way bridge for the networks.

(iv) Applications: It consists of units such as cloud/server, data analytics, smart devices (i.e. tablets, mobiles, and computers). The cloud acts as edge of the IoT architecture. The task of cloud is to collect and store the data accessed from various IoT devices, later for which it can perform analysis and mining of data to extract knowledge from it for better performance. It plays an important role in IoT technology and manages the devices, communication networks, machine to machine communication, perfect data and continuously monitoring system and predicts or forecast for making system simple, convenient and efficient. Any cloud can interact with other cloud whether it is private or public. The knowledge extraction made by cloud is further used for better performance of IoT devices through application available on the web or smart devices. Other than that these applications help in manipulating the data and providing positive feedbacks to the devices without the human consent. For example, home automation using IoT technology consists of sensors that can process the data and give commands through the help of knowledgeable data cloud to all the devices connected to it.

4.4.1 Layered Architecture of Internet of Things

There are so many ideas given by the researchers about the architecture of IoT globally. Different researchers bring different types of architectures. Two basic types of architectures are Three-layer and Five-layer architectures. Other two types of system architectures are Cloud and Fog architectures.

(i) Three-Layer and Five-Layer architectures: In three-layer architecture, the three layers are: application layer, network layer and perception layer as shown in Figure 4.4 (i).

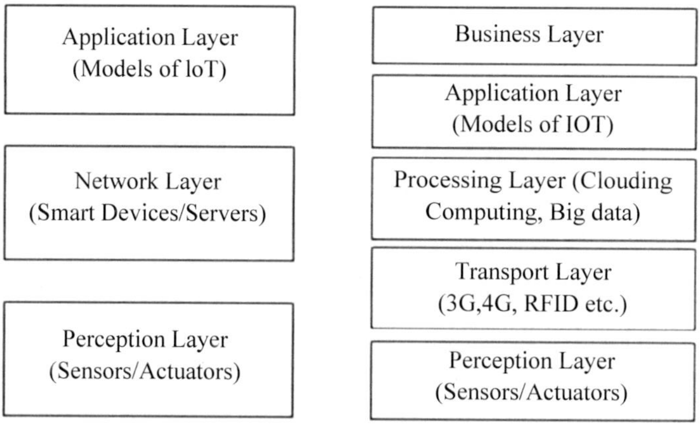

(i) **(ii)**

Fig 4.4: Basic architecture of Internet of Things (i) Three-Layer (ii) Five-Layer

a) **Perception layer:** It consists of physical objects and data collected by such objects, i.e. sensors, actuators. It senses the data of different parameters like temperature, pressure, flow rate and humidity, gathered by objects (sensors) from the physical environment and further process it in digital form and hand over to next layer which is networklayer.

b) **Network layer:** It assures about the connectivity of the IoT system. All objects are interconnected within this layer such as smart devices, gateways, servers, internet, cloud, routers, etc. Also data is transmitted, received and processed under this layer.

c) **Application layer:** This layer is capable of providing thedata about the specific task performed by dedicated application to the end user. IoT is deployed in various application specific fields such as medical, education, home automation, industry, automobiles, smart city infrastructure, etc., so the user can access any of these services via application layer.

Since three-layer architecture does not provide the complete idea about the utilization of this technology, researchers have proposed architecture based on five layers which has two more layers named as business layer and processing layer. This includes five layers which are business, application, processing, transport and perception layers, as shown in Figure 4.4(ii). Features of two newly added layers are explained below:

a) Transport layer: It manages the transport of sensor data between perception and processing layer, for example; 3G/4G, Bluetooth, NFC, RFID, etc.

b) Processing layer: Main task of processing layer is to process and analyze the data coming from transport layer. This layer is also named as middleware layer. It provides different services to layers present at lower level. Various technologies supported by this layer such as cloud- computing and big-data.

c) Business layer: The business layer performs as a manager for all applications and whole IoT system. It takes care of models of IoT, its applications and privacy of the end user. If in any case this layer becomes vulnerable, then there are chances of attacks (i.e. business logic attack and zero-day attack) on security and privacy because of the weak business logic.

(ii) Cloud and Fog based layered architectures: In previous section (i), layers of IoT architecture is based on protocols which barely gives the information about nature of data processing. So to know in detail about the data processing we require cloud based architecture. For this purpose, we need cloud computers as center of the system. In this system cloud is present in the center with application layer and network of things layer above and below it respectively. Cloud computing is used because of its two main features viz; flexibility and scalability. Due to presence of these features it can support variety of IoT services like storage of information, analysis of data, various software, platforms, and infrastructure. Cloud computing also supports machine learning, visualization, data analytics for better knowledge extraction and information gathering. IoT needs Cloud based architecture because of ambiguous type of data collected and sensed by IoT devices. The Figure 4.5

(i) Shows data processing nature in Cloud based layered architecture of IoT. Another six layered architecture based on fog computing shown in Figure 4.5(ii), where data processing and analysis is made by sensors and gateways. A Fog architecture of IoT has six layers which are transport, security, storage, pre-processing, monitoring, and physical layers arranged from top to bottom. One which monitors the system aspects like power, resources, services required by user, responses from the user, etc. is known as monitoring layer. The next layer which is pre-processing layer does all the filtration job for further processing and for analyzing the sensor data. This processed data is then stored on a temporary basis in storage layer in required format and then sent to the destinations according to their protocols. The security layer takes care of the security and privacy of the data throughout the transmission in a fog based IoT system with the help of encoding and decoding of the data. Before transferring the data to the cloud it is monitored and pre-processed at the edge of the network gateway just after the physical layer. Fog based architecture is more advance than cloudarchitecture.

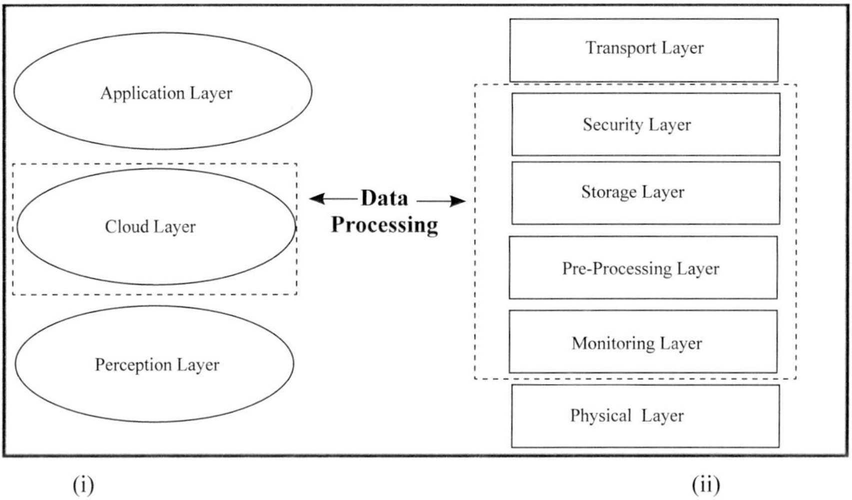

Fig. 4.5: (i) Cloud and (ii) Fog based layered architecture with Data Processing for Internet of Things

"Fog computing" and "Edge computing" both are similar, some companies like Cisco originally provides the name "Fog computing" which indicates smart sensors and gateways. The "Edge computing" term basically refers to the data's pre-processing in such smart devices which are available at the edge of the network. Therefore, the architecture of edge computing is similar to the fog computing, hence, the protocol based and system based architectures are not differentiated in any way, in fact they both are co-designed and go hand in hand. The five-layer architecture is considered as a base for both fog and cloud based architectures.

4.4.2 Classification of IoT Based on Communication Network

(i) Cellular Network (3G/4G/5G): Cellular networks use mobile networks for communication with IoT devices and these networks are used for smart phones. Since this network is specially designed for power consuming sources like smart phones, it is not considered good for IoT devices. More technologies were developed which were used for IoT cases since they were more suitable for IoT. Nowadays Cellular network becomes much prevalent and is considered safe, secured and reliable source of communication in IoT technology. So many sites in the U.S. are connected with wireless cellular networks such as Basements, Wardrobes, Shaft of Elevator because these are some important areas which are always out of connectivity, so with IoT devices one can get access of them anytime anywhere.

Latest wireless protocols like Long Term Evolution (LTE)-M and Narrow Band IoT (NB-IoT) are dominating the cellular network in the domain of low power devices. LTE-M network has already started in some countries like U.S.

The NB-IoT is also hyped all around the world for its better performance in low power devices, consumes less battery power, but it is costly in the recent times.

(ii) Local Area Network and Personal Area Network (LAN/PAN): Local Area Network (LAN) and Personal Area Networks (PAN) are those networks that cover short distance with low cost. These wireless networks are those commonly used with IoT technology for Bluetooth and Wireless Fidelity (WiFi). A large network with many access points in any locally distributed topology is considered as WiFi. The drawback of WiFi is that it only provides signal till you are closer to the access point and also it consumes more energy. Efficiency of Bluetooth is a more than WiFi. Although very less amount of data can be transmitted in Bluetooth technology as compared to WiFi. Establishing connection through Bluetooth and WiFi is easier as compared to other wireless network protocols. Security is still an issue in WiFi networks.

(iii) Low Power Wide Area Networks (LPWAN): This network is responsible for long distance communication by transferring small data packets. To overcome the challenges, present in cellular network, this network is well developed for that purpose. Its range is longer than WiFi and Bluetooth and it also consumes less power comparatively both. First LPWAN network was developed by Sigfox, a French venture that initiates the LPWAN technology. An IoT network protocol used for this purpose is known as"LoRa WAN (Long Range Wireless Area Network)" used for "LoRa (Long Range) Communication". The benefits of this IoT based network protocol LoRa WAN is that it requires less power, provides longer battery life, cost effective, provides range upto some kilometers in urban areas and in rural areas ranges from 15kms to 30kms.

(iv) Mesh Networks: Unlike star topology (where all devices communicate with centralized hub to send the data), in mesh networks all devices can do communication with one another, there is no central hub where nodes can send data to reach the gateway/ border router. An example of mesh network topology is Zigbee wireless technology. They are meant for short range communication. For long range transmission they need repeaters or extra circuitry. They consume some extra power but advantages of this network are that they are robust, reliable, get easily installed, most popularly used in buildings for communication.

4.5 Applications of Internet of Things

The potential of IoT applications is high as compared to other wireless network applications. The areas of applications covered under the IoT is shown in Figure 4.6. It includes Medical field, Industries, Transportation, Smart Environment (City, Infrastructure, Agriculture, etc.) and defense. These IoT applications also exhibit necessary features required for better performance such as Energy efficiency, Security, Scalability, Mobility and Reliability. Following are the general applications of IoT:

(i) Medical Field: The IoT has put a huge impact in the field of healthcare sector with great potential. Some examples of contribution of IoT in medical field are real time monitoring of patient's health status, ease of emergency services, detection of emergency situation at real time basis, monitoring of cleanliness in hospital, etc. Medical field has some requirements from IoT like security, mobility, real time monitoring, reliability, quick responses etc. Real time monitoring is necessary in emergency services and security is required when it comes to saving patient's general information and ongoing treatment. Mobility is also important factor while operating, when devices are mobile. The reliability of the system ensures correct judgment like detecting location of nearby clinics and hospitals, calling ambulance services, getting history of patients. Elderly care, disabled person care, abnormal person care, etc. are also important aspects of IoT enabled healthcare system. This system is also applicable for animal healthcare and vet services. Thus IOT can be used in medical field for testing, tracing, tracking, treatment and teamwork continuously on larger scale. Many scientists are working to judge future health of person based on present health status and parameters of a person by taking few tests and measuring parameters related to blood, cell, DNA and other general body parameters. For diabetic and heart patients, there is a need to continuously monitor health of human being so that any unforeseen circumstances can be overcome to a greater extent. In this context, IOT can play important role in monitoring and testing of health parameters of a patient.

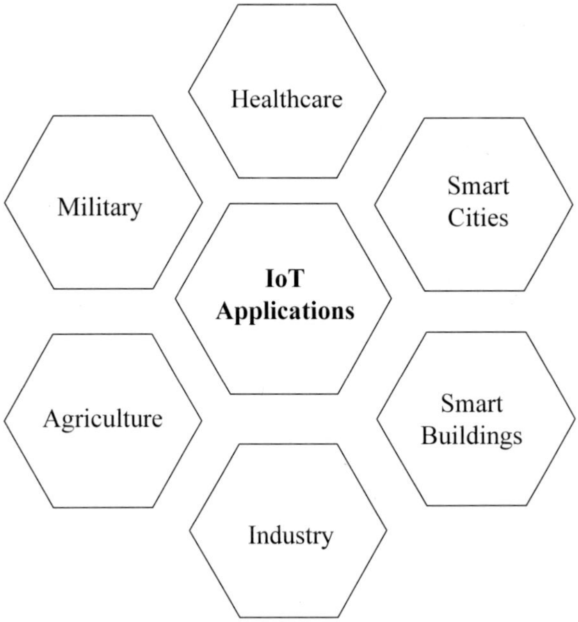

Fig. 4.6: Applications of Internet of Things

(ii) Smart Environment: Environment means land, air, and water. IoT can be used to supervise complete ecosystem of the environment. It includes smart infrastructure, agriculture, cities, etc. Area under these applications is very large that requires mobility management, reliability, security, energy consumption. Security is an essential feature used in applications related to smart buildings. In agriculture, IOT can be used for crop monitoring and forecasting crop yield and quality of crop produce.

(iii) Transportation: In transport sector sensors are deployed to control traffic so that heavy congestion could be avoided. IOTs can be used to give alarms to driver on road to get rid of nearby traffic. Sensor nodes need to collect data depending upon total number of vehicles, also their task is to sense the emergencies on the road like accidents, faults in street lights, traffic signals, pot holes on the surface of road. Latest technology trend evolved in transport sector is self-assisted driving cars which use IoT Technology including embedded devices for detecting the lane position, emergency brakes, touch sensors, cameras and auto parking enabled mode. In future, because of IOT, road accidents shall be minimized along with quick drive thereby shall saving of fuel and time.

(iv) Smart Industries: The IoT has been growing rapidly since last decade in the industrial sector. A lot of work in industries is done by automation and robotics technology. Industrial applications use control system in which sensor nodes monitor the environment of surroundings and then collect data for providing full automation with the help of actuators. IoT can be used for making industrial action simple, convenient and efficient. An example of this control system having closed loop is smart grid application. Smart Power grid is used with WSN as well IoT for power generation in renewable energy applications. Solar Panels, Smart metering and turbines play key role in Smart Power Grid Industries. Transparent services to users are provided with the help of remote sensing and real time monitoring which allow consumers to detect power supply usage by them. Power failures, energy generation, consumption, faults in grid line etc. can also be detected under this application of IoT.

(v) Defence: IoT plays a key role in Military or defence technology. Here saving energy is a main feature, because in a war field it is impossible to charge the battery in remote and dangerous areas. Deploying sensor nodes in the war zone helps military to detect position of enemies and weapons so that it can save energy and life of soldiers. Disaster Prevention, data Surveillance, Navigation, and Robotic intervention are some features of Military applications. Soldiers use the IoT enabled wearable's to detect physical state of the body as well as mapping and detecting hazardous situation. IOT is a step forward for fairness, effectiveness, transparency, objectivity, and inclusiveness in defense system, which is the present need for proper security, safety and surveillance.

4.6 IoT in Agriculture

Internet of Things (IoT) is an emerging digital technology which finds extensive applications in agricultural sectors. The IoT with hybrid of digital technologies has tremendous potential and scope for improving crop monitoring, yields, profitability, and farming techniques. The advancement and rapid growth of sensor technology and the availability of high accuracy sensors pertaining to farm machineries has further raised the scope of IoT enabled sensors for precision farming. The deployment of appropriate sensors on the farm and farm equipment, can provide real-time data of relevant farming operations, soil parameters, crop diseases, irrigation, fertilizers etc. These sensor data are analyzed using computer software tools and artificial intelligence algorithms for taking corrective and preventive actions. Precision agriculture, also known as precision farming, is one of the most well-known IoT applications in agriculture. Smart farming applications such as animal monitoring, vehicle tracking, field observation, and inventory monitoring help to make farming more precise and controlled. Precision farming's purpose is to analyze data supplied by sensors and react accordingly. Precision farming techniques like land preparation and sowing, irrigation management, intercultural operation and harvesting, livestock management, vehicle tracking, and many more help to increase the efficiency and effectiveness of the agriculture industry. Precision farming powered by IoT can assist farmers in generating data using sensors and analyzing that data to make educated and timely decisions. There are great opportunities in agriculture field for collection of data in different on-farm applications and subsequently analysis of data and finally inference of work for increasing its applications. The IoT has been applied at a number of places for fertilization and irrigation management and deciding when to irrigate, how to irrigate, and how much to irrigate. Results of crop monitoring and evaluation is not only useful for increasing productivity and production but also maintaining good quality of crop produce, higher remuneration, sustainable development, climate friendly agriculture and trading for more revenue per unit area.

The IoT enabled irrigation equipments will be able to monitor and control farm operations more efficiently in terms of resource utilization such as fertilizers, seeds, and water. Further, it can monitor farm conditions in real time using IoT sensors-based smart farming solutions. This helps farmers in detecting irregularities, reducing operational problems, and increasing efficiency. In IoT network, the data from sensors can be exchanged with stakeholders through a local server or the cloud in sensor-based precision agriculture. These data are accessed via smart phones, and user- friendly apps that can be used to represent it in a simple and clear format. The key benefits of using IoT are increased crop yields at a lower cost of production. According to research, adopting IoT on a farm increases agricultural output by 1.75 percent, reduces energy expenditures by 17 to 32 percent per hectare, and reduces irrigation water use by 8%. It is anticipated that by 2050, the Internet of Things will have increased agricultural production by 70%. India is a big country with enormous potential for sensor and IoT-based crop fields and the generation of massive sensor data that may be used for effective crop surveillance and management, soil health management, decision-making, and food supply chain management.

4.6.1 IoT Enabled Soil Health Monitoring

The physical and physiological changes that occur during an agricultural crop's journey from seed germination to harvesting are numerous. The soil parameters like soil moisture, temperature, nitrogen (N), phosphorus (P), potassium (K), sulphur (S), electrical conductance, organic carbon, micro-organism concentration, salinity etc determine the health of the soil and play a decisive role to get a healthy agriculture crop with maximal productivity. The real-time information of soil parameters revealing soil health may be of vital importance for the prognosis of adversity, if any, in soil parameters. The real time information of soil parameters to the end users (farmers) help avoiding over-use or under-use of resources like water and fertilizers, leading to optimal resource utilization. The Figure 4.7 shows block diagram of IoT enabled soil health monitoring system. It is powered by a solar panel mounted on its top, charging the battery through a controller. The sensors are buried in the soil at appropriate depth and are physically connected to an IoT subscriber identity module (SIM) card. The IoT SIM card is interfaced with IoT gateway module which transmits all sensor data to far end cloud server.

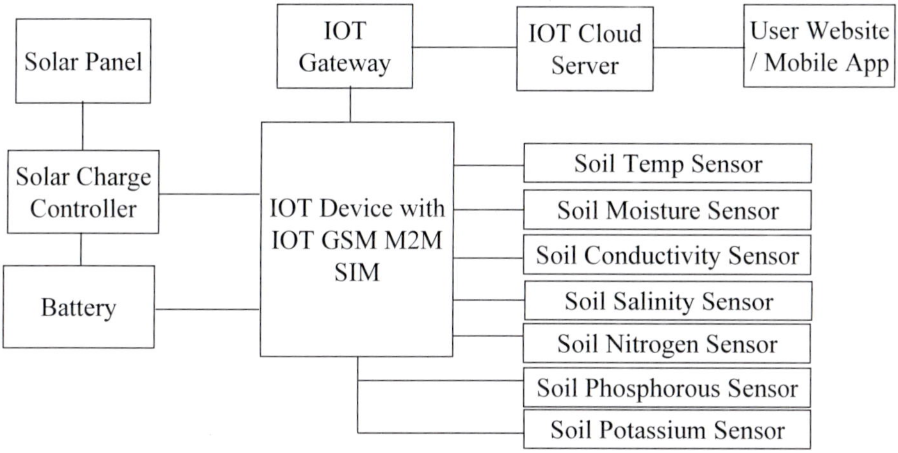

Fig. 4.7: Block diagram of IoT enabled Soil Health Monitoring System

Fig. 4.8: IoT enabled Soil Health Monitoring System [Courtesy: MPUAT, Udaipur]

The cloud server is accessed either by a 'Mobile App' or on its website to get real time information of soil and also is used to send advisories to the users. The Figure 4.8 shows the pictorial view of on-the-farm deployment of IoT enabled solar powered soil health monitoring system developed by Maharana Pratap University of Agriculture and Technology, Udaipur. It measures real time soil parameters: moisture, temperature, nitrogen (N), phosphorus (P), potassium, electrical conductance and salinity The system provides hourly soil data on mobile as well as on local server for further analysis. The cloud shares soil data to the users and is capable of sending alert messages and advisories. The real time soil data are extremely useful for research experiments exploring effect of soil status on the crop. Also it can give alert messages and advisories for over use or under use of water and fertilizers facilitating optimum resource utilization. Many scientists have predicted the attack of pests and insects on crops. The observations based on real time fertilizer monitoring in soil coupled with future pests and insects attack can decide efficient operation and way forward for higher yield.

4.7 Limitations of Internet of Things

(i) Security Challenges: If various types of nodes are added in any IoT network then there is possibility that some of them would be malicious and could distort and hamper the data packets. So many attacks on IoT network might be possible to hack the system. With the increase in security breaches in IoT, the security of system becomes major field of concern and research should be done on high level to reach the goal of having secure IoT network.

(ii) Connectivity issues: When there are numerous nodes want to connect within a network, the system model needed advanced network structure with stable connection. In recent times, there is dependency on a server which authenticates and authorizes the nodes which want to connect in an IoT network. As per required criteria and increment in users' population day by day, there will be a challenge of connectivity within IoT network to connect billions of devices without any intervention. In such cases the centralized server become an obstacle and slows downthe whole communication process. To overcome this hurdle, a major cloud server is required to tackle the situation. If the centralized server fails, then cloud server take over the communication process.

(iii) Longevity and Compatibility: As IoT is growing at very fast rate, various technologies want to become a part of it. In this situation, the extra hardware and software are needed for better compatibility with the IoT network. Some other requirements for new networks are protocol compatibility, good M2M communication, new cloud services, etc. which become the bottleneck for the IoT technology.

(iv) Functional innovativeness: As IoT is based on collection of reliable and valid data from wide spectrum of sphere and then incorporating appropriate analytical techniques for interpretation of data and finally, the biggest challenge is to go back to original system and presenting the developed technology based on decision and organisation of system to attain higher efficiency in a simpler and convenient manner. In this whole process, there are a number of functional and professional difficulties in real time arrangement.

5

Virtual Reality, Augmented Reality and Mixed Reality

5.1 Introduction

The human civilization and environmental eco-system are the two most important components of real world. The technology intervention to safeguard human civilization and the environment has always been the foremost priority of scientific and engineering community through their innovative expeditions. In real world, there are two aspects of reality: unseen reality which does exist but is not physically or economically accessible and cannot be experienced either due to its complexity, its microscopic nature or due to human or environmental limitations; and second, non-existing reality (fiction or animated) which is imaginary but constructive and creative, which illustrates a system or process hypothetically, and may or may not become a reality in future. The question is how to portray and sense an existing unseen (inaccessible) reality and non- existing reality to create a sensation of real world. The answer lies in immersive technologies called Virtual Reality (VR), Augmented Reality (AR), Mixed Reality (MR) or Extended Reality (ER). The VR serves as foundation of AR and MR, which are advanced versions of VR and give sensation of more closeness to the reality. With these technologies, it is possible to feel and sense experience of reality without physical presence in that real world. Such type of an artificial experience is of vital importance in understanding very complex systems in a simpler manner and also to experience a physically unrealizable or inaccessible environment or objects. It is a step forward for understanding a complex system in simple way for creating a real awareness and finally bridging gap between its reality and potential.

5.2 Virtual Reality (VR)

It is the creation of an emulated (or simulated) experience with sensation of reality which may be similar to or completely different from real world. The term "virtual" acronym of 'actual' has been used in the computer sense of "not physically existing but made to appear by software" since 1959. The term "artificial reality" coined by Myron W. Krueger, has been in use since 1970.

The word "virtual reality" was first used in a science fiction context by Damien Broderick's 1982 novel 'The Judas Mandala'. The virtual reality can be treated as an artificial world that is virtually created using combined techniques of optics, acoustics and computer software. A person using virtual reality equipment is able to look around the artificial world, move around in it, understand the process and interact with virtual features or items for the purpose of gaining knowledge, skill, ability, and sharing experiences relatedto particular subject matter.

The VR systems provide realistic visuals, sounds, and other sensations that imitate a user's physical presence in a virtual environment using virtual reality headsets or multi-projected settings. VR headsets with a small screen in front of the eyes are usually used to get this effect, but it can also be achieved in specially constructed rooms with several huge screens. The Common applications of VR includes: Video games, 3D cinema, Sporting Events, Fine arts, Agriculture, Manufacturing industry, Medical Sciences, Education, Training and extension, Flight simulators, Architectural design, Bridge inspection etc. It is also used in modelling of the real environment such as robot navigation, construction modelling, and airplane simulation. Image-based virtual reality systems have been gaining popularity in computer graphics and computer vision communities. It is critical to precisely register collected 3D data while creating realistic models; typically, a camera is employed to model small objects at a short distance. Simulation-based virtual reality is one way for achieving virtual reality. For example, 'Driving simulators' provide the onboard driver, the feeling of actually driving an actual car by predicting vehicular motion triggered by user input and providing visual, motion, and audio cues.

5.2.1 Components of VR Systems

The VR system is developed with the aim to replace real environment and objects by digital versions usually by means of head mounted display and spatial sound. The main components required for creating VR and to experience VR contents are: 360 VR Camera, VR Camera Software and VR Glass. The 360 VR camera as shown in Figure 5.1 which is a special 360 Camera having 8- Lens to capture 360 Videos and Photos and that can be transferred to VR Glasses for Virtual Experience.

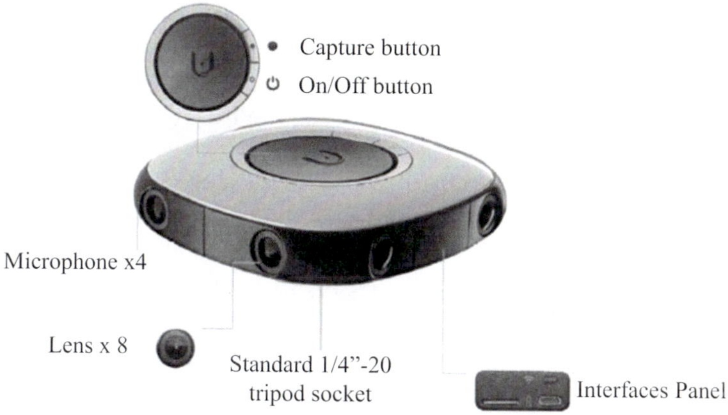

Fig. 5.1: VR 360 Camera (*Courtesy*: VUZE)

It is interfaced with a Mobile App and the switching ON and OFF functions is operated through 'Mobile App' by a remote user to capture video or images of the real world for which VR contents are to be created. The VR camera unit is embedded with large memory to record and store contents up to few hours.

Fig. 5.2: VR Camera Software (*Courtesy*: VUZE)

The second important component for creating VR contents is VR Camera Software as shown in Figure 5.2. It is a software tool used for mixing and editing the camera recorded files to prepare VR content ready for the display. The common types of the software used for VR editing and mixing are: Vuze VR Studio, Adobe Premier Pro, Filmora, Final Cut Pro X, Unity etc. The third and the most important component is the Head Mounted Display (HMD) or VR glass. A Head-Mounted Display is a display device worn on the forehead, such as a harness or helmet-mounted. It is a battery operated portable unit embedded with processor and having adequate memory as good as a small computer. Figure 5.3(a) shows a photograph and Figure 5.3 (b) and (c) show two isometric views of a VR glass. It appears like a head phone fitted with front lens assembly placed just in front of eyes, like binocular. Two embedded stereophonic speakers on left and right ears and a microphone in front are embedded with the VR glass to depict object virtually in more systematic manner. It is provided with USB port to interface with any other device. Touch pad buttons are provided for its different operations like volume control, selecting a VR file from the content list and displaying selected files. When a user wears VR glass on head, a screen is displayed just like a computer screen in front of eyes showing VR content files, Operating instructions and other information. It provides Three degrees of freedom (3DOF), a term often used in the context of virtual reality, refers to tracking of rotational motion in three orthogonal axes called as pitch, yaw, and roll.

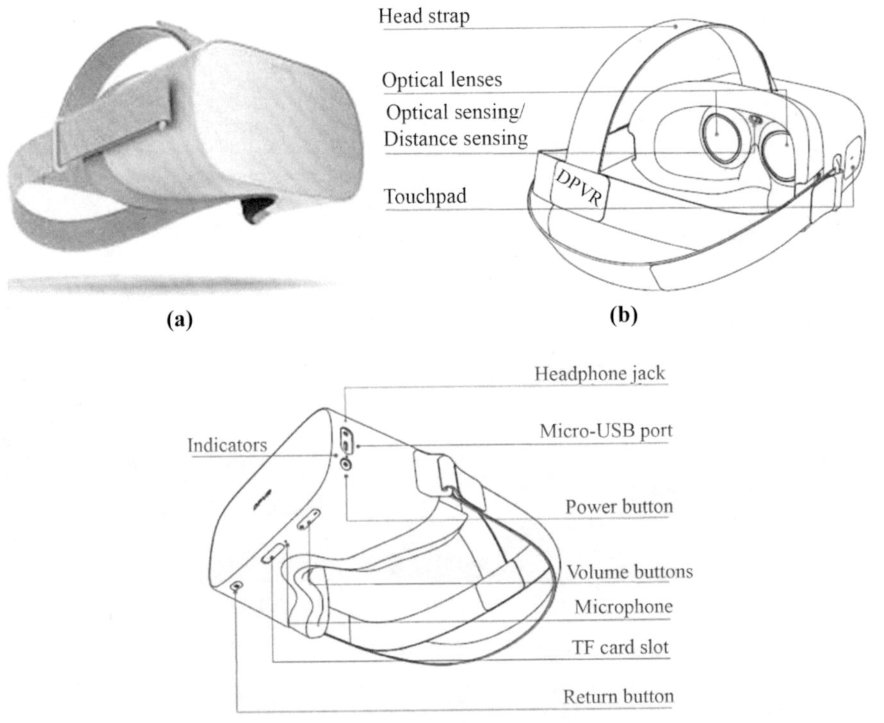

Fig. 5.3: VR Glass: **(a)** Photo View **(b)** Lens Assembly **(c)** Control Buttons (*Courtesy*: VUZE)

5.2.2 Steps to Create Virtual Reality Contents

Step-1: The 360 VR cameras is mounted on a tripod stand at appropriate height on real locations of which the VR contents to be created. The user moves away from the camera at a remote location and use Mobile App to switch ON camera to start shooting the real scene for the time already set in the cam as shown in Figure 5.4. The duration of recording may be adjusted as er requirement. The effectiveness of the camera of 360 degree arrangement is crucial for recording real scene and further processing.

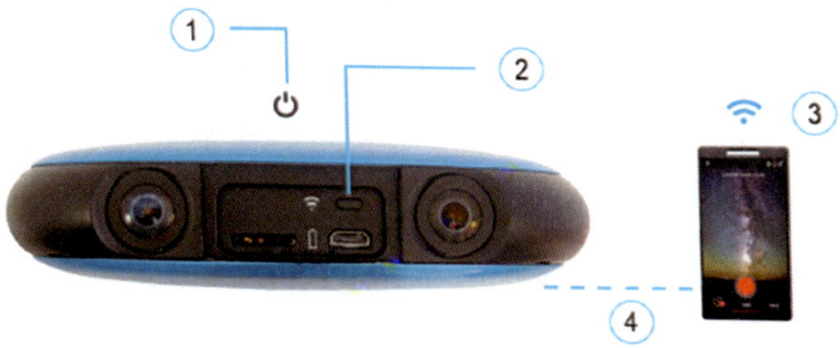

Fig. 5.4: Switching operation of VR Camera with Mobile (*Courtsey*: VUZE)

Step-2: After capturing the 360 video with camera, the process may be repeated at different relevant locations to create a sequence in the scene. Once the camera recording is completed the camera data are transported to Computer with a USB cable as shown in Figure 5.5.

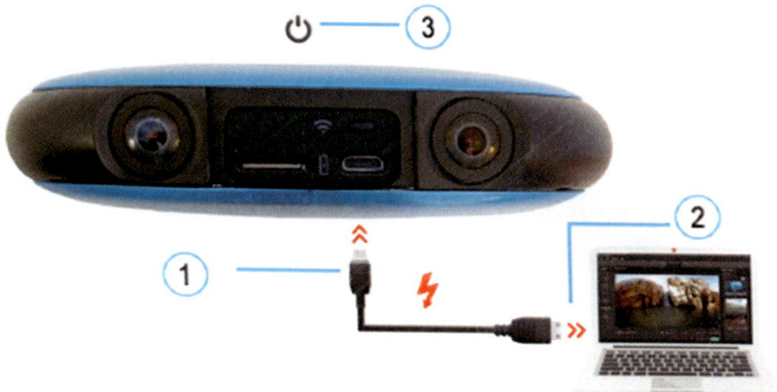

Fig. 5.5: Transportation of VR data of Camera to Computer (*Courtesy*: VUZE)

The camera data are stored in the computer memory and processed through a suitable software for mixing and editing the stored contents. Background voice or sound can also be added during this process to make content clearer and having a wide coverage. Now the VR content is ready for display.

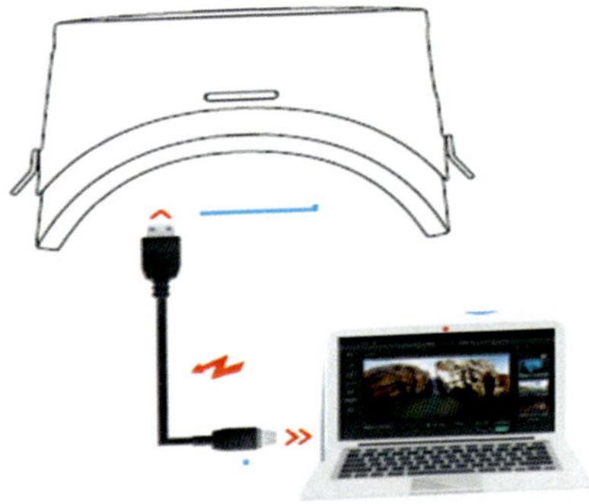

Fig. 5.6: Transfer of VR files from Computer to VR Glass

Step-3: The VR contents prepared through the software can be stored in computer memory similar to normal document files with a suitable title. The final step is to transport VR files from Computer to VR glass using a USB cable as shown in Figure 5.6. Even a SD memory card can also be used for this purpose. Once the files are transported from Computer to VR glass, it can be disconnected and now the VR glass is loaded with VR contents and ready to be used to experience virtual reality of the real world. At this stage VR glass can easily be transported from one place to user's choice.

5.3 Augmented Reality (AR)

Augmented reality (AR) is a type of virtual reality that aims to provide an interactive experience of a real-world environment in which objects in the real world are enhanced by computer-generated perceptual information, sometimes across multiple sensory modalities such as visual, auditory, haptic, and factory for demonstrating the entire system and its concept. The users' experience of reality in virtual reality (VR) is entirely reliant on virtual information based on digital settings. In augmented reality (AR), the user is given additional computer-generated information that improves their view of reality and allows them to track and forecast the future. The main benefit of augmented reality is how digital elements mix into a person's view of the actual world, not as a simple display of data, but as the integration of immersive sensations that are seen as natural features of an environment. The AR system combines real and virtual worlds, allows for real-time interaction, and allows for accurate multi-dimensional registration of virtual and real things. Basically, AR is overlaying of digital objects in to real environment. This is either made with a transparent screen on a head mounted display or by using a portable camera and monitor to render the object in to environment. Generally, it uses QR Code or floor sensing for placing the object in space. The superimposed sensory input might be beneficial (i.e., beneficial to the natural environment) or harmful (i.e., harmful to the natural environment) (i.e. masking of the natural environment). Augmented reality modifies one's continuing view of a real-world environment, whereas virtual reality totally replaces the user's real-world environment with a simulated one. AR contrasts from virtual reality (VR) in that some of the surrounding world is genuinely "real" in AR, whereas VR just adds layers of simulated things to the real environment. In VR, on the other hand, the environment is fully virtual. In a nutshell, virtual reality immerses users in a completely artificial digital environment, whereas augmented reality overlays virtual elements on the real-world environment with spatial registration that allows geometric persistence in terms of placement and orientation inside the actual world. The Common applications of Augmented Reality are: Archaeology, Architecture, Agriculture, Urban design and Planning, Industrial manufacturing, E-commerce, Visual Art, Remote collaboration, Healthcare, Flight training, Navigation, Broadcast and live events, Tourism etc. In addition to other digital technologies like AI, Bigdata, and IoT, farmers can use AR in agriculture to manage growing food demand, bridging gap between food demand and supply, increase production, productivity and profitability. Further, it can be used for training and capacity building to other farmers.

5.3.1 Components of AR Systems

The Figure 5.7 shows various components of AR system with functional interconnections. The Augmented Reality System is made up of three primary components: hardware, software, and a remote server. A processor, display, input devices, and sensors are the hardware component of AR-based devices. The processing sequence to create AR content is in the order:

(1) Sending real content captured by input device to the processor

(2) Processor requesting for virtual content from web server/cloud server

(3) Sending virtual objects from studio to processor

(4) Sending augmented contents to AR Browser/Application

(5) Display augmented content through display devices.

Hardware: The processor, sensors, input devices, and display devices are the essential hardware components of any AR-based system. A monitor, smart phone, mobile device, eyeglasses, or head-mounted displays might all be used as displays (HMD). The input device is either a Smartphone camera or a webcam that is connected to the internet. Sensors can include a mobile device's gyroscope or accelerometer, as well as an infrared sensor. A smartphone nowadays contains all of the gear required for augmented reality, including input and display devices.

The current generation of smart phones and tablet computers has all of the necessary specifications to run an AR application, including a camera and MEMS sensors such as an accelerometer, GPS, and solid state compass, making them ideal AR platforms. Capturing of real object configuration is very important in AR systems therefore choice of appropriate hardware is very important in its functioning.

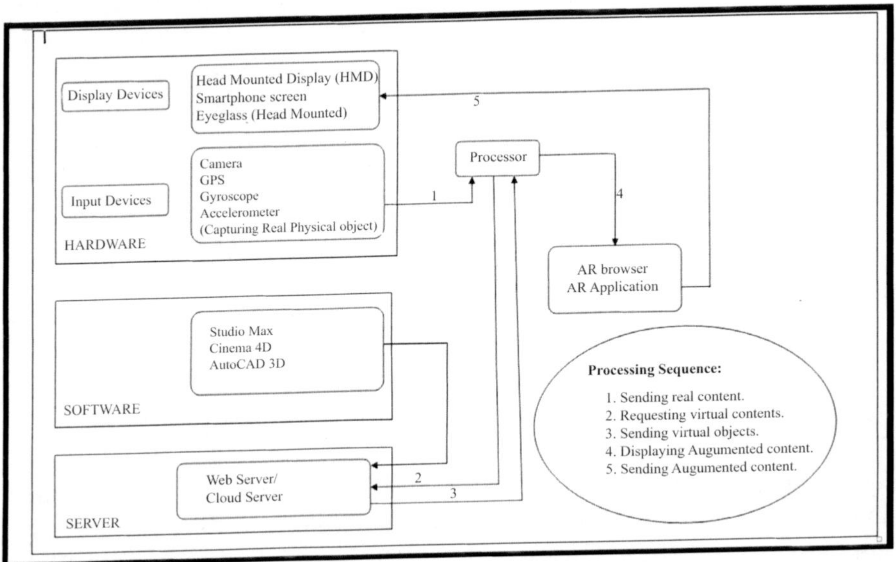

Fig. 5.7: AR System Components incorporating Hardware, Software, and Server arrangement

Software: Software plays a key role in the functioning of any device based on augmented reality technology which is essentially meant for creating computer generated virtual objects and mixing it with the real objects. In AR-based applications, special 3D augmented reality programs are used. The use of 3D software allows for the overlapping of digital projections over a real-life item for comparison and diagnosis. These programs are accessible for PCs, and the smart-phone app already includes all of the standard features. 3D software can be used to create virtual visuals that can be layered over a real-life image. The Software that is commonly used are: AutoCad3D, StudioMax or Cinema 4D. Further, the CT and MRI data can also be added to the real world in order to experience the augmented reality. The end-user of AR has to download a software application or browser plug-in. As software is essential to create virtual image, the choice is very critical for displaying augmented content.

Remote Servers: Apart from the hardware and software point of views, a web or cloud server is essential for storing the virtual image database. Virtual pictures are collected from the web or cloud server and sent to the AR application for additional processing based on the request received from the AR application. Virtual pictures and projections are downloaded from the web or cloud server and displayed via a smart-phone in response to the request received from the AR source. Because the amount of data generated during the process can be significant, employing a hosted service or cloud for storing, accessing, altering, transmitting, or receiving data is recommended.

Head Mounted Display for AR: In augmented reality, the Head Mounted Displays (HMDs) are different from that of virtual reality glasses. Such HMDs overlay the user's field of view with images of both the real environment and virtual items. Figure 5.8 (a) shows image of helmet type HMD with sensors. Sensors for six degrees of freedom monitoring are commonly used in recently developed HMDs, allowing the system to align virtual information with the physical world and modify accordingly with the user's head movement. In AR systems, six degrees of freedom (6DoF) is used, which refers to the freedom of movement of a rigid body in three-dimensional space, as shown in Figure 5.8 (b) and (d). The three degree of freedom as shown in Figure 5.8 (c) allows motion only in three orthogonal axes i.e. roll, yaw and pitch. On the other hands, in six degree freedom the body is free to change position in three perpendicular axes as forward/backward, up/down, and left/right translation, as well as changes in orientation through rotation about three perpendicular axes, commonly referred to as yaw (normal axis), pitch (transverse axis), and roll (longitudinal axis).

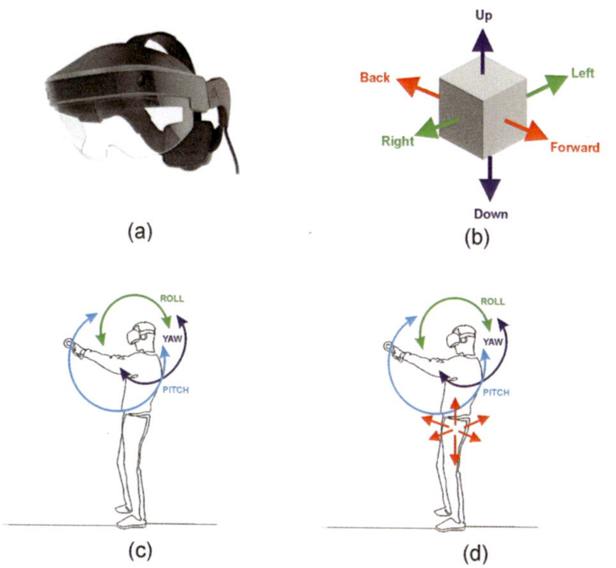

Fig. 5.8: : **(a)** Head Mounted Display **(b)** 6-Degrees **(c)** 3-Degrees of freedom **(d)** 6-Degrees of Freedom

Figures 5.8 (c) and 5.8(d) show comparison of freedom of movement 3DoF versus 6DoF. The virtual reality systems use three degrees of freedom (3DOF) which refers to tracking of rotational motion along only three orthogonal axes: pitch, yaw, and roll instead of six axes as used in AR systems. The rotational motion is confined to forward/back, up/down, and left/right axes.

5.3.2 Types of AR Systems

Augmented reality based applications work on the basis of two types of approaches, named as **Marker-based** and **Location-based.**

(A) Marker-based AR: Figure 5.9 illustrates working of marker based augmented reality application, in which QR code is used as marker. The most prevalent type of marker-based augmented reality is the QR code. The most basic type of AR marker is the 2D barcode; however, more complex types include brilliant colors and meaningful graphics. When a smart-phone with a Marker-based AR application scans a pattern with its camera, such as a bar code or a symbol, the software detects it and superimposes a digital image on the screen. For a better experience, a 3D or animated digital image is employed. The recognition-based augmented reality approach is also known as the marker-based AR approach.

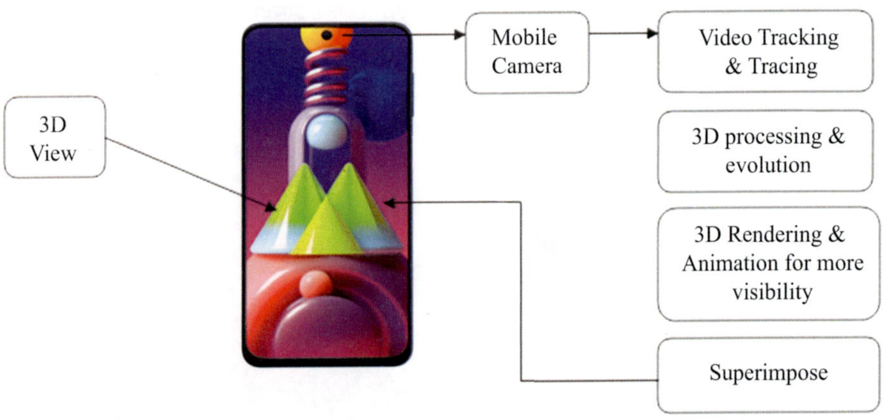

Fig. 5.9: Marker based AR

(B) Location based AR: The functioning principle of location-based AR applications is depicted in Figure 5.10. When the camera of a smart-phone with a location-based augmented reality app is directed at a real scene, the device's inbuilt GPS software determines its location in the world. Based on the device's recorded location and orientation (as determined by inbuilt sensors such as the accelerometer and gyroscope), the program provides info relevant to the precise location the user is looking for. These digital data are then placed on the real picture, which is visible to the device camera for comparison and diagnosis. The most extensively used AR application is the location-based method.

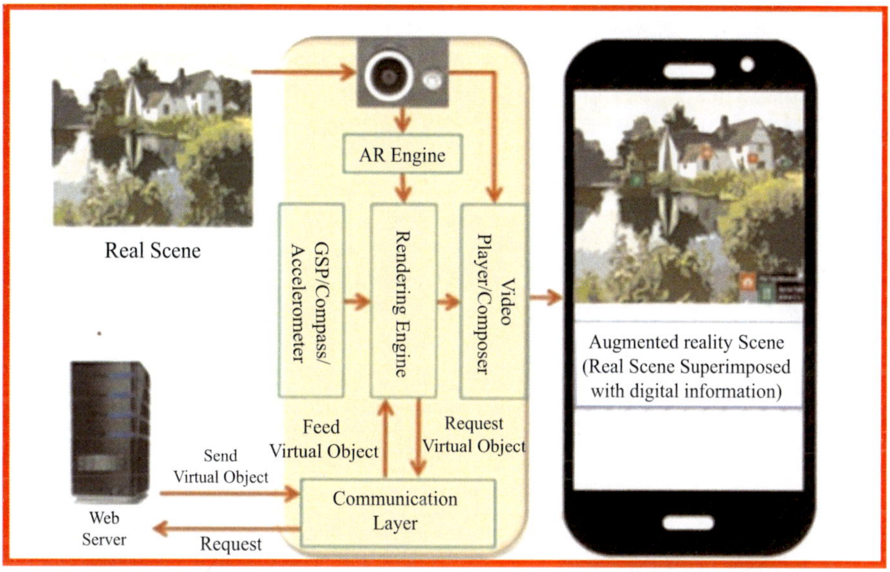

Fig. 5.10: Location based AR (*Courtesy*: Satish Kumar, AugReality Pedia)

5.4 Mixed Reality (MR)

The term Mixed Reality (MR), coined by Paul Milgram and Fumio Kishino in 1994, refers to the blending of actual and virtual environments, to create new habitats and representations in which actual and digital items reside side by side and interact in real time It is a combination of reality in terms of physical assets and virtual reality, encompassing both augmented reality and augmented virtuality via immersive technology, and it does not take place primarily in either the physical or virtual environment. Further, it is a blend of physical and digital worlds, unlocking the links between human, computer, and environment interaction, as shown in Figure 5.11. It is combination of traditional with technology for enhancing talent of different stake holders for federating them in trading to undertake a profitable business. Computer vision, graphical processing power, display technology, and input systems have all advancements to enable this new world. Human Computer Interaction is a discipline that studies the interaction between human and computer input (HCI). Human input is received via a variety of methods, including keyboards, mice, touch, ink, speech, and even Kinect Skeleton tracking. Sensor and processor advancements are opening up new avenues for computer input from the environment. Furthermore, because the interaction between computers and environments is referred to as environmental understanding or perception, the names of the Application Programming Interfaces (APIs) in Windows that reveal environmental data are referred to as the perception APIs. Environmental inputs include ambient illumination, environmental sound, object recognition, location, and other atmospheric parameters. as well as a person's position in the world (head tracking), surfaces, and boundaries (spatial mapping and scene interpretation).

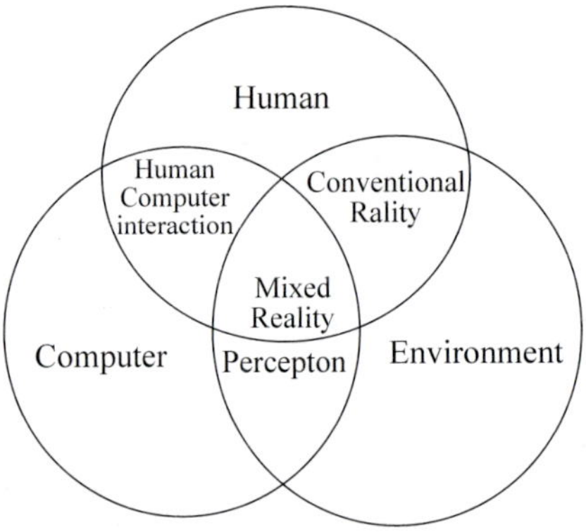

Fig. 5.11: The Mixed Reality Interactions between Computers, Humans, and Environment

As shown in Figure 5.12, the use of Mixed Reality goes beyond display technology to encompass environmental input, spatial sound, and locations and positions in both real and virtual areas. Because mixed reality combines virtual reality (VR) and augmented reality (AR) technology to create a space where actual and virtual items can coexist, exchange, and interact in real time. It has a wide range of applications in training, education, entertainment, and remote working for proper understanding, diagnosis and identification for remedial measures.

Fig. 5.12: MR experience with Microsoft Hologram Glasses (*Courtesy*: Microsoft)

There are two main types of devices that deliver Mixed Reality experiences:

(i) Holographic devices: These are characterized by the device's ability to place digital content in the real world as if it were there. It is helpful in sorting, screening and Characterization of different parameters of a system or process

(ii) Immersive devices: These are characterized by the device's ability to create a sense of "presence"-hiding the physical world, and replacing it with a digital experience which is helpful in monitoring and forecasting future actions. Unlike VR which is experienced by only wearing VR headsets, Mixed Reality can also be experienced through Smartphone.

5.5 Applications of Augmented Reality in Agriculture

Augmented Reality (AR) and the Internet of Things (IoT) are technologies that either add helpful information to the real-world environment or receive useful information from the real-world environment. In order to promote the creation of knowledge bases and intelligent applications related crops, VR, AR, MR, and IoT technologies can be deployed with enormous benefits in the agricultural industry. Crop monitoring and yield projections are possible with this technology. It can also be used in conjunction with Semantic Web, which is an extension of the World Wide Web (www) based on standards established by the World Wide Web Consortium (W3C). The Semantic Web's purpose is to make data on the Internet machine readable. Technologies like Resource Description Framework (RDF) and Web Ontology Language (OWL) are used to enable the embedding of semantics with data. These technologies are used to represent metadata in a formal way. Concepts, relationships between entities, and categories of objects can all be described using ontology. The Semantic Web, in short, is a platform that enables data to be shared and reused across application, corporate, and community borders. As a result, the Semantic Web is seen as a connector between various content and information applications and systems.

(1) Farm AR Ontology: The AR technology can be used for identification of plant species and plant diseases regularly on real time assessment mode. Each plant has data properties that describe it, such as its name, scientific name, use, plant care information, sowing irrigation, inter-culture operation, and harvesting. Also, there is a "may Diseased" object that refers to the concept of "Disease" and correlates it with the possible diseases and Pests future damage that may affect it. The plant diseases and pests are categorized into categories for example: Armyworms, Anthracnose, Bacterial canker, and Barley yellow dwarf, to name a few. Data variables such as symptoms and treatment are used to describe each condition. It also includes information on crop areas and climate data for these areas. The most important feature of this concept is the object property "fertile" corresponds to the concept "Plants" and associates the area with a plant and a crop index metric of that plant in same region. The ontology in the knowledge base can be used for innovative applications in the agriculture sector, such as advising farmers on how to optimize their cultivations while also providing them with useful information on whether maximizing the yield of a particular crop is economically feasible in their area. The augmented reality service matches a plant photo obtained with a mobile device camera to a recognized plant and displays relevant information for the detected plant from the knowledge base. By comparing these natural features against a specified target resource database, the Plant identification approach finds and tracks the features that are naturally found in the image itself, and thus diagnoses the anticipated diseases, etc. Similarly, the leaf image renders to the specific disease of the plant and drawing strategies for remedial measures. Further, with AR, farmers can visualize the entire farming a single dashboard and detect the presence of any pest or insect infestation, which saves time and energy in diagnosis and remedial measures. It is not only useful to detect plant diseases but also its timely disposal. Digital cameras and/or other optical sensors, accelerometers, GPS, gyroscopes, solid state compasses, radio-frequency identification (RFID), and other motion tracking technologies are used in modern mobile augmented reality systems. In a variety of terrains, these technologies provide various levels of accuracy and precision. All sensor data can be integrated with AR technology to give immersive display about fertility of land, soil health data, crop maturity indices, environment humidity and temperature parameters and productivity. This will help farmers to check the soil status and fertility of lands to select the crop they want to sow in that farm thus help in understanding soil-water-crop relationship. The AR can also augment fertility inspection, e.g. if a farmer wants to inspect land for any infestation, he would need to check each inch of the land manually. But with AR, farmers can visualize the entire farm in a single dashboard and detect the presence of any pest or insect infestation in his field. It is step forward for quick diagnosis and appropriate remedial measures, thus check the crop health intermittently.

(2) Training and Extension: The VR, AR and MR can be very effective in imparting training and capacity building of farmers and different stake holders such as growers, milk man and entrepreneurs about the latest technological developments in farming techniques and methodologies without carrying them to actual sights. The AR can enable new farmers to get familiar with agricultural equipment without actually having a need to operate it. It is very easy to give required inputs for all six useful dimensions of agriculture i.e.

soil, water, seed, mechanization, climate and farmers. With historical accident-related data and how they occurred, farmers can also train juniors on how to avoid such unforeseen casualties. These are the devices for integrating different technologies for empowerment of farmers. The AR will help new farmers to visually learn the use of complex agriculture tools including biotic and abiotic stress. These devices can be used to create awareness in the mind set of trainees to understand full theory and practice behind it. It also broadens the scope of work and bridge the gap between reality and actuality. It will also facilitate remote collaboration, coordination, cooperation, and networking with experts of agriculture and the farmers, to adopt advanced agricultural methods. Giving farming tips from such experts in their field can help new farmers to take an appropriate approach based on their land conditions to enhance yield and profit. For instance, an AR app allows farmers to get a glimpse of their farms' inner workings with the help of their smart-phones or tablets. With the help of these technologies farmers can increase their crop productivity thus more production and more profitability.

6

Communication Technologies

6.1 Introduction

Sending a message from one place to another place, which are physically separated from each other, is called Communication. The Communication Engineering or Communication Technology deals with the design and development of engineering systems to transmit information from its source, and at the same time, to receive the same information at a remote destination with reliability, accuracy and quality. The source end is called *transmitter* and the remote destination end is called *receiver*. Since the distances among transmitting and receiving users are very large, of the order of hundreds and thousands kilometers, it is also called telecommunication engineering in place of simply communication engineering. A network or facility which establishes and ensures reliable means of communication for exchanging information among multiple users is called *communication network or telecommunication network*. We are living in *Information and data* age, where the *users* and *things* (machines, devices) spread over the entire globe are interconnected irrespective of geographic location. In other words, we can say, the entire world is connected to a universal information and telecommunication grid for exchanging all type of information or messages viz voice, video, multimedia, text, pictures, raw data, etc. A single type of technology is not adequately capable to provide and fulfill requirements for global connectivity, rather, a mix of technologies including satellite communication, optical fibre communication, microwave terrestrial communication, cellular (mobile) communication are collectively and collaboratively used to perform this task more effectively.

An elementary block diagram of a communication system is shown in Figure 6.1, illustrating transmitter and receiver separated by a transmission medium called communication channel. The channel may be a wired channel or wireless (radio) channel. The information signal may be an analog signal or a digital signal, depending on the type of source and associated electronic circuit. The output of a microphone is example of analog signal and output from a RS-232 port of a computer is example of a digital signal. The input transducer as may be microphone, a video camera, sensor, etc, which acts as source of generating and collecting information signal. The output transducer may be radio speaker, a TV display, a computer monitor, etc.

The communication channel (wired or wireless) is exposed to several types of inherently generated noise and distortions, which tend to corrupt the originality of information during the process of transmission. It is communication system designer's job to develop robust systems for compensating the adverse effects of noise and distortion added in the channel so as to receive reliable and accurate information at the receiving end.

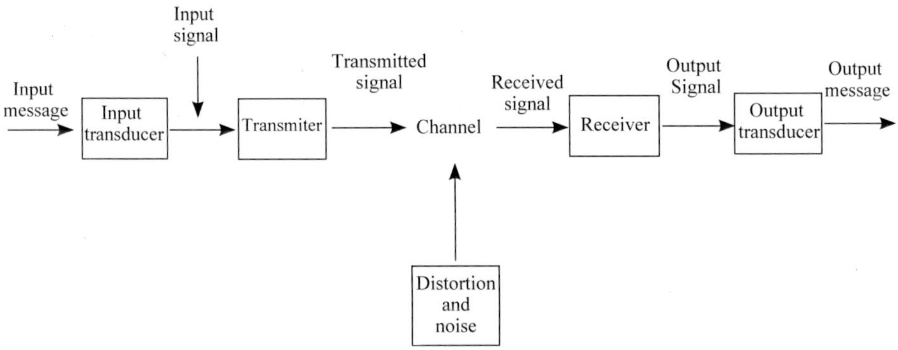

Fig. 6.1: Elementary block diagram of a Communication System

6.2 Wireless Technologies

When communication channel between transmitter and receiver is tether less or do not have any physical connection but connected through a radio wave it is called wireless communication. In most of the day to day communication, we can observe wireless communication e.g. mobile phones, cordless landline phone, WiFi, Bluetooth, TV reception at home, AM and FM radio, etc are all examples of wireless or radio communication. In precision agricultural applications, a number of things, devices, sensors, appliances etc need to be interconnected using standard communication technologies and protocols. It is an example of Internet of Things (IoT) since it is device-to-device or machine-to-machine communication. Due to the increasing growth of IoT devices and WSN technologies, which are also employed in agricultural applications, a variety of communication protocols have been developed in recent decades. The bandwidth, number of free channels, data rate, battery timing, price, and other factors all influence the parameters of each protocol. The most widely utilized wireless communication protocols in IoT-based agriculture applications include:

Cellular Technology: It is the most adaptable telecommunications technology, suited for a wide range of applications requiring high data rates. It can provide stable high-speed Internet connectivity via GSM, 3G, 4G, and 5G cellular communication capabilities. It necessitates the deployment of infrastructure as well as the cost of operation and backup personnel with a centralized management authority. Cellular technology is a good alternative in underground wireless sensor networks, such as security systems in smart home projects and agriculture applications, and can be utilized as a core network to support many applications in the agriculture domain. With the use of cellular technology, a smart crop management system can be created in which numerous sensor nodes are put on-farm utilizing a local network, and sensor data is transferred over the cloud to end users using cellular networks.

6LoWPAN: It is an IP-based communication protocol that was the first protocol used for IoT communication. It stands for IPv6 over Low-Power Wireless Personal Area Networks. It's a low-cost, low-bandwidth, and low-power technology that supports a variety of topologies, including star and mesh. Between the network layer and the MAC layer, there is an adaption layer that handles interoperability between IPv6 and IEEE 802.15.4. 6LoWPAN has applications in health equipment monitoring, environmental monitoring, and security and home automation systems. In addition, a 6LoWPAN-enabled wireless sensor network is employed to track soil conditions and crop metrics.

ZigBee: It's a wireless communication protocol based on the IEEE 802.15.4 standard for wireless communication. The ZigBee alliance designed it primarily for personal area networks, and it's widely used in Precision Agriculture to monitor soil health, ambient factors, and crop health indicators. Although ZigBee networks have a lower data throughput, a shorter range, and are less secure than WiFi networks, they have a more flexible network structure, a longer battery life, and allow mesh, star, and tree topologies with multi-hop data transmission. In smart agriculture applications such as smart green houses and smart irrigation systems, ZigBee is widely used. The ZigBee protocol uses a single 2.4 GHz frequency and has a wireless range of 70 meters indoors and 400 meters outdoors. It provides networking versatility by supporting different networks such as point-to-point and point-to-multipoint mesh networks, which can cover residences of any size. Low latency and low duty cycle result in decreased power consumption, allowing sensors to survive up to 7 years on a single charge. The mesh-network operability of ZigBee minimizes the likelihood of node failure, while ad-hoc routing provides more stability.

Wireless Fidelity (Wi-Fi): As a Wireless Local Area Network, it is the most prevalent communication protocol that allows devices to communicate over a wireless signal (WLAN). IEEE 802.11, 802.11a, 802.11b, 802.11g, and 802.11n are supported by the Wi-Fi protocol. It has the ability to connect millions of sites, including homes, offices, and public spaces. Agriculture systems, such as smart irrigation, crop health monitoring, and greenhouses, employ Wi-Fi extensively in IoT-based applications. Wi-Fi networks can offer data transmission from several sensors to the gateway in Precision Agriculture applications.

Bluetooth: Bluetooth (BLE) is a low-power short-range communication technology that runs on the 2.4 GHz ISM band. The term ISM band stands for 'Industrial Scientific Medical' band for personal, portable, and handheld electronic devices. Bluetooth is generally used to replace connection cords between varieties of personal devices, such as notebook computers, cellular phones, personal digital assistants (PDAs), digital cameras, and so on. It's optimized for low- bandwidth, low-latency, and short-range applications, and it's also a good fit for IoT applications like agriculture. Bluetooth wireless technology aspires to replace the multiplicity of proprietary cords that people must carry and utilize to connect their own devices with a universal low-cost, user-friendly air interface. It's a great protocol for wirelessly delivering little amounts of data over a short distance (less than 100 meters), and it's a great wireless replacement for serial communication interfaces. Bluetooth is named after the Danish king Haruld Blitund (Bluetooth). During the 10th century, King Bluetooth is credited with uniting the Scandinavian people.

Radio Frequency Identification (RFID)

The wireless non-contact use of radio frequency waves to transport data is known as Radio Frequency Identification (RFID). It employs electromagnetic fields to identify and track tags affixed to items automatically. A radio transponder, a radio receiver, and a transmitter make up an RFID tag.

The tag transmits digital data, usually an identifying inventory number, back to the reader when triggered by an electromagnetic interrogation pulse from a nearby RFID reader device. This number can be used to keep track of your inventory. Users may automatically and uniquely identify and track inventories and assets by tagging them with RFID tags. RFID advances auto-ID technology by allowing tags to be read without requiring line of sight, with read ranges ranging from a few centimeters to over 20 meters depending on the kind of RFID. The RFID has gone a long way since its first use in World War II, when it was used to determine whether planes were friendly or hostile. Not only is technology improving year after year, but the cost of adopting and operating an RFID system is also decreasing, making RFID more cost-effective and efficient. While RFID and barcode technology are both used to track inventory in similar ways, there are three key differences that make each one a superior option in certain situations:

1. RFID tags can be read without requiring a direct line of sight.
2. An RFID tag's data can be updated in real time. Bar code data, on the other hand, is read-only and cannot be modified.
3. RFID tags need to be powered. Bar codes, on the other hand, only require a power source from the technology that reads the bar code.

RFID Tags: RFID (radio-frequency identification) is a technology that employs electromagnetic fields to identify and track tags attached to items. The tag transmits digital data, usually an identifying inventory number, authentication number of the object on which it is tagged, or registration number of the vehicle, back to the RFID reader when triggered by an electromagnetic interrogation pulse from a nearby RFID reader device. The RFID tags are made out of three parts: a microchip, antenna, and a substrate as shown in Figure 6.2. Microchips are integrated circuits that store and process data as well as modulate and demodulate radio frequencies signals. For receiving and transmitting the signal, a tiny microstrip antenna is used. Both are attached to a surface. The information about the tags is saved in a nonvolatile memory.

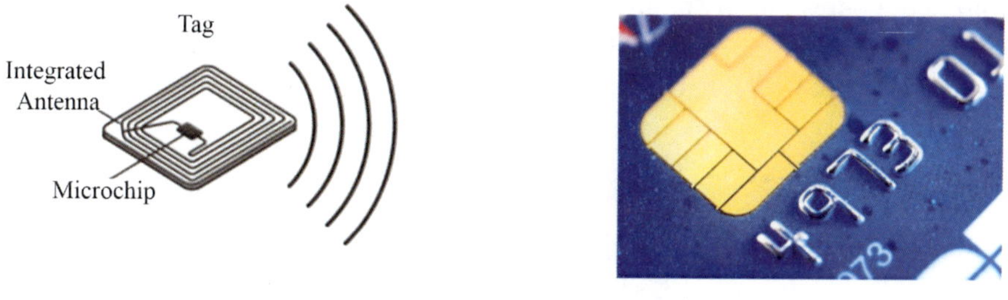

(a) **(b)**

Fig. 6.2: (a) Components of RFID tag **(b)** RFID chip on Banking card (*Courtesy*: MDSCOTT)

For processing transmission and sensor data, the RFID tag incorporates either fixed or programmable electronics. RFID tags can be attached to objects and used to track and manage goods, assets, people, and other information. It can be attached to cars, computers, books, mobile phones, and other items, for example.

RFID tags can be passive, active, or passive with battery backup. An active tag has a built-in battery and emits its ID signal on a regular basis. A battery-assisted passive contains a tiny battery that is activated when an RFID reader is present. Because there is no battery in a passive tag, it is less expensive and smaller. Instead, the tag consumes the radio energy transmitted by the reader. A passive tag, on the other hand, must be lighted with a power level a thousand times higher than an active tag in order to transmit signals. This has an impact on interference and radiation exposure.

Tags can be read-only, with a factory-assigned serial number that serves as a database key, or read/write, with the system user able to write object-specific data into the tag. Write-once, read-many tags are available; "blank" tags can be written with an electronic product code by the user.

After receiving the message, the RFID tag answers with its own identity and other data. It could just be a unique tag serial number, or it could contain product-specific information like a stock number, lot or batch number, manufacture date, or other details. Because tags contain unique serial numbers, the RFID system can distinguish between many tags that may be within the RFID reader's range and read them all at the same time.

RFID Reader: The RFID reader sends electromagnetic wave pulses to a nearby RFID tag to receive its information to process the application for which it is designed and applied. Figures 6.3 and 6.4 show two different types and applications of RFID reader.

Figure 6.3 shows RFID handheld reader designed for keypad and touch based applications. Figure 6.4 shows a complete electronic toll collection system where UHF long range RFID reader is used.

Fig. 6.3: RFID Handheld Reader (*Courtesy*: ZEBRA)

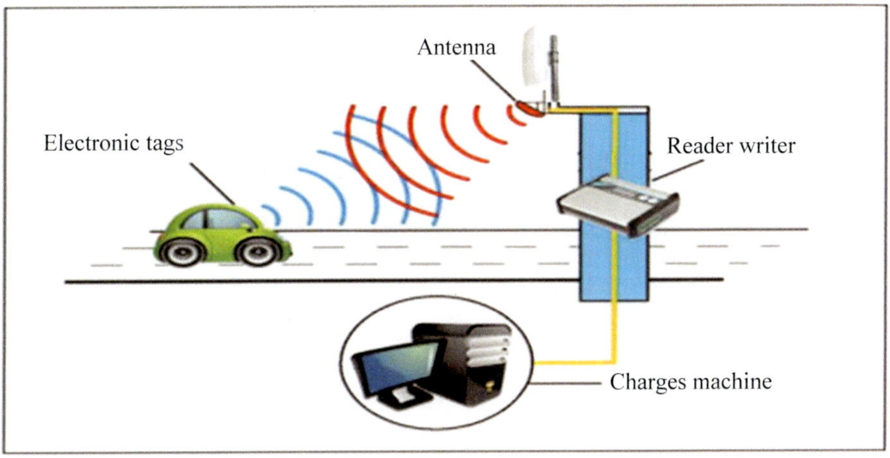

Fig. 6.4: RFID Reader at Electronic Toll Collection

The type of tag and reader used in RFID systems can be categorized. A passive reader receives only radio signals from active tags in a Passive Reader Active Tag (PRAT) system (battery operated, transmit only). The PRAT system reader's reception range can be varied from 1–2000 feet (0– 600.m), giving it versatility in applications like asset protection and supervision. An active reader broadcasts interrogator signals and gets authentication responses from passive tags in an Active Reader Passive Tag (ARPT) system.

Active tags are used by an interrogator signal from the active reader in an Active Reader Active Tag (ARAT) system. A Battery-Assisted Passive (BAP) tag, which works like a passive tag but has a small battery to power the tag's return reporting signal, might be used in a variant of this system. Fixed readers are set up to produce a defined interrogation zone that can be regulated precisely.

This allows a highly defined reading area for when tags go in and out of the interrogation zone. Mobile readers may be handheld or mounted on carts or vehicles.

Bar Code

A barcode, is a machine-readable visual representation of data. Figure 6.5 (a) shows how barcodes used to represent data by altering the width and spacing of parallel lines. These barcodes, also known as linear or one-dimensional (1D) barcodes, can be scanned using special optical scanners known as barcode readers, as seen in Figure 6.5. (b). Later, two-dimensional (2D) variations using rectangles, dots, hexagons, and other geometric patterns were developed, dubbed matrix codes or 2D barcodes, despite the fact that they do not use bars.

On mobile devices with built-in cameras, such as smart phones, 2D barcodes can be read or disassembled using application software.

(a)

(b)

Fig. 6.5: **(a)** Bar Code and **(b)** Barcode Scanner (*Courtesy*: Honeywell)

Quick Response (QR) Code

A QR code (short for Quick Response Code) is a sort of matrix barcode (or two-dimensional barcode) that was first developed in 1994 for the Japanese car industry. A barcode is an optical label that provides information about the item to which it is attached and can be read by machines. In actuality, QR codes frequently include information for a locator, identifier, or tracker that directs users to a website or application. To store data efficiently, a QR code uses four defined encoding modes (numeric, alphanumeric, byte/binary); extensions may also be employed. Because of its faster readability and larger storage capacity than ordinary UPC barcodes, the Quick Response system gained widespread outside of the automobile industry. Product monitoring, item identification, time tracking, document management, and general marketing are some of the applications. Consumer advertising has become increasingly reliant on QR codes.

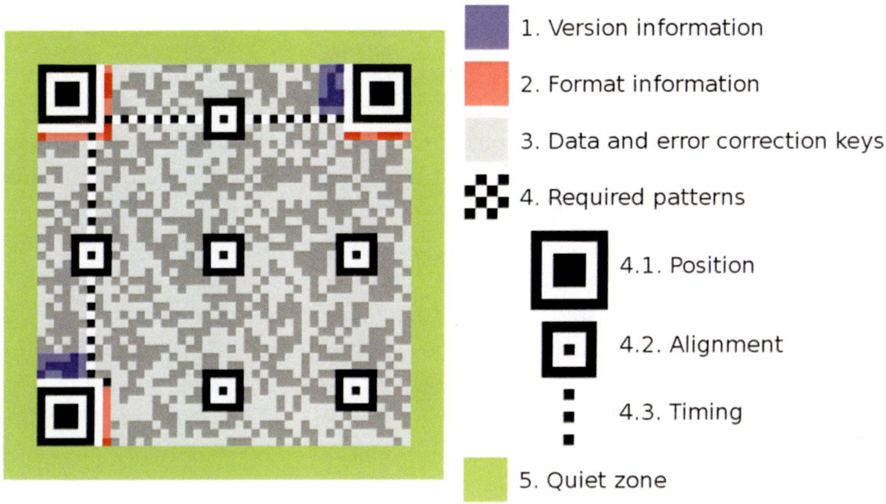

Fig. 6.6: Structure of a QR code (*Courtesy*: Bobmath)

As depicted in Figure 6.6, A QR-code is made up of black squares placed in a square grid on a white backdrop that can be scanned by a camera and then processed using Reed–Solomon error correction until the image can be properly interpreted. The essential information is then derived from patterns in the image's horizontal and vertical components. A QR code scanner is typically a smartphone or RFID reader that displays the code and converts it to a useable format (such as a standard). A website's URL, which eliminates the need for a user to type it into a web browser).

LoRa Protocol: Long-range network (LoRa) is a wireless technology for M2M and IoT applications that provides long-range, low-power, and secures data transmission. LoRa is based on chirp spread spectrum (CSS) modulation, which, like Frequency-shift keying (FSK) modulation, has low power characteristics, but can be utilized for long-range communications. Sensors, gateways, machines, gadgets, animals, humans, and other objects can all be wirelessly connected to the cloud via LoRa networks. It is marketed as an infrastructure solution for the Internet of Things, with end- devices communicating with gateways linked to the Internet, which act as transparent bridges and relay communications between these end-devices and a central network server over a single wireless hop. In different places, these technologies operate in distinct frequency bands. It operates in the 915 MHz range in the United States, in the 868 MHz band in Europe, and in the 865 to 867 MHz, 920 to 923 MHz spectrum in Asia.

Long Range Wide Area Network is a modified version of LoRa (LoRa WAN). It is a LoRa Alliance-developed Low Power Wide Area (LPWA) networking protocol that connects battery-powered 'things' to the internet in regional, national, or global networks, addressing key Internet of Things (IoT) requirements like bi-directional communication, end-to-end security, mobility, and localization services. LoRa WAN defines the network's communication protocol and system architecture using unlicensed spectrum in the ISM bands, while the LoRa physical layer establishes long-range communication links between remote sensors and gateways linked to the network. This protocol aids in the rapid establishment of public or private IoT networks utilizing hardware and software from any location. Table 6.1 compares all of the wireless communication protocols discussed. 6LoWPAN and ZigBee are considered to be the most suited wireless communication technologies for precision agricultural applications since they are both based on mesh networking, which allows them to cover a broad area.

Table 6.1: Comparison of Wireless technologies for Precision Agriculture

S.N.	Communication Protocol	Standard	Physical Range
1	6LoWPN	IEEE 802.15.4	2–5 km urban 15 Km suburban
2	ZigBee	IEEE 802.15.4	10–100 m
3	Bluetooth	IEEE 802.15.1	30 m
4	RFID	RFID	10–20 cm
5	LoRa	IEEE 802.11ah	5–10 km
6	Wi-Fi	IEEE 802.11	50 m

6.3 Applications of Communication Technologies in Agriculture

i. Automation in Farming using wireless communication protocols.

ii. Precision Agriculture.

iii. Monitoring crop from far away i.e. monitoring facility is easy by using wireless technology protocol in agriculture field.

iv. Soil moisture information is received in farmer smart phone.

v. Monitoring and controlling of different parameters in green house irrigation system.

vi. Controlling of the devices like water sprinkler and water pumps etc.

vii. The ZigBee technology has a wide range of agricultural uses. Temperature, soil moisture, humidity, water level, pH, and other volatile compound detection are all monitored using the sensors.

viii. The ZigBee can obtain the temperature, humidity and illumination information in real time.\

ix. The ultimate goal of the LORA is to gather, monitor, and efficiently use important data for agricultural processes in order to achieve a more efficient and environmentally sustainable agriculture.

x. Cattle monitoring.

xi. Smart soil sensor.

Fig. 6.7: Lora Gateway for Smart Irrigation

RFID-based Spray Movement Monitoring: Radio Frequency Identification (RFID) is a technology that aids in the management of information flow within the supply chain and security in the agro-food sector. RFID has been used in animal identification and tracking, as well as in the food chain for traceability control, for many years. Animal identification and tracking have been done with RFID for years, and it's a routine practice on many farms. It is also been utilized to control traceability in the food chain. Sensors in tags allow for the monitoring of perishable food products' cold chains as well as food the development of new applications in domains such as environmental monitoring, irrigation, speciality crops, and farm machinery etc. In addition, RFID monitoring devices have the potential to transform many agricultural processes. It enables data collection in difficult areas like greenhouses and farms. Figure 6.8 depicts an RFID-based method for tracking sprayer movement in an orchard or vineyard.

Fig. 6.8: RFID based Spray Monitoring System [*Courtesy*: C. Zhai, A. Landers, B. Zhang]

The extremities of tree or vine rows are sometimes too narrow for a sprayer to make a U-turn to the next adjacent row during pesticide spraying in an orchard or vineyard. In these situations, the operator frequently skips the row, sprays the next one, and then returns later (often referred to as alternate row or row skips). This necessitates him memorizing the spraying routes accurately; otherwise, he risks over- or under-spraying. A spray monitoring and guiding system for orchards and vineyards that records the amount of pesticide applied and the path the sprayer travels, then displays the data on a screen in real time, can be extremely beneficial to the sprayer operator in terms of increasing efficiency. Identifying sprayer movement, including its position and direction of travel, is critical in the spray guiding system.

RFID Livestock identification: RFID livestock tagging can be a valuable tool in a farmer's armory for identifying each animal, as well as providing pedigree and medical information. During veterinary checkups or inventory counts, an LF reader or wand scans the animal and, with the help of software, uploads significant information about each animal to a database, as shown in Figure 6.9.

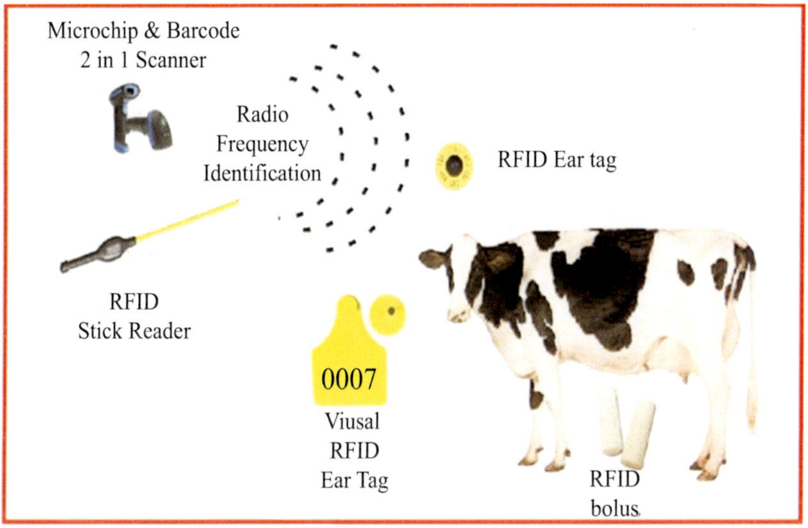

Fig. 6.9: RFID based Livestock Tracking

Animals including farm animals are being traced with RFID. In order to build a system to identify lost and found pets, veterinarians are now pushing for all domestic animals to be tracked using RFID. When all family animals are tagged with LF RFID chips, vets may scan their tags to view information like identification and the owner's contact information when they are located. Lost pets can be reunited with their owners using RFID chips that identify all pets on a national database. The management of exotic and endangered animals in preserves or other wildlife habitats is another key reason for using RFID to tag animals. In animal management, LF RFID, UHF RFID, and GPS technologies are all used. The type of system chosen is usually determined by the information required and the animals' safety.

Smart Farming with Bluetooth Mesh and IoT Network: Bluetooth mesh with IoT network hybrid communication technologies is also used in Integrated Smart Farming to Supply Chain of agricultural products. Such an integrated system makes use of IoT and Bluetooth technologies to revolutionize farming. Sensors allow calibration of irrigation and fertilization based on crop type, growth phase, soil and environmental conditions. The traceability allows monitoring of the movements of food products from the field, through storage to end consumers. Bluetooth LE sensor tags are used for monitoring conditions during storage and transportation so as to assess freshness, integrity, as well as to provide for traceability. It provides informations for optimum water and fertilizer use, better quality and yield of crops, increased safety, reduction in production costs, reduction in negative impacts on the health and environment, smart traceability etc.

7

Sensor Based Imaging for Crop Management

7.1 Introduction

One of the major goals in agricultural crop management is to achieve maximum yield with minimum investment while maintaining a good quality of the crop produce. Crop infestation due to insects, diseases, and weeds are some of the major factors responsible for loss in crop yield. Further, an efficient Precision Agriculture Crop Management System is one, which is capable of precisely detecting the crop yield indicators (or crop health parameters) at an early stage and can predict the yield at any point of time of the crop cycle. The early detection of crop infestations followed by instant remedial and correcting measures to counter the factors can minimize yield losses. This can help to increase crop yield and hence subsequent profit. The crop yield prediction is an important exercise to estimate the farming economics in advance. This chapter covers introduction to multispectral and hyper spectral sensor based crop imaging that can be used for yield predictions. The imaging sensors provide real time data about temporal, spatial and spectral characterization of the crop. These data can be analyzed to predict the crop yield and at the same time can generate prognostic tools to counter the adverse effects, if any.

7.2 Temporal Characterization and Variability

When a crop is mapped with imaging sensors of specific band or bands of wavelength, at a certain periodicity of time intervals, then the variation in sensor data of the same object with respect to time is called temporal information of the crop for that specific band of spectrum. The images may be captured on any predetermined time scale, may be of seconds, minutes, hours, etc. The statistical variations in these images with respect to time, is called temporal variability. The temporal characterization gives correlation between the images which is used to monitor the dynamic change in the crop field with respect to specific time interval. The minimum time gap between two successive sensor images of the same object is called as temporal resolution.

7.3 Spatial Characterization and Variability

The imaging of the crop field or any object with reference to space (distance, area, direction etc) gives spatial characterization of crop field for a given band of spectrum. The variation in crop parameters across the crop field with space, is termed as spatial variability of the crop. The qualitative and quantitative modelling of spatial variables of the crop is a critical exercise to accurately predict the crop yield. The spatial characterization of the crop field gives correlation between sensor images to monitor the spatial variability. The minimum distance between two consecutive pixels of image is called spatial resolution. In an image, larger the number of pixels, higher will be its spatial resolution and vice-versa.

7.4 Spectral Characterization and Variability

The imaging of crop field or any object at discrete wave bands of the spectrum is called spectral characterization of the object. It gives vital information about the reflectance and absorption of spectral bands, to estimate the vegetative growth of the crop and also to detect the presence of insects and pests on the crop. The minimum spacing (usually in Nanometers) between two closest spectral points of the image, is termed as spectral resolution. The spectral variability and spectral correlation between two images is used to monitor the dynamic change in the object.

7.5 Multispectral and Hyper Spectral Imaging

The multispectral imaging is a technique of crop field mapping field that gives temporal, spatial and spectral response at discrete bands of the electromagnetic spectrum. The common spectral bands used in multispectral imaging are Red (R), Blue (B), Green (G) and Near Infrared (NIR). The multispectral imaging can be done by remote sensing satellite. The multispectral sensors are deployed on-board satellite orbiting the earth, in lower earth orbit (about 1000 km from earth surface). The sensors on board are directed towards the desired region of the earth to be mapped. The images captured by the sensors are sent back to the earth stations for processing the data for further analysis. The multispectral sensors can also be mounted on-board drone or Unmanned Aerial Vehicle (UAV), called as aerial imaging. The drone mapping allows much closer mapping of the crop as compared to remote sensing satellite based imaging. More recently, aerial or drone images have been widely used for yield predictions before harvesting the crop. Such UAV born sensor images can provide cloud free information of crop's spectral characteristics with high spatial resolution for analysis of vegetation patterns. A strong absorption of red energy and strong reflectance of NIR energy is an indication of healthy crop characteristics. The strong contrast of absorption and scattering of the red and near-infrared bands can be combined into different quantitative indices of vegetation conditions. These mathematical quantitative combinations are known as vegetation indices. The multispectral sensing generally captures limited number of images at 3-15 discrete broadly spaced wave bands.

The hyper spectral imaging on the other hands is a special type of multispectral imaging technique that analyses a wide spectrum of light instead of just 3-5 colours to each pixel. A wide spectrum of wave bands maps each pixel of the image. A typical hyper spectral Imaging System (HIS) is as shown in Figure 7.1. The sensor bands are: Red (R), Blue (B), Green (G), Near Infrared (NIR) and Thermal, mounted on UAV or drone. The narrow spacing between wave bands of the order of 1-5 nanometer is normally used to give complete spectral characterization of the crop field being mapped with a hyper spectral resolution. More than thousand images are sent to the IoT gateway through radio frequency link. The big data of crop mapping from gateway is sent to the cloud sever for processing and analysis using computer vision models based artificially intelligent engines.

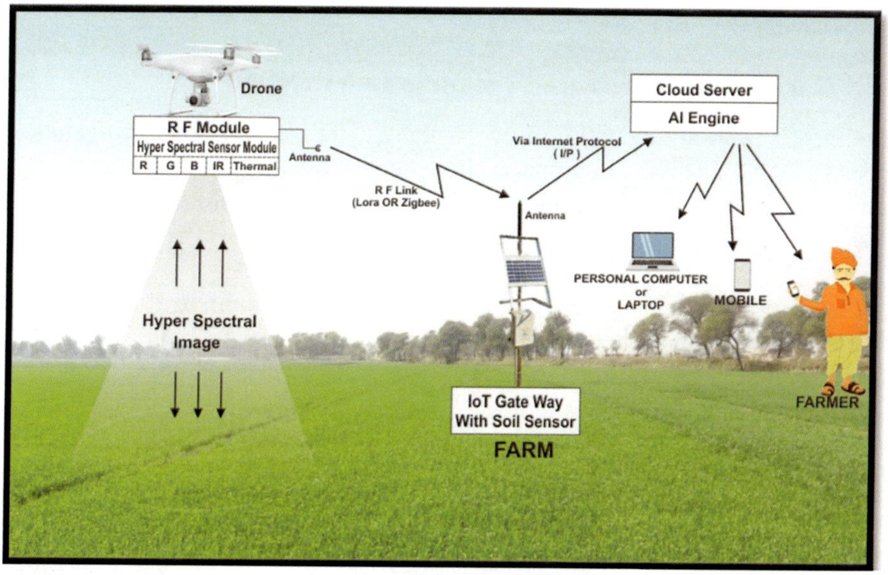

Fig. 7.1: Hyper spectral Imaging based Crop Management System

The magnitude of reflectance, scattering and absorption of different spectral color is a measure to model various vegetation indices for yield predictions. The AI engine performs analysis of big data of high resolution images, using neural network approaches and computer vision models. It generates realtime accurate information about crop health, maturity indices and yield predictions. Based on these observations, prognostic advisories are sent to the end user/ farmer to take corrective measures for efficient crop management.

7.6 Vegetation Indices for Yield Predictions

The vegetation indices are the spectral transformation of the crop in to mathematical models of spatial and temporal variability that accentuates the spectral response of vegetative properties of plants so that they appear distinct from other image features. It is a single number that quantifies vegetation biomass and/or plant vigor for each pixel in a multispectral or hyper spectral image. The index is computed using few spectral bands of wide spacing (multispectral) or a large number of narrow spacing bands (hyperspectral) that are sensitive to plant biomass and vigor. The quantitative information of vegetation indices as applied to Precision Agriculture provides a basis for macro- and micromanagement of agricultural production. Further, it can also be used for yield estimation of crops. However, the applicability of multispectral and hyper spectral imaging and computation of its different Vegetation Indices extracted from these techniques usually relies on the sensors, instruments and analytical platforms.

7.6.1 Normalized Difference Vegetation Index (NDVI)

The most common vegetation index is the normalized difference vegetation index (NDVI). The NDVI compares the reflectance values of the red and near-infrared regions of the electromagnetic spectrum using the following formula:

$$NDVI = (\alpha_{NIR} - \alpha_{RED}) / (\alpha_{NIR} + \alpha_{RED})$$

α_{NIR} is the pixel's reflectance value in the near-infrared band, α_{RED} is the pixel's reflectance value in the red band. The NDVI value, typically ranges from -1.0 to 1.0 for each pixel in an image, helps identify areas of varying levels of plant biomass/vigor. Higher values indicate high biomass/high vigor.

7.6.2 Green Difference Vegetation Index (GDVI)

This vegetation index is similar to NDVI except that it measures and compares the reflectance values of near infra-red and the green spectrum (540 to 570 nm) instead of the red spectrum. This index is more sensitive to chlorophyll concentration than NDVI. It is given by formula:

$$GVI = (\alpha_{NIR} - \alpha_{GREEN}) / (\alpha_{NIR} + \alpha_{GREEN})$$

7.6.3 Green Chlorophyll Index(GCI)

The green chlorophyll index is used to estimate the leaf chlorophyll content in different species of plants. The chlorophyll content reflects the physiological state of vegetation. In case of plants under biotic or abiotic stress, the value of GCI is lower, hence it is direct measure of plant health. It is given by formula:

$$GCI = (\alpha_{NIR} / \alpha_{GREEN}) - 1$$

7.6.4 Soil Adjusted Vegetation Index (SAVI)

Due to soil wetness, soil color, and high saturation plants, NDVI measurements can be unreliable. The Soil Adjusted Vegetation Index (SAVI) is a modified version of the Normalized Difference Vegetation Index (NDVI) that includes a soil correction element. The difference in red and near- infrared extinction via the forest canopy is accounted for by this index. The SAVI is a transformation approach that reduces the effects of spectral vegetation indices in the red and near-infrared (NIR) wavelengths on soil brightness. In places with little vegetative cover, it is used to compensate the Normalized Difference Vegetation Index (NDVI) for the influence of soil brightness. It is calculated using a formula:

$$NDVI = (1+L)(\alpha_{NIR} - \alpha_{RED}) / (\alpha_{NIR} + \alpha_{RED} + L)$$

Where, 'L' is canopy background correction factor, and its typical value is nearly 0.5 to minimize soil brightness variations and eliminate the need for additional calibration for different soil.

7.6.5 Enhanced Vegetation Index (EVI)

It's an improved vegetation index that decouples the canopy background signal and reduces atmospheric influences to improve the vegetation signal with improved sensitivity in high biomass regions and improved vegetation monitoring. The EVI is more responsive to canopy structural variables, such as leaf area index (LAI), canopy type, plant physiognomy, and canopy architecture, than the Normalized Difference Vegetation Index (NDVI), which is chlorophyll sensitive. In global vegetation research, the two vegetation indices work together to increase the detection of vegetation changes and the extraction of canopy bio-physical data. Another distinction between the Normalized Difference Vegetation Index (NDVI) and the Environmental Variation Index (EVI) is that NDVI drops in the presence of snow, but EVI increases.

The vegetation indices explained in above sections are generic and applicable to large crop area management. However, presently site specific crop management (SSCM) has become an important component of precision agriculture vigorously applied for enhancing crop production. It involves spatial referencing, crop and climate monitoring, attribute mapping, decision support system, and differential action. The SSCM demands more advanced image processing algorithms to derive high end vegetation indices for accurate site specific yield prediction and crop management.

8

Robotics

8.1 Introduction

The term *robot* is czech word, first time used by play write Karel Capek, in year 1920, applicable to the forced labour or serfs or slaves. The first commercial, digital and programmable robot, named 'Unimate' was built by George Devol in 1954. The robot may be defined as an automated reprogrammable engineered machine that can autonomously perform multiple tasks and a series of complex operations without human intervention. Robotics is a branch of science and technology that deals with design, development, operation and applications of robot. The robotics involve multi-disciplinary fields like electronics engineering, mechanical engineering, computer sciences, artificial intelligence, machine and deep learnisng etc. When a robot is made to perform some of the tasks as performed by a human being, it is called a humanoid robot. A humanoid robot can perform face recognition, human interactions, voice communications, body gestures, navigation etc. Whereas, industrial robots are designed to perform various typical tasks and complex operations which are either dangerous to human operators or less precisely performed by the operators. These complex operations are generally specific to manufacturing, automobiles, textile, heavy engineering etc. The specifications and design of a particular robot depends on the specific demand, requirement and its applications. The robots can replace human operators to perform repetitive and dangerous tasks or to perform the tasks having size limitations. It can replace human operators, specially, when the operations are to be performed in extreme environment like high temperature furnaces, fires, outer space, or bottom of sea in extreme low temperature etc. In modern time, the commercial robots are available for various applications including industrial, agricultural, medical, automobile, space, domestic, civil etc. It finds extensive applications in agriculture sector for crop management, weed control and precision farm management. This chapter introduces a brief theory of robot operations followed by its classification and major agricultural applications.

8.2 Basic Components of a Robot

The Figure 8.1 shows block diagram of an industrial robot and its various components. The major components of a robot are:

(i) Manipulator or robotic arm

(ii) Endeffector

(iii) Actuators or Motors

(iv) Processor and Controller

(v) Sensors

(vi) Power supply

(vii) Software

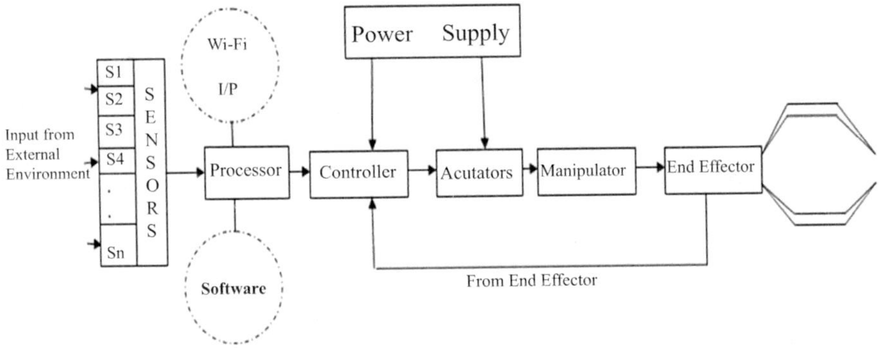

Fig. 8.1: Basic Components of a Robot

(i) Manipulator

The manipulator also called robotic arm, which is an electromechanical system formed by sequence of mechanical link and joint combinations. It is a hardware assembly of joints, axes, links etc that assist physical interaction of the robot with the surroundings. In other words, these are the hands and arms of a robot to physically interact with the environment and nearby objects. The links are the rigid members connecting the joints, or axes.

The axes are the movable components of the robotic manipulator that cause relative motion between adjoining links. It is an arm-like mechanism that grips and move objects with a number of degrees of freedom, without direct physical contact by the user. These are mainly used for various purposes like controlling and handling dangerous hazardous and radioactive materials, handling the welding automation, robotic surgery and in space.

(ii) Endeffector

The endeffector is a gripping assembly just like fingers attached to Palm of human hands. It is attached to the end of manipulator or robotic arm. The manipulator's base is fixed to the base support, and the end effector is attached to its other free end. These are basically gripping tools of robot that act as the fingers and palms of a robot.

(iii) Actuators and Motors

The locomotion and arm movement of a robot are performed by devices called actuators. Actuators convert one form of energy in to another form i.e. linear motion. It gives mechanical movement to robot and causes body of robot to move forward or backward. Actuators are generally embedded with sensors and controllers for making process simple and convenient. The commonly used actuators in robots are electric actuators that convert electric energy in to linear or rotational movements.

The rotational movement of robot and its arms is performed by use of ac/dc driven motors, which are connected to controller unit through relays. Motor converts electric energy in to rotational movement. The switching operation of appropriate motor is performed and controlled by the signals as received from the controller of the robot. The motor is part of driving mechanism of robot. It is connected with other components of driving mechanism including gears, chains, pulleys, and belts. The gearboxes are for the transmission of rotational movement from one place to another for operational mode. In a humanoid robot the role of motor is similar to the human muscles of arm, palm, legs, fingers etc. Three types of locomotion devices are used in robots depending on the source of energy they use, such as electricity, hydraulics, and pneumatics. In robots, servomotors are also used as a powerful means of converting the rotational motion into the linear motion. These motors are easily programmable and are perfect for repeating a robot's movement. Also, these motors come in radio-controlled versions, called R/C servo motors. In some of the robotic applications, pneumatics is also used as actuators to produce motion. These systems typically use air cylinders to generate rotary and linear motion. Pneumatic robots are widely used in manufacturing work.

(iv) Processor and Controller

The processor and controller of a robot is generally an embedded unit and acts as robot brain. It is a computer with a robotic software and adequate memory. The role of processor and controller is analogous to the human brain. The embedded software and algorithms enable the robot to think and generate necessary commands to perform an assigned task by its controller unit. The controller directs and controls the movement of the Manipulator and the Endeffector. The processor calculates the motions of the robot's joints, determines how much and how fast each joint must move to achieve the desired location and speeds, and also tracks the coordinated actions of the controller and the sensors. It requires an operating system, programs, peripheral equipment like a monitor, and has the same limitations and capabilities. In some systems, the controller and the processor are integrated together into one unit. In others, these are separate unit for performing their individual work.

(v) Sensors

The sensors in robot play the important role of its perceptual system. A robot is generally operated in different physical environment depending on its applications. It is exposed to light, heat, obstacles, strain, pressure, magnetism etc and also to other surrounding objects of the environment. Further, it has to fix up its geometrical coordinates by defining its physical

position or location before it navigates to perform a task. The Sensors are devices for sensing and measuring geometric and physical properties of robots and the surrounding environment – position, orientation, velocity, acceleration, distance, size, force, moment, temperature, luminance, weight etc. All such information is extracted by a variety of sensors deployed on the robot. Sensors are critical in detecting heat, light, obstacle etc by converting them into digital form, which is understandable by machines. The processor of robot processes the sensor data and control the robot operation to act accordingly. Some of typical physical parameters sensed by robot sensors from its interacting environment are contact, distance, inclination, light, temperature, sound, strain, rotation, magnetism, smell, inclination, pressure and altitude.

(vi) Power Supply

The robot is an electro mechanical machine comprising various electronic and electrical hardware components like motors, relays, switches, processor, and the controller. An appropriate voltage and driving currents are required for these hardware components to operate and work as per designed task. A central power supply source is used which is normally a rechargeable battery. The source of energy for the robots is the power supply, which is needed to make the robot fully operational. Power supplies include batteries, hydraulic, solar power, or pneumatic power sources.

(vii) Software

The robot is a computerized machine and all its operating instructions to achieve a task are stored in the form of specific programming language like

C++ and python. In early generation robots programming languages are used to store the instructions to the robot. Present generation robots are driven by cloud based artificially intelligence and machine learning algorithms. Many programming languages are used to program robotic systems, e.g. VAL, Robo ML, ROBOFORTH, ROSSUM, XRCL etc.

8.3 Advantages and Disadvantages of Robots

The advantages of robot applications in industries and other sectors are as follows:

a. The use of robot in industry can add new dimension to process automation and manufacturing for increasing productivity, safety, efficiency, quality, and precision of the products.

b. Robots can work in hazardous conditions such as fire, radiation, bottom of deep sea, darkness, extreme hot and cold, space, other planets, and so on without the need for life support, or critical safety requirements.

c. These can efficiently work round the clock without specific environmental conditions like lighting, oxygen, air conditioning, ventilation, and noise protection.

d. In some of the engineering process and medical surgery applications, the robots can be even more accurate than humans. The sensors and accessories of current generation robot have capabilities beyond those of humans, with linear accuracy of micro scale. It is a step forward for getting more accuracy, reliability and precision.

e. Robots can process multiple stimuli or tasks simultaneously, whereas human can only process one active stimulus, hence it can replace human workers, causing economic hardship, worker dissatisfaction and resentment, and the need for retraining the replaced workforce.

Although the robot is extremely useful for the reasons explained above, however, there are some disadvantages as follows:

a. It lacks in capability to respond in emergencies, unless the situation is predicted and the response is included in the system.

b. Safety measures are needed to ensure that these do not injure operators and other machines that are working with them. This includes: inappropriate or wrong responses, lack of decision-making power, loss of power, damage to the robot and other devices, injuries to humans.

c. Robots, although superior in certain senses, have limited capabilities in cognition, creativity, decision-making, and understanding.

d. Further, these have limited degrees of freedom and dexterity, sensors and vision systems, real-time response.

e. Robots are costly due to its initial cost of equipment and installation, need for peripherals, need for training, need for skilled programming.

8.4 Robot Classification

The robot is an automated computerized machine that can be programmed to carry out certain complex actions automatically with the help of machine support. It can be driven and controlled either by an external control device or by the controller embedded within the machine. The robots can be classified on the basis of its autonomy, power source, work envelope, size of the robot, type of drive system, and uses etc.

8.4.1 Autonomous and Automated Robots

Autonomy of a robot is defined as the degree of freedom to perceive (sense) and make independent decision and action to achieve a task with available support. A robot is called autonomous robot if it is so developed to perceive and make its own decisions and then perform an action accordingly with minimal human intervention. A true autonomous robot is one that can **perceive (or sense)** its environment, **make decisions** based on what it perceives and/or has been programmed to recognize external environment and then **actuate a movement or manipulation** within that environment. On the other hands, automated robots are robotic vehicles that require some sort of external control for guidance and are largely dependent on human intervention to perform various sets of tasks. The guidance can include to a beacon, remote control, tape strips on the floor, or any other method of guidance. An automated robot has negligible degree of freedom and it operates with human control through a remote control unit as per requirement. The automatic robot is remote controlled machine which does not perceive nor make decision or action independently. The decision based actions with respect to robot mobility, include but are not limited to some elementary tasks like start, stop, and obstacle avoidance that are obstructing its path.

8.4.2 Classification based on the Power Source

On the basis of the power source used to drive a robot, it can be classified into five major types namely electrical, hydraulic, pneumatic, nuclear, and green powered robot.

(i) Electrical Powered robot: The robots are driven with motors of different types and size depending on a specific application and the operation to be performed. Robots operating with the electrical power source can further be subdivided as alternating current (AC) or direct current (DC) driven robots. The DC power robots usually provide greater torque but these often require more maintenance for the motors. The use of such motors generates dust and spark that can cause hazards to the process. The DC power driven robots are common for the hobby robotics and are usually mobile, battery-powered robots. The AC powered robots are common in industries and for heavy applications use Servo motors. Stepper motors are also used for these systems for various applications.

(ii) Hydraulic Powered robot: Hydraulic power generates a large amount of force and it is used for heavy loads in robotics. The system uses some other form of energy for generating hydraulic pressure. The robot uses this hydraulic force for performing its tasks. However, due to the improvements in servo motors, the hydraulic powered robots are losing ground. Hydraulic robots have some drawbacks such as-as a hydraulic leak, fire hazard, increased noise, increased maintenance and the cost of oil etc.

(iii) Pneumatic Powered robot: Pneumatic robots are powered by compressed air or compressed inert gases. Such robots are generally used for high speed and high load carrying capabilities. Such systems are very fast and the industries use it as a ready supply of cheap pneumatic pressure. However, the biggest problem with these robots is drifting. This causes difficulty in maintaining its position. The only way to make it stable and hold its position is to use hard stop and constant pressure. Pneumatic robots also suffer from the issue of noise and leaks.

(iv) Nuclear Powered robot: Nuclear-powered robots make use of its own nuclear reactor that is smaller in size and capacity than the reactors of nuclear power plants. The nuclear powered robots are generally used in space missions for deep space exploration. Nuclear powered robots are operational for years and decades without the need for human interaction suitable for the space missions.

(v) Green Powered robot: The robots which are powered by non conventional methods of energy generation are called green powered robots. The green power source refers to a wide variety of power generation techniques that do not adversely affect the environment. The potential green power sources for powering the robots include solar power, wind power, organic biomass sources, natural heat sources etc.

8.4.3 Classification based on the Workspace Geometry

The workspace of robot is the set of geometric coordinates or points that can be reached by its endeffector or robotic arm. In other words, the workspace of a robot is the geometrical space in which the entire system is working. On the basis of work envelope formed by geometric coordinates, robots can be classified as Cartesian, Cylindrical, Spherical, Articulated, SCARA, and Delta type.

(i) Cartesian Geometry robot: It is the most commonly used robot in the industries and in service sector. Such robots are user friendly, easy to use and program. The kinetic structure of such robot arm is made up of three mutually orthogonal prismatic joints. The wrist position of the robot is defined in three Cartesian coordinates: X, Y, and Z. The X-axis is for forward and backward movement, Y-axis to move in side to side, and Z-axis to move up or down. The robot forms a rectangular or cube shaped workspace by linear movement of Cartesian elements. However, these robots have the drawback of complexity of assembly.

(ii) Cylindrical Geometry robot: As the name reveals, work space of such robots resembles a cylinder. It has a rotary axis on the base for spinning the robot and two linear axes for moving the tool in the general work space. The cylindrical geometry robots are suitable for entering in the machines, and have rigid structure as suitable for large payloads. These are comparatively simple and similar to the Cartesian robots in their axis of motion. Such robots require minimal assembly complexities hence the installation of the robots is easier compared to its counterparts.

(iii) Spherical Geometry robot: It is a mobile robot with spherical external shape. Such robots are also called ball shaped robot because one of the joints of a Cartesian robot is replaced by a revolute joint. It is made up of a spherical shell serving as the body of the robot and its movement is enabled by an internal driving unit. The work envelope of this robot is a ball which is cutoff where this robot mounts. It can operate autonomously, or as remotely controlled automated robot. In general, wireless communication is used between internal driving unit and external control unit because of the mobility and closed nature of the spherical shell. A battery located inside the robot is used as power source of the robot, but some spherical robots are designed to make use of solar power. The spherical geometry gives the user a large range of options for positioning the robot and also has long reach with a smaller size compared to the the cylindrical robots.

(iv) Articulated Geometry robot: In articulated robot, all three joints are revolute to access its work space. Generally, these revolute joints are arranged in a chain sequence, supporting each other in a chain. The workspace of such robots is very complex and has a crescent shaped cross section. The mechanical movement and configuration of articulated geometry robot closely resembles a human arm. The arm is mounted to a base with a twisting joint. The arm itself can feature anywhere in workspace from two rotary joints up to ten rotary joints, with each additional joint allowing for a greater degree of motion.

(v) Selective Compliance Articulated Robot Arm (SCARA): The SCARA is a combination of Cartesian linear motion robot and an articulated geometry robot. It consists of two revolute joints followed by a prismatic joint. All these three joint axes are parallel to each other and point towards the direction of gravity. Such type of robot is faster than its counter parts, used in electronics manufacturing industry and also in assembly of the parts of air plane. Because of its geometry SCARA has smaller work space and can handle lighter loads up to few Kilograms. These robots have the easiest integration system and are best for the majority of applications.

(vi) Delta robot: A delta robot is a parallel arm robot with three vertically parallel arms connected to pyramid type joint at the base. The key feature of its design is that the orientation of endeffector is maintained by use of parallelogram in the arms. The geometry of robot resembles the nose cone of any rocket due to formation of a cone during the sweeping motion of the three axes. The majority of the work envelope of this robot is closer to its base. When the tooling moves farther from the overhead unit, the work envelope becomes narrow. Such type of robots are extensively used in picking and packaging in factories because they can be quite fast, executing up to few hundred picks per minute.This type of robot is also used in 3D printing industry due to its speed, design and unique geometry. These are the fastest and most expensive robots.

8.4.4 Classification based on Movement

(i) Fixed robots: The robots which are stationary or fixed at a single location and perform the given task without human intervention are called fixed robots. Such robots are more commonly used in the industries where the robots work in well defined environment. Robots are generally mounted on stable platforms. These can compute their positions on the basis of their internal configuration. In automobile and other heavy engineering operations fixed robots are used.

(ii) Mobile robot: This type of robot is not stationary or fixed at a point, instead are capable of free movement over the surface in work space. Mobile robots can be of various types such as legged robots, wheeled robots, swimming robots, and flying robot etc.

(a) Wheeled robot: As the name indicates, such robots are fitted with wheels at the bottom of robot for its movement, and are guided by the kinematics models that rely on motion. Wheeled robots can either be single wheeled, two wheeled or multi wheeled. Single wheeled robots use a single wheel for balancing itself and for navigating to surrounding places. The example of single wheeled robot is the Murato girl (Seiko). In two wheeled robot, two parallel wheels are fitted in the base of robot with its centre of gravity below the wheel axle. In order to maintain wheel balancing, such robots make use of a tilt sensor for detecting the tilt of the robot. The example of two wheeled robot is the NBOT. In case of three wheeled robot, the wheels arranged in the triangular shape which makes it balanced. The front wheel of the robot acts as the steering wheel while the two rear wheels provide the motion. In the four wheeled robots, the first two wheels provide the steering and the rear wheels provide the movement. The example of four wheeled robot is the Scarab, the rover used by NASA. Multi wheeled robots have more than four wheels for motion. All the wheels must have the same speed for movement and perfect synchronization, which makes it critical to design. The example of multi wheel robot is the Mars rover with 6 wheels.

(b) **Legged robot:** Such type of robot is walking type robot that use limbs for motion. These robots are critical to design and are mainly used for movement in a highly unstructured environment. Legged robots are capable of moving in any kind of path and terrain. These can either be bipedal, tripodal, quadrupedal or hexapod, provided the number of legs are two, three, four, six respectively. For example, the robot namely ASIMO by Honda, and Sony's QRIO are bipedal robots. The example of the tripodal robot is the STRIDER robot from RoMeLa. The example of the hexapod robot is the OSU Adaptive Suspension Vehicle of the Ohio State University.

(c) **Swimming robot:** The robots which are designed and developed for working under deep ocean surface or for assisting navigation to submarine and ships, are called Swimming robots, which can swim or can go deeper in to the water. The example of swimming robots are the ' PacX Wave Glider' and the ' Swumanoid robot'.

(d) **Flying robot:** Flying robots are generally light weight and micro sized robots that mimic the morphology of an insect or the larger unmanned aerial vehicles (UAVs). Such robots find variety of applications in land mapping, crop monitoring, aerial photography, remote imaging etc. The example includes the drone of DRDO, namely 'Rustom'.

8.5 Humanoid Robot

A robot that is so developed to perform some of the actions and tasks as performed by a human being and its physical structure looks like human body, it is called a humanoid robot. A humanoid robot can perform face recognition, human interactions, voice communications, body gestures, navigation etc.

Figure 8.2 (a) shows image of a two wheeled humanoid robot and the Figure 8.2 (b) shows its line diagrams. It is a wheeled robot having spine based centre of gravity (CG) balancing, integrated with sensors and AI algorithm. The shape of the robot looks like human structure that provides a good experience to a person while interacting with it.

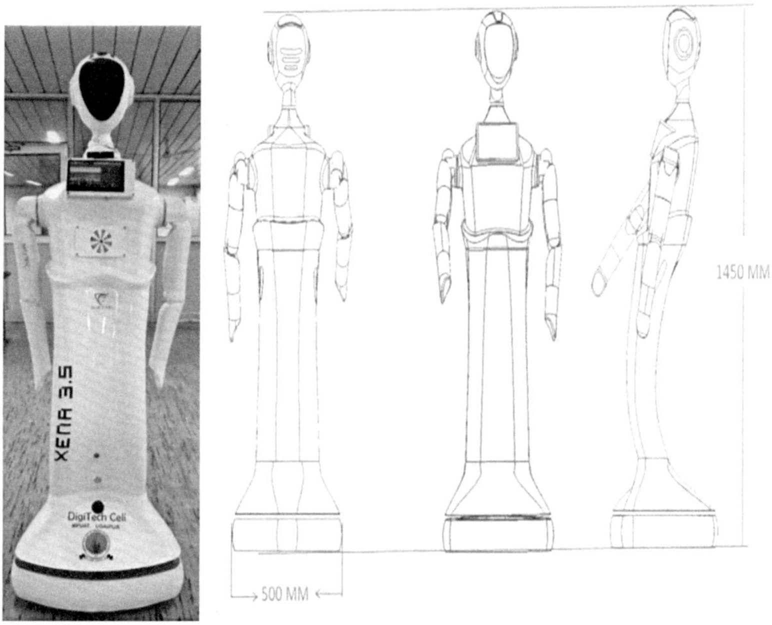

(a) (b)

Fig 8.2: (a) Photograph of Humanoid robot **(b)** Line diagram with dimensions (Courtesy: MPUAT, Udaipur and ClubFirst Robotics)

The inbuilt sensors and control system enables the robot to detect object and human in its path and provide collision avoidance when it is navigating from one place to another. Such type of robot is specifically designed as help desk to meet and interact with the visitors. The robot can register the visitor and interact through face recognition and voice communication. It can also register complaints and feed back of the visitors and can answer the frequently asked questions (FAQs) about the company/institute by voice, video and pictures. It can perform Laser based navigation in a complex environment providing the autonomous, smooth and collision free movement with a speed of about 0.7 meter per second. It can also perform self-mapping and navigation with the help of Laser, Digital Compass and Digital Gyro. Such robots operate with rechargeable battery of typical 40,000 mAh rating and once fully charged, can work for 5-6 hours.

System Working: The functional block diagram of the humanoid robot system is as shown in Figure 8.3. The major functional blocks are: central processing unit, control unit, motors, and robot operating system (ROS) server.

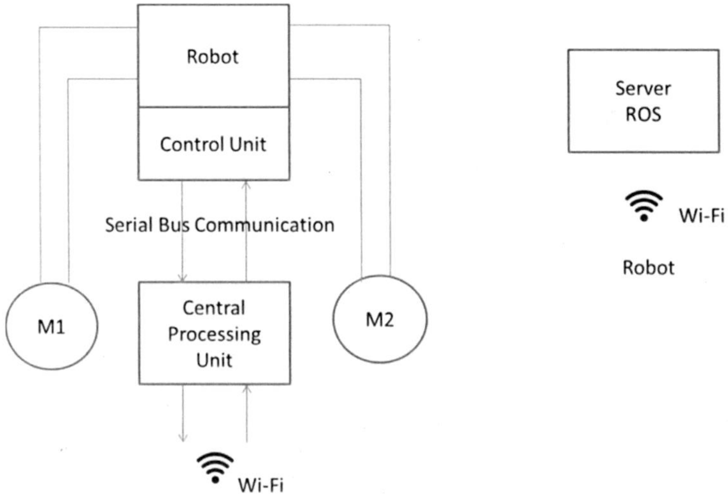

Fig. 8.3: System Block Diagram of Humanoid Robot

The ROS has been installed on server side of robot. It has its own control unit that is called the base controller via which encoder motors are connected. The control unit of robot is communicating with the central processing unit with serial bus communication. The base controller is ARM ATSAM3X8E controller that serves as a communication bridge between main computer and hardware peripherals of the robot. The base controller communicates via serial communication with CPU at a frequency of 10Hz. It receives motor request RPM and time stamp from CPU transmitter pin and send actual RPM and sensors data to CPU receiver. A Wi-Fi static IP is required to access the functions of robots. The base controller performs the tasks like: processing of motor encoder data, maintaining PID controller, processing IMU data, processing sensors data, and sending formatted data to various units of robot. The ROS are environments where multiple nodes communicate with each other via ROS topics. Some nodes publish the data to particular topic and other nodes subscribe the published data. The ROS packages possess user friendly functionality and carry nodes and ROS libraries.

Communication System: The block diagram of internal communication system of robot to establish communication among various units and nodes is shown in Figure 8.4. The Inertial Measurement Unit (IMU) of the system is a specific type of sensor unit that measures angular rate, force and sometimes magnetic field. The IMUs has important function in robot operation and comprises a 3-axis accelerometer and a 3-axis gyroscope, considered as 6-axis IMU. These can also include an additional 3-axis magnetometer, considered as 9-axis IMU. It works by detecting rotational movement of the three-axis, commonly known as Pitch, Roll, and YAW. Technically, the term "IMU" refers to sensor, but IMUs are often paired with sensor fusion software which combines data from multiple sensors to provide measures of orientation and heading. In common usage, the term "IMU" may be used to refer to the combination of the sensor and sensor fusion software; this combination is also referred to as an AHRS (Attitude Heading Reference System). The IMU is providing the angular data to the base controller of robot and proportional integral derivative (PID) controller is used to maintain the RPM of robot motors by publishing and subscribing the data of RPM of motors, Goal, Time and value of Yaw i.e. angular data. The PID controller objective is to reduce the error by the adjusting the RPMs.

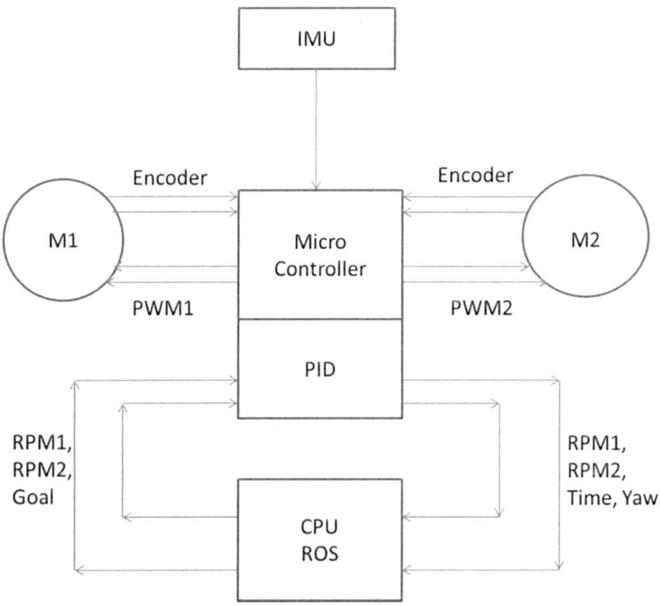

Fig. 8.4: Communication System of Robot

Simultaneous Localization and Mapping (SLAM): The robot localization means computing the robot's position or coordinates and the mapping of robot means building a self map of surrounding area and objects or the environment with reference to its home location. SLAM is one of the most widely researched subfields of robotics. Determining the location of objects in the environment is an instance of mapping, and establishing the robot position with respect to these objects is an example of localization. The SLAM subfield of robotics attempts to provide a way for robots to do SLAM autonomously. A solution to the SLAM problem would allow a robot to make maps without any human assistance whatsoever.

Detection of surrounding objects of the robot is performed with the help of light detection and ranging (LIDAR) method. It is a method that primarily uses a laser sensor to detect the presence of surrounding object and to find its range/distance from the robot. It scans the surrounding objects in the vicinity of robot. Compared to cameras, and other sensors, lasers are significantly more precise, and are used for applications with high-speed moving vehicles such as self-driving cars and drones.

Fig 8.5 (a): Lidar Sensor

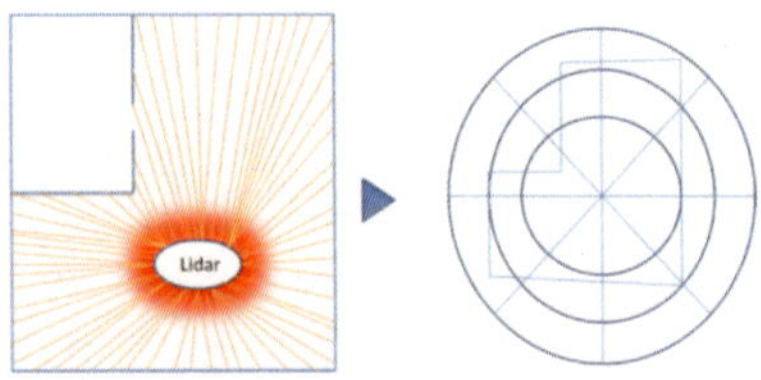

Fig 8.5 (b): Scanning Process of Surroundings

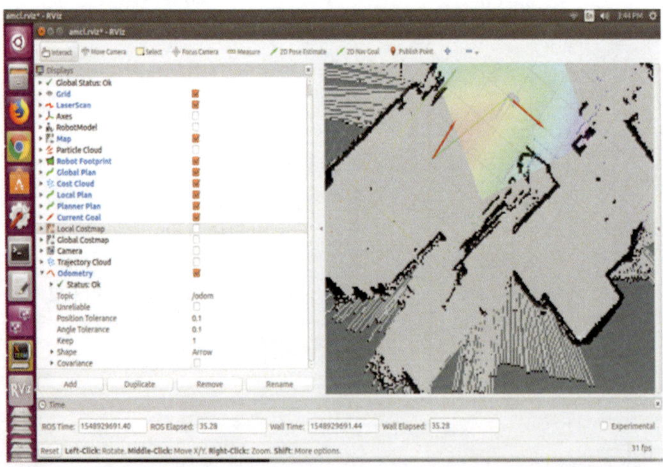

Fig 8.6: Indoor Map using Simultaneous Localization and Mapping

The output values from laser sensors are generally 2D (x, y). Figure 8.5 (a) shows image of a Lidar sensor and Figure 8.5 (b) indicates the scanning by robot Lidar for building the map. Figure 8.6 demonstrates self created 2D map by humanoid robot using SLAM process. The autonomously created map of robot environment helps in determining the location of various objects in the navigation path of robot, so that the robot can move around the obstacle by collision avoidance.

8.6 General Applications

In present scenario, technology intervention is observed in almost every aspect of day to day life. With the advancement in robotic technology, the scope of robot applications is also increasing in a wide variety of areas including agriculture, medical, industry, space, defence, security, entertainment, business, domestic works and service sectors. Some of the applications are listed below:

1. Robots with fixed manipulators are widely used in industries for performing different repetitive tasks in the various working environment. These can be used for performing different tasks such as welding, painting, machining, drilling etc.

2. In Medical science, robots are extensively used for different purposes such as performing surgery, rehabilitation and training etc. Medical robots do not replace the medical surgeon but work as a surgical assistant to the surgeon in performing different medical surgeries. During Covid-19 pandemic, service robots are used to carry water, meals, medicine etc. for serving the patients kept under isolation wards of hospitals.

3. Robots are now widely used in defence and security systems. Specially designed security robots are used for bomb disposal. Further, surveillance and transport operations are performed with the help of robotic drones. The sensors used in defence robots are have fast response time, highly sensitive, and accurate. Hence such robots react more quickly than humans during an emergency. Robots are also used for surveillance and guarding large civilian facilities, nuclear power plants, oil refineries etc.

4. The day-to-day domestic work and activities have become very easier now by the use of robots. The domestic robots are used for performing various daily tasks at home. For example: robotic vacuum cleaner, robotic dishwasher, robotic window cleaner, robotic coffee maker etc.

5. Robots have found their applications in various space explorations and space missions. Robotic rovers are used for the study of various celestial bodies such as planets, stars etc. Examples of the use of robots in space exploration include Yyommitra of ISRO, Curiosity, Pioneer, Robonaut, RASSOR etc.

6. The Entertainment industry also finds use of robots for various purposes. The specially designed robots are used for entertainment purposes in various places such as amusement parks, sports etc. Examples of

entertainment robots include KUKA Robocoaster, Honda's Asimo, Sony's Aibo, etc.

7. Robots are also being used in Agriculture on farm applications such as interculture operations, safety and security of farms and other post harvest operations etc. Its details are given in subsequent heading.

8.7 Applications of Robots in Agriculture

The agriculture sector has tremendous potential of technology intervention including the use of robotic technology for increasing the efficiency and accuracy of on farm operations and hence to increase the overall crop productivity with minimal investment on the crop. The crop harvesting, seed planting, soil analysis, insect and pest control, weed control etc are some of the major areas of farming that find robot applications to improve the overall efficiency and crop production with significant reduction in labour requirements. These applications cover almost all relevant farm operations during the crop cycle from sowing to the harvesting stage. In order to provide a feasible and more viable alternative to the conventional techniques, the agricultural robots are specifically designed and developed using suitable manipulator or robotic arm and gripper or end effector.

8.7.1 Crop Harvesting Robots

The basic concept of crop harvesting robot is to design an AI/ ML enabled robotic arm to detect the ripening of fruit and to pick the ripened fruit from the tree. The robotic arm mounted on a robotic vehicle carries sensor modules and gripping and picking tools. The sensor provides inputs of ripening parameters to the robot's processor to analyze the ripening status using AI/ ML algorithms and computer vision models. The controller of the robot gives control command to the gripper and picking tool to take away the ripened fruit. The speed and accuracy of harvesting robot are important performance parameters. The accuracy and the response time of the sensor modules and gripping tools determine the efficiency and accuracy of crop harvesting. An automated fruit harvesting robotic arm using deep learning is developed by Yuki Onishi is as shown in Figure 8.7. It comprises a stereo camera, detection unit and harvesting unit. The major operations performed by this robotic arm are: fruit detection, localization, and harvesting without damaging the fruit and its tree. A colour camera and a Single Shot MultiBox Detector (SSD) are used to detect the two-dimensional (2D) position of the fruit.

Fig. 8.7: Crop Harvesting Prototype Developed by Yuki Onishi, Takeshi Yoshida, Hiroki Kurita, Takanori Fukao, Hiromu Arihara and Ayako Iwai

The SSD is one of the commonly used object detection methods that can comprehensively estimates colour and shape of the object using Convolution Neural Network (CNN) approach. The knowledge about three-dimensional (3D) position of object is necessary for high order accuracy of the robotic arm. Hence a stereo camera is used to measure the 3D position of the fruit detected by the SSD. The route and path flow of the movement of the robot arm to the fruit location is determined by applying inverse kinematics. The robot arm can harvest a fruit by gripping and rotating it without damaging it and its tree. Such type of prototypes can be extended to develop automated farm vehicles fitted with such type of robotic arms for harvesting different types of crops.

8.7.2 Robots for Weed Control

The weed control or intercultural operations in the field of agriculture has been a standing issue for last many decades. The use of agrochemicals like pesticides and herbicides to control weed is although effective, but, is detrimental to human health and pollutes the environment. The automated weed control through weed detection and removal can be a very useful and effective precision farming technique to improve weeding efficiency and also protecting the environment. The accuracy and effectiveness of weed control depends on resolving weed image and discriminating it from surrounding objects. The weeding robots make use of robotic arm fitted with multi camera to detect the weed and a gripping and cutting tool to remove the weed without damaging the trees. The AI/ML algorithms based on CNN are used to analyze the images of multi camera for accurately detecting the weeds. The application of chemical spray to kill weeds onto fields is not only wasteful but it can severely harm the environment. Robots provide much more efficient method of weed control. The concept of micro spraying using robot significantly reduces the amount of herbicide used in crop growing. Micro-spraying robots make use of computer vision technology to detect weeds and then spray a targeted drop of herbicide onto them. The Figure 8.8 shows weed control robot and its working principle. The navigation of robot is through GPS and its operation is controlled using smart phone. The robot is solar power driven with adequate battery backup. The robot camera captures the high resolution images of weed and analyzed to take a decision followed by action to target the weeds. The robot works without being constrained by a human administrator. It makes the progress just by getting its heading and situating itself with the assistance from its camera, GPS and sensors. Its arrangement of vision enables it to follow crop lines, and to recognize the presence and position of weeds in and between the columns. Two automated arms then, at that point apply a micro-dose of herbicide, methodically focusing on weeds that have been recognized. The robot speed also adjusts it-self depending on the density of weeds. Such robots are recommended to be used after an underlying standard use of herbicide. The machine can be totally controlled and arranged through a smart phone application.

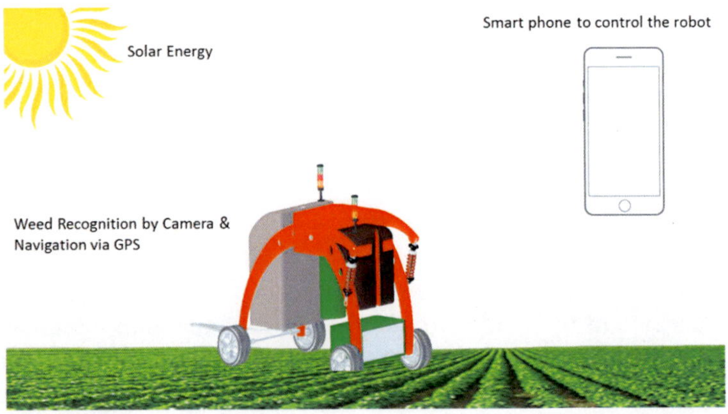

Fig. 8.8: Working Principle of Weed Detection and Spraying Robot

8.7.3 Seed Planting Robot

The planting of seed or sowing is the most important process of the farming. It is time consuming and requires lot of human efforts to maintain appropriate depth and seed to seed spacing. The robotic vehicles for seed plantation are widely used in precision farming to assist farmers. Such robots perform planting of seeds more accurately than the human operators and also save human energy, lobour cost and time.

A seed sowing robot consists of a robotic arm to sow the seeds. The arm captures seed from a seed container attached with the machine. The movement of robot arm is controlled through the mobile application to set the desired positions of the arm. Once all the positions are set, the robot is switched on through mobile application and the robotic arm sows the seed automatically. The robot moves on wheels which are controlled through the mobile application. Thus, such a robot completely automates the seed sowing process and reduces the efforts and the total cost of sowing.

8.7.4 Pesticide and Insecticide Spraying Robots

The use of agro chemicals is inevitable to control the insect and pest attacks on the crop. Conventionally, human operated spraying machine is used to spray the insecticide and pesticide. Such manual spraying practices are not only inefficient but also harmful for the health of the farmers. The spraying robots are automated spraying machines which can be controlled remotely with mobile applications. The robotic arm of such robots is fitted with spraying nozzle. The height of nozzle can be set according to the average height of trees. A high resolution stereo camera mounted on the robot can capture the images of tree leaves. The AI based computer vision models are used to detect the presence of insects and pests on the tree. Accordingly, the Controller Unit of the robot switch-on the spraying nozzle to spray a controlled quantity of the chemical at the desired portion of the tree. This reduces wastage of the chemicals hence reducing the cost and also saves time and labour cost. In addition, a direct the exposure to chemicals can be avoided, hence protect the farmer from harmful effects of the chemical exposure.

9

Geospatial Technologies

9.1 Introduction

The term '*geo*' is a Greek word, it means the earth, and the term '*spatial*' means parameter/feature measured, mapped or modeled with reference to distance or space. The geospatial technology refers to the technology that measure, model, analyze, map, or predict the features or phenomena that occur on earth and its surface. The geospatial technologies also known as '*geomatics*' deal with the science and technology for gathering, storage, processing, analysis, mapping and distribution of geographic data for some specific applications. These applications may include meteorological, agricultural, environmental, tactical, natural resource exploration etc. There are three technology domains categorized under geospatial technologies. These are namely Remote Sensing (RS), Global Positioning System (GPS), and Geographical Information System (GIS). This chapter introduces three types of geospatial technologies, explains working principle of each one and also gives an insight of its general and agricultural applications.

9.2 Remote Sensing Technology

Remote Sensing (RS) refers to the science and technology of identification, imaging, mapping, modeling, classification of earth's surface features/objects from a remote distance and without being in physical contact. This is performed by detecting and recording the reflected or emitted electromagnetic radiations from the earth's surface or objects using highly sensitive sensors deployed on aircraft or unmanned vehicle (UAV or drone) or on satellite. The remote sensing accomplished using aircraft or drone is called airborne remote sensing and that by satellite is called space-borne remote sensing. In both cases, some portion of electromagnetic radiations is used as the medium of interaction with the earth surface and its atmosphere. The electromagnetic spectrum interacting with earth surface may be visible or infrared, near infrared, mid infrared, thermal infrared and microwaves. The RS system records the energy reflected or emitted by earth surface. The amount of electromagnetic radiation from an object (called radiance) is influenced by both the properties of the object and the radiation hitting the object (irradiance).

9.2.1 Electromagnetic Spectrum for RS

The Electromagnetic (EM) spectrum is defined as complete range of EM radiation bands in which each band is ordered or grouped according to its wavelength or frequency. Sun is universal source of EM radiations with complete spectrum of radiations. Figure 9.1 shows EM spectrum grouped in to different bands in the order of wavelength and frequency.

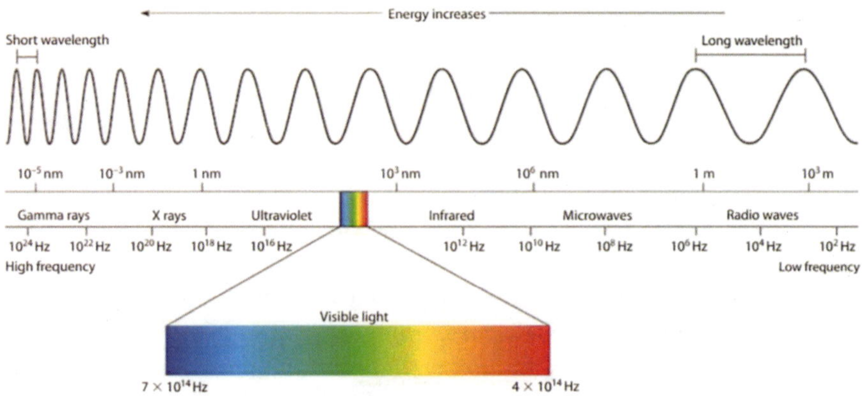

Fig. 9.1: EM Spectrum

In Figure 9.1, as we move from left to right, the wavelength is increasing and frequency is in decreasing order. At the same time, the energy of EM waves (E=hf, f is frequency, h is plank's constant) increases with the increase in frequency and with the decrease in wavelength. It means the gamma rays possess the highest frequency and highest energy and the lowest wavelength in the entire EM spectrum. In earth's remote sensing, the EM bands of importance are visible light (400 nm-700nm) infrared light (700 nm- 1000nm), near infrared light (800-2500nm), and microwave bands (10mm or 10000 nm). The term 'infra' means 'below', so, 'infrared' means the EM waves having frequency below the frequency of 'red' band of visible spectrum. The microwaves are also called centimeter waves because of wavelength of the order of centimeters (10mm or lower). The term 'micro' means small, on account of its smaller wavelength in centimeters as compared to other radio waves having wavelength in meters.

9.2.2 Principle of Remote Sensing

The remote sensing is based on detection, recording, processing and analysis of EM radiations reflected and emitted from various natural and manmade objects on earth surface. As shown in Figure 9.2, sun is source of radiations incident on earth. The object reflects some portion of EM energy and the remaining energy is absorbed by the object and the atmosphere. The wavelength of the reflected radiation from a specific object depends on its colour. The wavelength corresponding to the colour of object is reflected and the remaining wavelengths are absorbed by the object. In other words, the colour of an object as seen by human eye or any other sensor represents wavelength of reflected light from the object. For example, a green object reflects green wavelength and absorb lights of all other wavelengths. Similarly, it is also true for objects having other colours. The amplitude and wavelength of reflected radiations varies for different types of objects like vegetation/forest, sand, rocks, hills, land, water, building, roads etc.

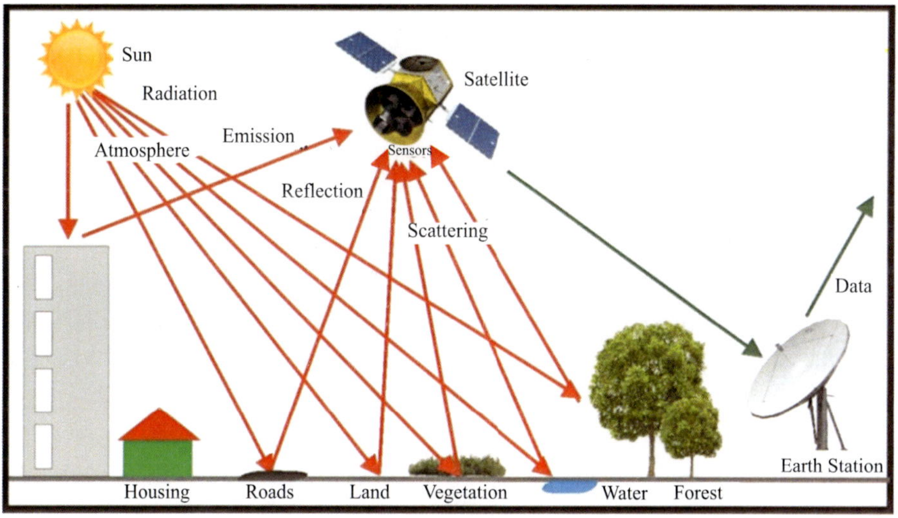

Fig. 9.2: Principle of Remote Sensing

The RS sensors are deployed on the satellite onboard in case of satellite based or space borne remote sensing. On the other hands, the RS sensors are fitted on drone or aircraft in case of aerial remote sensing. In both the cases, the sensor detects and stores the reflected radiations in the form of digital data, called remote sensing data. These data are sent to earth station located on the ground station through wireless communication link. The ground station is also called as remote sensing earth station. At the RS earth station, the received data are processed with image processing software to prepare false colour composites (FCC) and prepare a complete map of that part of the earth highlighting earth features in different colours.

9.2.3 Passive and Active Remote Sensing

The magnitude, phase, polarization and wavelength of the reflected EM radiations from earth surface, and its accurate detection plays decisive role in accurate mapping of earth's surface. When remote sensing is undertaken with sun light as the primary source of energy or radiations as shown in Figure 9.3, it is called passive remote sensing. Here, the solar radiations incident on the earth surface and the reflected or backscattered from earth are detected and analyzed by the sensor on aircraft or drone or satellite. Obviously, such RS systems rely on the availability of sun, and difficult during night. On the other hands, in active remote sensing, sun light is not used as source of EM radiations. A specially designed source of energy emitting EM radiations is used in the sensor. The EM radiations of specific bands from the sensor are allowed to target and fall on desired portion of earth surface and the backscattered or reflected radiations are recorded and analyzed. Such type of remote sensing is based on the principles of Radio Detection and Ranging (RADAR) and Light Detection and Ranging (LIDAR). In RADAR, generally microwaves are used for remote sensing, whereas, in LIDAR optical waves or light waves are used. The arrow '1' in Figure 9.3 indicates incident radiation; arrow '2' indicates the reflected or backscattered radiations. The sensor records the reflected or backscattered energy and processes it to produce encoded signal in the form of data, called remote sensing data. The remote sensing data are sent to earth station as indicated by arrow '3', for further processing and analysis.

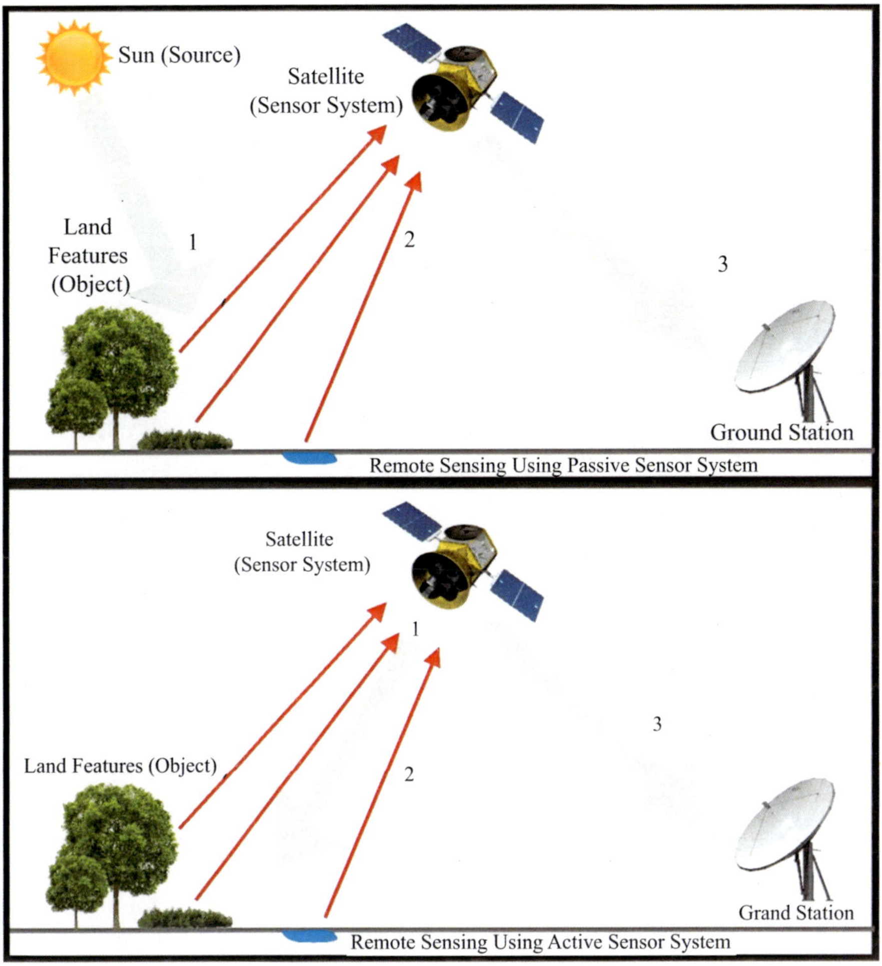

Fig. 9.3: Passive and Active Remote Sensing

9.2.4 Image Resolution in Remote Sensing

The earth's mapping data as acquired by remote sensor are sent through wireless link to the remote sensing earth station. These data correspond to the targeted objects of earth, are converted to an artificial image, called False Colour Composite (FCC). The FCC is different from True Colour Composite (TCC) or the actual colour image. It is combination of red, green and blue, different from natural colours of the objects. The commonly used FCC represents near infra red as red, red as green, and green as blue. Figure 9.4 (a) and (b) show FCC and TCC images respectively of Landsat-8 satellite. The advantage of using FCC instead of TCC is that it allows visualization of the wavelength near infra red range, that human eye cannot see. The vegetation appears in different shades of red depending on the condition of vegetation. This allows vegetation to be readily detected in the image. The FCC graphics encompasses vast information about the targeted area of the earth. Such composites can be understood and analyzed only by highly skilled and specialized experts or dedicated software tools.

(a) **(b)**

Fig. 9.4: Images by Satellite Landsat **(a)** TCC **(b)** FCC [Courtesy: NASA]

The accuracy of analysis and interpretation of such images depends on the image resolution. There are four type of resolutions used to describe the output image of a remote sensor. These are called as spatial, spectral, temporal and radiometric resolution.

(i) Spatial Resolution: The term spatial means a function described in terms of the linear dimension either space or distance as a variable parameter. The spatial resolution gives the number of pixels in an image, and it determines the smallest feature of earth surface or an object that can be detected or resolved from its surrounding objects. In an image, larger the number of pixels, higher will be its spatial resolution and vice-versa. The spectral response of the earth surface or object with reference to space or distance gives spatial characterization of the object for a given band of spectrum. The variation in spectral response of earth surface with space or distance is termed as spatial variability. The spatial characterization gives correlation between sensor images to monitor the spatial variability. The latest generation satellite based remote sensors can exhibit spatial resolution of less than 5m, that means, it can resolve or distinguish earth features or objects separated by 5m or even less. In case of aerial or drone based remote sensing, on account of lower altitudes of sensor as compared to the satellite sensors, it is possible to attain spatial resolution of 5cm or even less.

(ii) Spectral Resolution: The remote sensing and imaging of earth surface or any object by a sensor at discrete bands of the EM spectrum is called spectral characterization of the object. The smallest wavelength spacing (usually in nano-meters) between two closest spectral points of the image, is termed as spectral resolution. The spectral variability and spectral correlation between two images is used to monitor the dynamic characteristics of image of any object. It gives vital information about the reflectance and absorption of spectral bands by the objects. The spectral characterization and also the spectral resolution is very useful parameter to accurately distinguish closely spaced objects of different colour and texture. For example it helps in estimation of the vegetative growth of the crop and also to detect the presence of insects and pests on the crop.

(iii) Temporal Resolution: The term temporal is a function described with reference to time as variable parameter. The remote sensing data of the same object or region of earth surface obtained at regular intervals with some periodicity of time is called temporal information. The statistical variations in these images with respect to time, is called temporal variability. The smallest time interval between two successive sensor images of the same object is called as temporal resolution. The RS images may be acquired on any predetermined time scale, in interval of seconds, minutes, hours, days etc. The temporal characterization gives correlation between the images which is used to monitor the dynamic change in the features of earth surface. It gives temporal information like rate of crop growth, or rate of forestation or rate of deforestation etc.

(iv) Radiometric Resolution: In remote sensing, the radiometric resolution of image data represents sensitivity of the sensor to distinguish different grey-scale values. It is measured in bits. Higher the number of bits an image has, the more will be the grey-scale values that can be stored, and, thus, more differences in the reflection on the land surfaces can be spotted. For example One bit stands for a sensor that represents only black and white, 2-bit equals 4 grey-scale values and 4-bit 16 values.

9.3 Microwave Remote Sensing

The microwaves are EM waves or radio waves having frequency range from 3 GHz to 30 GHZ, and the wavelength range from 1cm to 1m. Since the wavelength of microwaves are longer than that of visible and infrared waves used in optical remote sensing, microwaves exhibit special properties that are important for remote sensing. The **longer wavelength of microwave radiations** are not susceptible to atmospheric scattering, therefore**, can penetrate through cloud cover, rain, dust, haze, dust, and fog.** The optical remote sensing on the other hands, having shorter wavelength are susceptible to atmospheric scattering and cannot penetrate under the mentioned atmospheric conditions. The microwave RS is therefore, advantageous as compared to its optical counter part because detection of microwave energy is possible under almost all weather and environmental conditions so that RS data can be collected at any time. The Microwave RS is performed using satellites called remote sensing satellite. The RS satellites are launched from earth station and placed in earth's orbit. The satellite revolves around earth in lower earth orbit (LEO) typically at an altitude of 800km - 1000km. The RS sensors are pointed or directed towards the desired region of the earth, of which remote sensing data are to be acquired. Figure 9.4(a) shows typical RS satellite orbiting the earth in sun synchronous orbit at an altitude of about 800-1000km, also called lower earth orbit (LEO). Another orbit shown in the Figure 9.4(a) is geostationary earth orbit (GEO). The GEO is satellite orbit at an altitude of 36000Km in the equatorial plane of earth. Generally, telecommunication and broadcasting satellites are placed in GEO. Figure 9.4(b) shows RS satellite acquiring remote sensing data from earth by emitting microwave radiations towards the desired portion of earth and detecting the backscattered or reflected radiations.

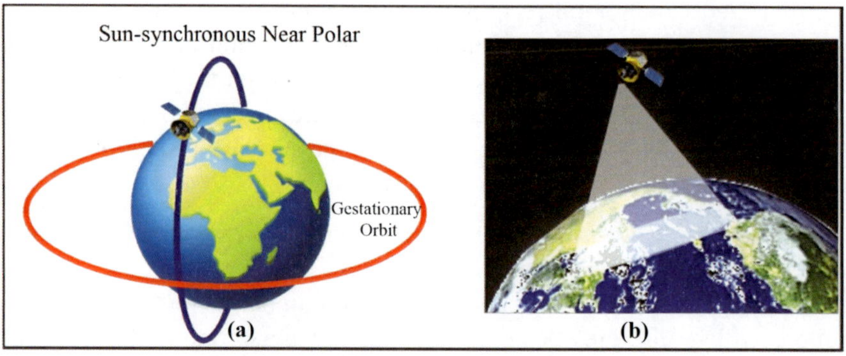

Fig. 9.5: Microwave Remote Sensing **(a)** RS satellite in LEO **(b)** Imaging by RS satellite

Although microwaves are naturally emitted from earth surface features, atmosphere and objects, but the energy detected by the satellite sensor is too low to infer or extract any information. Therefore, passive microwave remote sensing is not much popular. The active microwave remote sensing, on the other hands, makes use of microwave source fitted on the satellite. This microwave source on satellite emits microwave radiations towards the desired part of the earth surface to be mapped. The remote sensing data are acquired through the reflected microwave radiations as detected by the sensor on the satellite.

9.4 Global Positioning System (GPS)

Global Positioning System (GPS) is a worldwide multi-satellite RF wireless navigational system to track and determine real time geographic location of an object or user and to guide its navigation or movement from one place to another. The GPS is originally an American service technology, accessible worldwide depending on the availability of satellite connectivity from that part of the earth. The GPS provides position, velocity (if object is in motion) and timing information of GPS user. It finds extensive scope in military, civil, aviation, marine, space and agricultural applications.

9.4.1 Components and Working of GPS

In GPS, there are three major segments or components. These are space segment, control segment and user segment as shown in Figure 9.6(a). The space segment of GPS comprises 24 satellites arranged in 6-orbital planes at an altitude of about 20200 km from earth surface, having 55- degree inclination. Each satellite completes one revolution around the earth in about 12 hours (one-half of a sidereal day). With this orbital position and number of satellites, a user at any location on earth will have 24 hours connectivity at least with four GPS satellites.

The control segment also called operational control segment of GPS consists of master control station (MCS), ground antenna, and remote monitoring earth station. The monitoring earth stations track each of the GPS satellites and relay its navigational and tracking information like range, elevation, and azimuth data of respective satellite to the MCS.

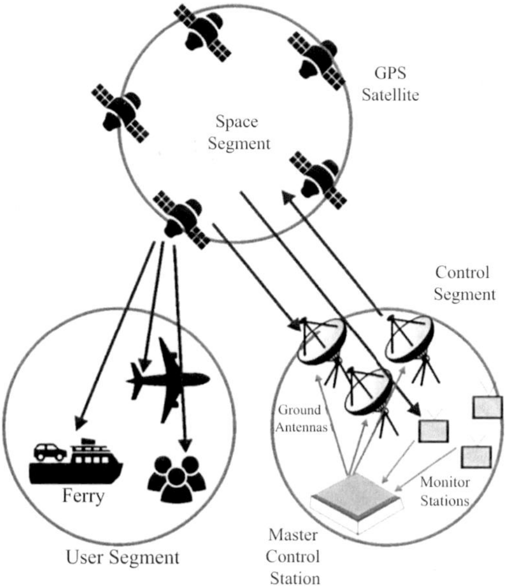

Fig. 9.6: GPS Segments

The user interface mainly consists of low noise high sensitivity receiver that receives tracking and navigation information of the user. Generally a GPS receiver consists of three basic components: (i) an antenna, which receives the signal and sometimes has anti-jamming capabilities; (ii) a receiver-processor, which converts the radio signal to a useful navigation solution; and (iii) a control/display unit, which provides receiver control interface and also displays the positioning, velocity and timing information.

Each satellite of GPS transmits a continuous radio signal with a unique code. The unique code includes data about the satellite's position and the timing synchronization using on-board atomic clock that gives exact timing when the coded signal was transmitted. In general, three-dimensional position of a user can be determined by simultaneously measuring the ranges by three satellites. However, because the GPS satellites and receiver clocks are practically not perfectly synchronized, a fourth satellite in GPS orbit is used to eliminate the receiver clock bias that is common to all measurements. Such type of ranging is termed as GPS pseudo ranging. The pseudo ranging technique improves the tracking and navigation information of the user.

9.5 Geographical Information System (GIS)

Geographical information system (GIS) is an integrated computer hardware-software based geospatial technology that captures, compiles, stores, manipulate, analyze and display patterns and maps of spatial information of the earth surface. The remote sensing data acquired by RS satellite or UAV or aircraft are used as input to the GIS. These data correspond to land mapping and other features of the earth surface. The GIS with its image processing software tools, provides patterns and trends of spatial details of local terrain. It helps users to view, understand, question, interpret, and visualize the geospatial data in many ways. The GIS maps provide patterns, trends and relationships of geospatial features in the form of maps, charts and reports. The GIS technology can be integrated into any enterprise information system framework.

The GIS maps can be used to explore earth features of a specific region or location that provides details of dynamics and spatial variability of local terrain useful in exploration and estimation of natural resources, vegetation, deforestation, water, urban and rural topography, soil maps, crop surveillance, road and buildings, rivers, ponds, lakes, oceans, mountains etc.

9.5.1 GIS Components

A GIS comprises five key components namely hardware, software, data, people and methods, integrated together as shown in Figure 9.7. The hardware comprises a high speed computer with graphical processing unit (GPU). It uses a wide variety of standalone or networked computer configurations including centralized computer servers or desktop computers.

The GIS software is an important component that provides functions and tools to store, analyze and display geographical information. The key functions and operations of GIS software are data base management, manipulation of geographic information, support geographic query, visualization and analysis etc permits easy access to tools using graphical user interface (GUI).

The people in GIS are the technical specialists who design and maintain GIS software and the geosciences experts who can interpret the GIS maps to effectively attain the objectives.

The GIS methods are the sequence of well designed procedures belonging to a strategic plan and rules. It includes models and operating practices unique to specific service or application.

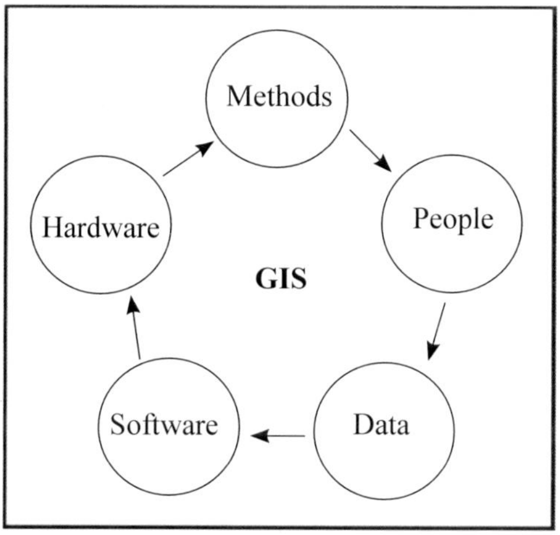

Fig. 9.7: GIS Components

The most important component of GIS is the geographical data as obtained from remote sensing techniques already explained. The DBMS of GIS create and maintain a data base to properly organize and manage data. The advancement in the collection and classification of data and its accuracy has helped creation of standard digital base-maps at different scales. The data used in GIS can be captured from multiple sources like manual digitalization of scanned images of aerial photographs, paper maps, existing digital data sets, remote sensing satellite imagery, drone imagery and data from GPS.

9.5.2 Applications of GIS

The GIS finds wide range of applications in different sectors. Some of the major applications are as follows:

Urban and Town Planning: The GIS can be very useful and effective in infrastructural development of urban and rural areas, town planning, building smart cities, development of sub urban area etc. The GIS maps facilitate builders, engineers, town planners and architects to make use of spatial data sets to plan on the futuristic township. It becomes easier for engineers and architects, to plan a complete architectural solution with help of granular information provided by GIS. A number of mega projects for development of metro cities make use of GIS data and tools for planning out the projects. The GIS is used to remodel the existing drainage system of metro cities and help to tackle the water clogging issues during floods and burst in monsoons.

Disaster Management: The GIS technology can be very useful in disaster management to prepare and effectively implement strategies to tackle with disaster caused by natural calamities like flood, earthquake, pandemic, volcanic eruption etc. The geospatial data sets and databases help organizations to store data at all levels. The GIS database contains all essential and vital information related to risk-prone areas like history and effects of calamities in that area, presence and location of hospitals, habitation, and isolation centres in the vicinity of high risk-prone zones etc to plan for further contingency plans. This helps authorities to take corrective measures to minimize its adverse effects and also to prepare for the future.

Mapping and Navigation: The GIS is also used in mapping and navigation applications. In present scenario, Google maps are the best example of GIS applications in mapping and navigation, the most widely used service of Google by people of entire world. Humans around the world use it while travelling to a new place and also to review any place. It has also become a popular and extensively used tool by Cab and carpool service providers. The GPS and GIS technology adds crisper and edge to the experience of navigation, in which users are also allowed to post any unknown or unnamed information in the map data set. Google accepts user map edits and also has its map maker. However, maps also collect data from local users and people in its proprietary tool, which is known as Map creator.

Deforestation and Vegetation Management: The surveillance and monitoring of aforestation or vegetation projects can be very effectively assessed periodically using GIS. The geospatial data of forest lands allows authorities and organizations to keep a close watch and track of the rate of deforestation. The past data sets of the same land area captured during different periods is used for analysis and to plan for reducing deforestation and also for reforestation and vegetation. Due to the increasing number of deforestation, government bodies are also keeping track of forest and vegetation data. The datasets are used for the further analytical purpose of reforestation.

Agriculture: As we know agriculture is one of the important segments of human civilization and plays a key role in the economy of a country. The use of modern digital technologies like GIS in agriculture can be beneficial in a number of applications.

a. **Drought:** In rain dependent farming, GIS can play a key role in providing the patterns of rains and drought affected areas to guide the local farmers to identify the drought area or land to avoid further damage of plant seeds, human effort, and costly fertilizers. This information is very useful for planning and executing contingent plan of area.

b. **Pest control:** The early prediction of pest attacks like locust and rodent is possible from the available spatial data sets of particular agricultural lands. This will allow the governing body and farmers to plan and take corrective measures to minimize the possible damage to the crop.

c. **Land and Soil Analysis:** From the periodic compilation, comparison and analysis of geospatial data of land and soil it is possible using GIS to predict and accurately quantify the soil erosion, soil nutrients, monitoring of soil health parameters etc. Such information is extremely important to assist farmers to decide the crop type on the basis of soil health status.

d. **Crop Surveillance:** The real time GIS data of a crop field and its analysis can monitor the crop growth and accurately predict the crop yield. This helps in identification of infestation and early detection of plant disease so that corrective measures can be taken by the farmers or the governing body to overcome the causes of crop adversities.

10

Big Data Analytics

10.1 Introduction

Big Data refers to extremely large, very fast, highly diverse, and complex data that cannot be managed with conventional data management systems, tools or processes. In the perfect world, Big Data may include all kind of data, which can deliver the right information, to right person, in the right quantity, at the right time, to help in making the right decisions.

Organizations today are facing the challenge of having the availability of wealth of huge data but are not in a position to get value out of it as all data being in its most raw form or in a unstructured or semi structured format. These data are generated from online transactions, emails, videos, audios, images, click streams, logs, posts, search queries, health records, social networking interactions, science data, sensors and mobile phones and their applications. Such huge amount of data generated continuously in real time challenges the current businesses to capture, store, manage, share, analyze and visualize these huge unorganized and unstructured data via conventional data processing procedures and tools. Big Data has its origins in the medical and scientific domains, where the complex analysis of enormous amounts of data has been made for physics modeling, drug development, and other forms of data intensive research.

Big Data and Big Data analytics are the terms which are used interchangeably these days. More profoundly Big Data analytics may be defined as the advanced analytic techniques used against voluminous, diverse and rapidly increasing big data sets that include raw, unstructured and semi-structured data from different sources, and in different sizes ranging from terabytes (2^{40} bytes) to zettabytes (2^{70} bytes).

International Data Group (IDC) predicts that global data volume was expected to grow exponentially from 4.4 zettabytes(approximately $4.4 * 10^{21}$ bytes) to 44 zettabytes (approximately $44 * 10^{21}$ bytes) between 2013 and 2020. By 2025, IDC anticipates that there shall be 163 zettabytes ($163 * 10^{21}$ bytes) of data. Consequently there is a great need of the tools and techniques to store, analyze and derive intelligence out of such rapidly produced huge data sets.

10.2 Characteristics of Big Data

The data growth in Big Data domain is perceived as being three dimensional referred as "3 Vs" model of describing Big Data. The "3Vs" can be defined as High Volume, Velocity and Variety of data occurring simultaneously. However, these days the Big Data Characterization as "3Vs" is upgraded to "4Vs" to signify High Volume, Velocity, Variety and Veracity/Value of data as elaborated below:

1. Volume: The quantity of data generated in the world has been doubling every 12 to 18 months. Conventionally data is measured in Gigabytes (2^{30} bytes or approximately 10^9 bytes) and Terabytes (2^{40} bytes or approximately 10^{12} bytes), but big data is measured in petabytes (2^{50} bytes or approximately 10^{15} bytes) and exabytes (2^{60} bytes or approximately 10^{18} bytes). This data is so huge that it is almost impossible to find any specific thing in it or make meaning of it in a reasonable period of time. The cost of storing data is decreasing approximately at the rate of 30% to 40% per year leading to dramatic increase in growth of data. Due to decreasing cost of storage, there is tendency to record everything that can be observed leading to '*datafication*' of the world. The other reason for the dramatic increase in the data can be attributed to the vast increase in the number of forms and functions of data.

2. Velocity: Big Data is like a fast flowing river. Big Data is being generated by billions of devices and communicated at hypersonic speeds via internet. The principal reason for this high velocity of data is because of the increased speed of the internet. Internet speeds are in general having been increased from 10 million bytes per second to gigabytes per second, which is 100 times faster. Moreover increased variety of internet sources such as mobiles, which can access internet on the go are also adding to the increase in the velocity of data.

3. Variety: Big Data will be required to deal with different variety of data. Broadly the Big Data can be categorized into three categories. The first category can be classified as the form of data. Data can be in the form of numbers, text, video, audio, maps, graphs etc. Moreover there can be composite form of data where multiple form of data are embedded in one form such as text documents may have pictures and graphs embedded in it and similarly audio may be embedded with video in a video file. All these form of data may require different storage format as video and audio storage format, which may be hugely different than storage formats for text and numbers.

The second category can be classified as the **function** of data. Data can be from anywhere such as business transaction records, human dialogs or conversation, videos, audio songs, recorded or archived, data from sensors etc. All these data may have different functions and hence needing different treatment.

The third category can be classified as the **source** of data. Mobile phones, laptops and computer systems support wide-ranging series of applications, moreover in case of mobile phones the data can be generated anytime anywhere. Business systems generate massive amount of business transaction information. Sensors on machines and RFID (Radio Frequency Tags) on assets generate a lot never-ending repetitive data. Therefore principally there are three types of sources of data that can be categorized as human-human communication, human-machine communication and machine-to-machine communications.

4. Veracity/Value: Veracity narrates to believability, truthfulness and quality of data. In Big Data domain there is considerable misinformation and erroneous data. The reason for this bad quality data can be due to human error, technical error or malicious intent.

Therefore, the Big Data need to organized and quantified by quality for it to be put to any good use, Figure 10.1 elaborates characteristics of Big Data as "4Vs".

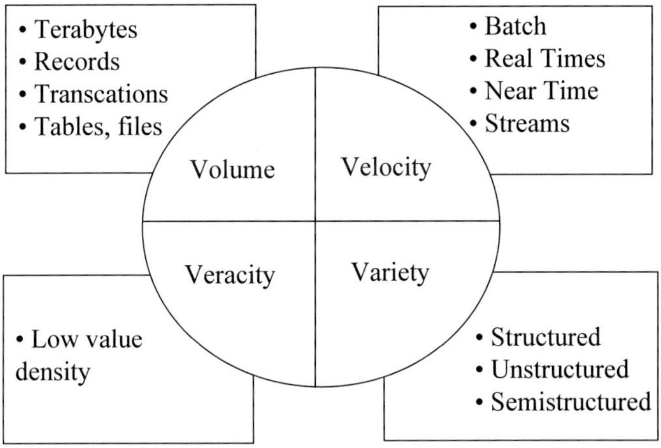

Fig. 10.1: "4Vs" characteristics of Big Data

10.3 Types of Big Data

As discussed in the previous section Big Data can be categorized based on volume, variety, velocity and veracity but the data in these categories shall broadly belong to three type as elaborated below.

1. Structured Data
2. Semi Structured Data
3. Unstructured Data

10.3.1 Structured Data

These are the data which can be mapped to pre-designed structure. Generally speaking all data that can be stored in table of rows and columns or in table of database, SQL lie in this category. Structured data is often managed and queried using SQL (Structured Query Language) in relational database management system. Structured data was a huge improvement over strictly paper based unstructured systems.

However, structured data first depends on creating a data model elaborating how the data will be stored, processed and accessed. This may include defining fields of data storage, type of data for each field be it alphabetic, numeric, currency or date and may be also restrictions on each field such as number of characters per field or restricted values per field as Male, Female or Mr. or Ms., etc. A sample relational database table exhibiting structured data is shown in Table 10.1.

Table 10.1: Sample Relational Database Exhibiting Structured Data

Employee ID	Employee Name	Gender	Department	Salary
2301	Ramesh Jain	Male	Finance	100000
2302	PriyaRajpurohit	Female	Admin	150000
2303	Vijay Gupta	Male	Admin	100000
2304	Naveen Roy	Male	Finance	125000
2305	Anju Sharma	Female	Finance	170000

Although the structured data has the advantage of being easily stored, quarried and analyzed but all data cannot be mapped to a pre-defined design and therefore in the domain of Big Data only 5 to 10 percent of data can fall in this category.

10.3.2 Semi Structured Data

Semi structured data can be defined as the information that cannot be stored in a relational database. However such semi structured data is expected to have some organizational properties to enable logical analysis of such data. Generally such data with some processing can be stored in a relational database but that may not always be possible.

Examples of semi structured data may include CSV, XML and JSON documents. Moreover NoSQL databases are also considered as semi structured. An example of semi-structured data represented in an XML file is demonstrated in Figure 10.2

<rec><name>RaviRay</name><sex>Male</sex><age>40</age></rec>

<rec><name>Priya Sharma</name><sex>Female</sex><age>30</age></rec>

<rec><name>Vijay Sharma</name><sex>Male</sex><age>50</age></rec>

<rec><name>Naveen Gupta</name><sex>Male</sex><age>51</age></rec>

<rec><name>Rahul sexana</name><sex>Male</sex><age>32</age></rec>

Fig 10.2: A sample semi-structured data represent in an XML

10.3.3 Unstructured Data

Unstructured data refers to the data that cannot be mapped to a predefined data model. This results in ambiguous and irregular data and is very difficult to get meaning out of it from such data using conventional data modeling tools as in relational database systems for structured data.

Techniques such as natural language processing, data mining and text analytics can be used to find patterns and interpret the information from such unstructured data. Examples of unstructured data may include audio, video, images, analog data, books, articles, health records and unstructured test such as body of an email messages, web pages and word processor documents to name a few. More than 80 percent of data in the domain of Big Data is of type unstructured data.

Unstructured data can be either human generated or machine generated. The examples of machine generated unstructured data may include data such as satellite imaging data, scientific data, images, videos, radar or sonar data etc. similarly the human generated unstructured data may include text documents, logs, surveys, emails, social media data generated from platforms such as youtube, facebook, twitter etc or data generated from mobiles and websites in the form of messages, location or unstructured web contents.

10.4 Big Data Analytics Techniques

Data Analytics is the discovery of meaningful patterns in data. Analytics generally relies on coherent application of computer programming, statistics, probability, and operation research to measure performance. Analytics along with data visualization can be used to present the insight on data in an easy to understand and communicable form.

Basically Data analytics in gist can be defined as the scientific process of transforming data into insight for making better decision based on the data in hand. The objective of small and big data analytics is to get actionable insights resulting in smarter decisions leading to better business and or scientific outcomes. The data analytics can broadly be classified as under.

1. Predictive data analytics
2. Descriptive data analytics
3. Prescriptive data analytics

(1) Predictive Analytics

Predictive analytics uses data to convert it into actionable and valuable information. Predictive analytics uses combinations of statistics, probability, data mining and machine learning to analyze the available data to predict the future outcome and recommendations. For example the business use predictive analytics to analyze customer purchase data to predict customer's future purchase behaviors. Predictive analytics is a challenging field requiring a good amount of data and skilled implementation to obtain accurate and actionable predictions.

(2) Descriptive Analytics

The descriptive analytics analyze and describe the features of a data. Descriptive analytics basically try to summarize the available data into valuable information. Generally all management reporting such as finance, marketing, operations and sales along with visual analytic reports uses this type of analysis to improve businesses. In businesses, descriptive analysis is applied for evaluating the key performance indicator for determining the business performance. Unlike predictive models that focus on predicting a single customer behavior, descriptive models identify many different relationships between customers or products.

(3) Prescriptive Analytics

Prescriptive analytics synthesizes data, mathematical sciences and business rules with machine learning and artificial intelligence to predict and prescribe the correct and careful business decisions for the future. Prescriptive analytics also uses the insight from predictive analytics and descriptive analytics to predict and prescribe correct information and recommendations.

Prescriptive analytics rise above just predicting future outcome by also proposing actions to benefit from the prescribed forecasts and presenting the decision maker with the consequences of each decision option. Therefore prescriptive analytics not only anticipates what will happen and when it will happen, but also why it will happen. Prescriptive analytics in general continuously processes incoming data in real time with preexisting data to continuously improve the accuracy of prediction and to provide better decision options.

Top information technology businesses like Google, Amazon, Netflix, Facebook uses prescriptive analytics to provide better customer satisfaction and to improve business with better business decisions. Other business sectors such as healthcare, financial institutions, energy and utility sector are also leveraging the power of prescriptive analytics techniques to achieve better business decisions and outcomes.

10.5 Standard Big Data Architecture

Broadly speaking a generic Big Data systems architecture can be thought of having multiple processing layers such as big data source layer, data ingest layer, batch processing layer, stream processing layer, data organization layer, infrastructure layer, distributed file system layer, data consumption layer. A block diagram elaborating the same is shown in Figure 10.3.

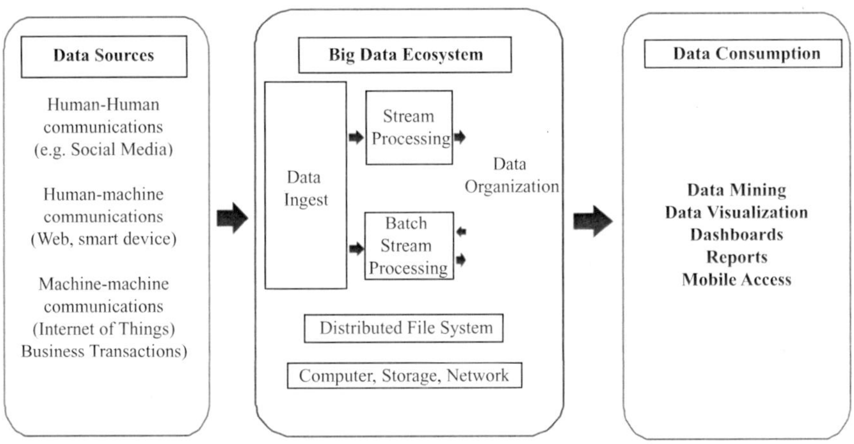

Fig 10.3: Generic Big Data Architecture

A Big Data solution typically comprises these as logical layers. Each layer can be represented by one or more available technologies, which is described as below:

(1) **Big Data Source Layer:** The choice of sources of data for an application depends upon what type of data analysis is desired and what kind of data shall be required to accomplish the desired analytics. Big Data will very in volume, velocity, variety and veracity/value as described earlier as "4Vs". The source of big data can be internal or external to the

organization. The scope of access to data available could be limited. The level of structure as well as the speed of data and its quantity could be high or low depending upon the data source.

(2) **Data Ingest Layer:** The job of this layer is to acquire data from the numerous data sources. Incoming data is received through numerous input points that can acquire data at various speeds and in various quantities. The data is sent to a batch processing system, or real time processing system, or to a storage file system such as *Hadoop*.

(3) **Batch Processing Layer:** The layer receives data from the ingest point or from the file system or from *NoSQL* database engine. Data is processed using parallel programming techniques such as *MapReduce* to process it and produce the designed results. This batch processing layer thus must understand the data sources and data types, the algorithms that would work on the data and the format of the desired outcomes. The output of this layer could be sent for instant reporting or be stored in *NoSQL* databases for an on demand report by the clients.

(4) **Stream Processing Layer:** This layer receives data directly from the ingest point. Data is processed using parallel programming techniques such as *MapReduce* to process it in real time to produce the desired results. This layer thus should understand the data source and data types extremely well, and the real time algorithms that would work on that data to produce the desired results.

(5) **Data Organization Layer:** This layer receives data from both the batch and stream processing layers. Its objective is to organize the data for easy access. It is generally represented by some non-relational database system such as *NoSQL* databases. Moreover SQL like languages such as *Hive* and *Pig* can be used to access data and generate reports from these databases.

(6) **Infrastructure Layer:** This layer manages the raw resources of storage, computation and communication. This is increasingly provided through cloud computing paradigms.

(7) **Distributed File System Layer:** This is the core of a Big Data system. It would store huge quantities of data and make it quickly and securely available and accessible to the other layers. Hadoop Distributed File System (HDFS) is the primary technology in this layer. It would also include the supporting applications such as *YARN* (Yet Another Resource Manager) that enable the efficient access to data storage and its transfer.

(8) **Data Consumption Layer:** The job of this layer is to consume the output delivered by the analysis layers directly or through the organization layer. The outcome could be standard reports, data analytics applications, visualization applications, recommendation engines.

The other way of understanding Big Data process flow is to describe the information flow within a Big Data system as a series of steps needed to generate value and useful insights as shown in Figure 10.4. This is generally referred as value chain of Big Data.

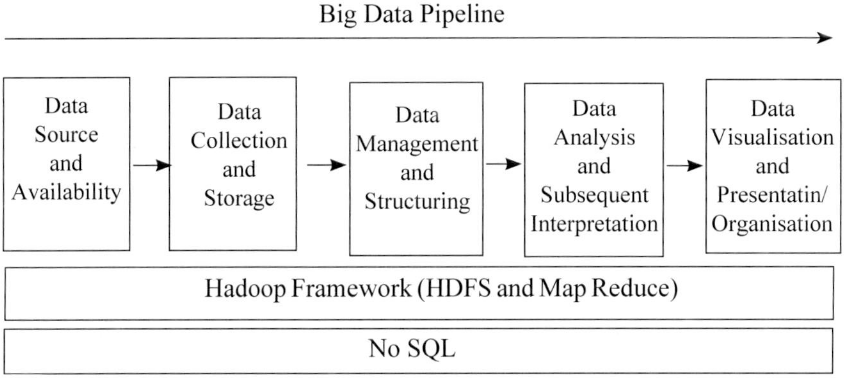

Fig 10.4: The Big data Value chain

10.6 Big Data Applications

Big data analytics involves insight from huge data sets, which can lead to better planning and monitoring, improved design, better risk mitigation and better output. Therefore the Big Data analytics has a role to play in all type of technology and business sector such as banking, communication, media, entertainment, healthcare, education, manufacturing, insurance, retail and whole sale trade, transportation, energy, utilities and agriculture etc. Some examples of role of big data in technology and business industries are elaborated in this section.

(1) Fraud Detection: Business which involves any type of claims or transaction processing, big data analytics can be of great help in detecting the anomalies in real time. Traditionally, the fraud is discovered long time after it has occurred, at which point the damage has been done and all that is left is to minimize the damage and may be adjust policies to prevent it from happening again. Big Data platforms that can analyze claims and transactions in real time, identifying large scale patterns across many transactions or detecting anomalous behavior from individual users, can change the fraud detection scenario all together.

(2) Call Center Analytics: The call center analytics can be a good example from consumer specific business domain. The communication with the customers in call center is a great indicator and influencer of market sentiments, but without real time big data analytics much of the insight that a call center can provide will go unnoticed or will be discovered too late. Big Data solutions can help identify recurring problems or customer and staff behavior patterns on the fly not only making sense of time and quality response resolution but also by capturing and processing call content itself.

(3) Social Media Analytics: These days social media is being used as a powerful tool for product advertising. Consumer goods companies use social media for majority of their advertising in preference over traditional media such TV, hoardings, etc. Consumer goods companies use Big Data processing platforms for sentiment analysis where social media data streams are filtered and analyzed based on certain keywords to gage customer sentiments for the desired region or demographics. This type of analytics can help provide vital information to the concerned companies to improve their product or marketing strategies.

The big data analytics for social media these days is extensively used for '*sentiment analysis*', which can lead to valuable insight regarding the sentiments of social media users. Such '*sentiment analysis*' can be useful for many industry domains such as communication, media, entertainment, healthcare, education, trade and service. These days '*sentiment analysis*' is also used by prominent political parties to gage the sentiments of the people regarding any issues or policies.

(4) Health Care and Medicine: Big Data Analytics can help decode DNA strings for better understanding of the human genetics leading to better understanding and predictions on disease patterns. Big Data along with smart watches and other wearable devices can be used for recording and analyzing blood pressure, blood sugar, heart rate and other biological parameters of millions of persons with different diseases to predict any cause of concern early before any physical symptoms appear in the patients.

One of the main limitations with medicines and pharmaceutical industry today is the precise understanding of biology of the disease. Big Data can help in aggregating more and more information around multiple scales for what constitutes a disease from DNA, proteins and metabolism of cells, tissues, organs, organisms and its ecosystems. Therefore a model build based on such Big Data analytics can help the pharmaceutical industry to synthesis better and more effective medicine in relatively quick time.

(5) Science and Technology: The sciences and technology have always been data hungry with the added challenge of analyzing data from various perspectives to deduce comprehensive understanding and results. For example the Large Hadrons collider (LHC) experiments represent about 150 million sensors delivering data at the rate of 40 million times per second. There are nearly 600 million collisions per second. After filtering and refraining less relevant data and recording only say 0.001% of the data produced by all the sensor streams in the LHC, the cumulative recorded data after filtering from all the four LHC experiments shall be approximately 25 petabytes (2^{50}) annually before replication and approximately 200 petabytes after replication. If all sensor data were recorded in LHC, the data flow would be extremely hard to work with. The data flow would exceed 150 million petabytes at an annual rate before replication, which will be more than all the data produced in the world annually from other sources. Therefore in such experimental setup Big Data analytics play a key role in not only making the meaning out of the data produced but also filtering and rejecting the less important data in such a way that final outcome is not compromised in terms of accuracy and quality.

Similarly in astronomy large amount of data is collected continuously in the form of images and other astrological parameters from advance telescope. This is huge stream of data being captured in real time, to make any meaning out of it, advance Big Data analytic techniques are required to capture and understand the various astrological phenomenon based on these captured data. Similar is the case with remote sensing from satellites for observing and analyzing data from earth. Recent Big Data techniques for data storage, data processing, data analytics, and data visualization play an important role in interpreting such huge amount and type of data.

(6) Design and Manufacturing: Big Data can help in information visibility and process automation in the domain of design and manufacturing. Big data can be helpful in analyzing and predicting trends based on manufacturing, inventory and equipment use and life time data.

Industrial systems and operations frequently produce a continuous stream data from sensors, events from smart equipment and machines. In a manufacturing unit, data sources may include Computer-Aided Manufacturing (CAM) models, Computer-Aided Design (CAD) models, Computer-Aided Engineering (CAE) models, instruments, sensors, and simulators. The data is invariable quite large, high velocity and variety. The data can be unstructured, semi-structured and structured or combination of these data types, which may including documents, logs, test data, CAD/CAM/CAE data, product failure data, product and process performance data, data pertaining to CAD drawings and specifications etc. The data from company's enterprise systems and manufacturing execution systems are generally structured and can be processed using standard relational database systems. Data from sensors and events such as vibration, pressure, valve and acoustics are generally of semi-structured nature. Moreover data such as log or shift reports or data from CAD/CAM/CAE are of raw or unstructured nature.

Therefore in a design and manufacturing enterprise, the high velocity and increasing volume of data with veracity needs to be stored, managed and analyzed with precision and perfection to remain competitive in the market. Big Data technologies with smart analytics can produce the desired results from such varying types of data from design and manufacturing process to predict and recommend the accurate and efficient outcomes.

(7) Big Data and Agriculture: The demand of food in the world is rapidly growing with population explosion. More over the situation is becoming even more challenging due to climate change and urbanization leading to adverse climate conditions and reduced land to grow more food. Big data along with other digital technologies can play a pivotal role in mitigating the ever increasing demand challenge for increasing yields from our farm lands. It can be useful for increasing productivity and profitability at farmers end.

The Big Data technologies along with Internet of Things (IOT) and cloud computing can be the key players for future agriculture to increase food production and addressing the increased food demand of the world. Sensors in soil, plants, fields, and agricultural equipment can help in collecting real time data from the farm land. Therefore IOT acts as the first phase of the Big Data analytics playground as a data collector. The real time information collected from the all the sensors are collected on some cloud platforms. The cloud will be collecting sensor data from a large number of farm fields leading to storage of huge agriculture data on the cloud. Most of the data collected on cloud from sensors are of high velocity, real time and semi-structured type. Since data from a single farm land may not be that large, applying Big Data analytics on a single field data may not be viable option. However on cloud since huge agricultural data will be collected from numerous farm fields, this is the appropriate place to apply big data analytics on data pertaining to a demography or region to predict and prescribe appropriate results and recommendations. The scope of Big Data in agriculture can be large; following are some of the examples to highlight the applicability of Big Data in Agriculture.

- To increase yield, Big Data can provide vital insights regarding rainfall patterns, fertilizer requirements, water cycles, etc. enabling the farmers to appropriately decide when to harvest and what to harvest for better yield and profitability.
- Big data can also give an insight regarding the pesticide uses suggesting how much, what type and when to use the pesticide for a particular crop, demography and region for minimized use of pesticides while still achieving the high profitability.

- Big data can also be useful for farm equipment for better maintenance and optimized uses of the farm equipment with the help of data analytics on the data received from the sensors fitted in the farm equipment.
- It is well known fact that one third of the food produced is wasted due to short coming of the supply chain and inappropriate time to market the produce. Big Data can help regarding the same by optimizing the time and routes of supply chain deliverables.

(8) Application of Big Data in other fields: Given below are some of the other fields that come under the umbrella of Big Data.

- Stock Exchange Data: The stock exchange data generally contains the information pertaining to 'buy' and 'sell' decisions on stocks of different companies along with other attributes of the of the companies. Big Data analytics can help predict the long term market scenarios for the company in view of the predicted forthcoming business challenges.
- Financial Service Organizations: Financial service organizations are using data mined from customer interactions to slice and dice their users into finely tuned segments. This enables these financial institutions to create increasingly relevant and sophisticated offers.
- Energy Sector: Big Data is also playing key role in energy sector specially having the smart grids and advance metering infrastructure. Big Data analytics is helping such energy companies in fault detection, preventive maintenance, ensuring electric power quality and load management.
- Insurance: Insurance companies are using Big Data analytics to see which home insurance applications can be immediately processed, and which one need a validating in-person visit from an agent.
- Retail: By embracing social media, retail organizations are engaging brand advocates, changing the perception of brand antagonists and even enabling enthusiastic customers to sell their products.
- Hospitals: Hospitals are analyzing medical data and patient records to predict those patients that are likely to seek readmission within few months of discharge. The Hospital can then intervene in hope of preventing another costly hospital stay.

10.7 Big Data Technology Landscape

The Big Data technology needs to address four major challenges that are storage, mining, analytics and visualization to handle Big Data. Different technology platform are used to address each of the challenges mentioned above. As the Big Data deals with large volume data set and computationally expensive algorithms, it is generally preferred to use professional cloud platforms supporting huge storage and massive processing power.

The Big Data technology landscape is growing rapidly and some of the fundamentally important technology platforms for Big Data are briefly discussed in this section.

10.7.1 Apache HADOOP, YARN and MapReduce

The first and foremost requirement for Big Data is the need to cater to very high volume, velocity, variety and veracity of data. Having a centralized system for such Big Data may prove to be a performance bottleneck. Therefore having distributed file system for storage, retrieval and processing on a networked collection of commodity machines seems to be a viable alternative for Big Data. This could be accomplished by storing sections of data at different machines and internally managing the lower level jobs of integrating and replicating data set across the computer network. The Apache Hadoop is a popular distributed computing platform to address the challenges of Big Data especially the requirement of providing limitless distributed file storage, computing power and handling of very large number of concurrent tasks.

The Apache Hadoop distributed Computing framework consists of the following four main modules.

1. Hadoop core/common: Hadoop core or as usually referred as hadoop common is the set of libraries and utilities needed by other hadoop modules.
2. HDFS (Hadoop Distributed File System): A distributed file system that is capable of providing very large storage of data on commodity machines with high aggregate bandwidth for storage and retrieval of data. Therefore the major objectives of HDFS may include hardware failure management, handling high volume, velocity, variety and veracity of data for storage on various clusters of hadoop, and network efficiency.
3. YARN (Yet Another Resource Negotiator): YARN is large-scale, distributed operating system for big data applications. It is basically a job scheduler and resource manager with the responsibility of allocating system resources to various tasks and scheduling tasks to the various cluster nodes of the hadoop.
4. MapReduce: MapReduce is a concurrent programming model to access Big Data stored in HDFS. MapReduce enables concurrent processing by fragmenting Big Data into smaller portions and processing them in parallel on Hadoop computing framework. To expedite processing in MapReduce, rather than sending data to where the logic resides, the

logic is sent to the server where the data resides. Finally all the data is aggregated from multiple servers and this consolidated result is returned back to the application.

(1) HADOOP Architecture

To enable scalability in processing, the hadoop organizes computers in master-salve configuration as shown in Figure 10.5. The master node is referred as Name Node and slave worker nodes are referred as Data Nodes. The Hadoop may contain many clusters and each small hadoop cluster may include a single Name Node (Master Node) and multiple Data Nodes (worker Nodes). A large Hadoop cluster may consist of a single Name Node and thousands of Data Nodes. The Name node basically manages the complete file system, its namespace and also the access to the files by the applications (clients). The name node has full knowledge of data nodes regarding which blocks of which file are stored in which data node. Since there is a single name node per cluster, it can become single point of failure and therefore generally backup name nodes are kept per cluster, which can take over the role of name node of the cluster if the original name node happens to fail. Master Node also keeps the log of each transaction in the file system to recover from failures.

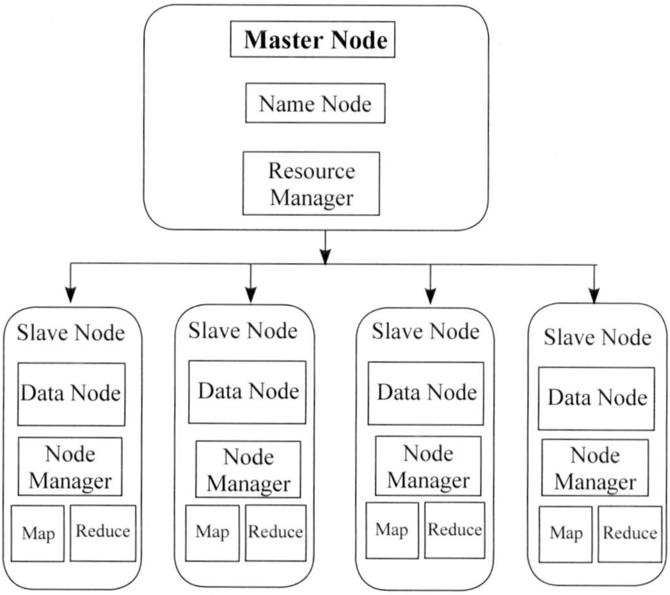

Fig. 10.5: HADOOP Master Slave Architecture

Each Data Node store data blocks in their storage space. The storage space of a data node may contain many disks (storage devices). Each Data Node has its own file system but is not aware of the distributed file system as a whole (i.e. HDFS). The Data Node stores and retrieves block of data from its storage space as guided by the name node. The block of data is sent and received by data block to and from the network with the help of something called block protocol. Each Data Node may have one or more of their replica node and therefore if a data node fails there is no serious problem as such. The Name Node receives heart beat signals from each of its Data nodes periodically, the consistently non-receipt of this signal by the Name Node from a particular Data Node may help Name Node to presume that this particular Data Node has failed and Name Node in response to this observation may shift its focus on the replica of the failed Data Node.

The Hadoop HDFS hides the intricacies of the working of the HDFS including the splitting and scattering of the data to various nodes of HDFS and provides a logically convenient interface to deal with data at logically high level for effective use of HDFS by the user. It is the responsibility of the Name Node to balance the storage and computing load among its Data Nodes to provide efficient service to its client applications. The Figure 10.6 exhibits the working architecture of HDFS.

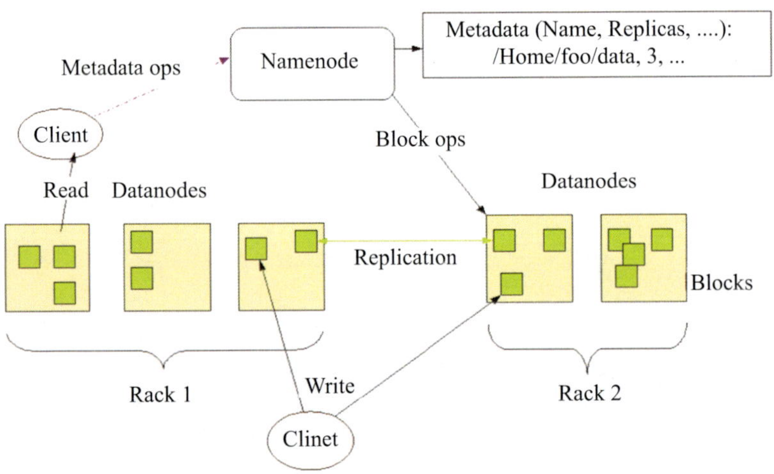

Fig. 10.6: Hadoop HDFS working Architecture

Every file in HDFS is organized as a sequence of blocks. The block size is generally a configurable parameter with size ranging from 16 to 128 MB. The default size of block invariable is 64 MB. The blocks of a file are typically stored across multiple machines (Data Nodes). Files are read and written in block wise granularities. This scheme provides the HDFS necessary mechanism for quick storage and retrieval of files from the Hadoop distributed computing framework.

(2) Yet Another Resource Negotiator (YARN)

YARN can be described as comprehensive distributed operating system for Big Data management. YARN monitors and manages workload of hadoop. The job of the YARN is to bring necessary flexibility as a common platform to run multiple tools and applications, while ensuring high availability across numerous hadoop clusters. The YARN provides the necessary base to run important applications such as interactive SQL (e.g. Hive), real time streaming (e.g. Spark) and batch processing (MapReduce) to work on data stored on HDFS platform as shown in Figure 10.7. The other popular tools running over YARN and HDFS may include Tez (batch and interactive data processing applications), Hbase (non-relational database), storm (distributed real-time computation system for processing large volumes of high-velocity data), Giraph (graph processing application on big data), Flink (distributed processing engine and a scalable data analytics framework), etc

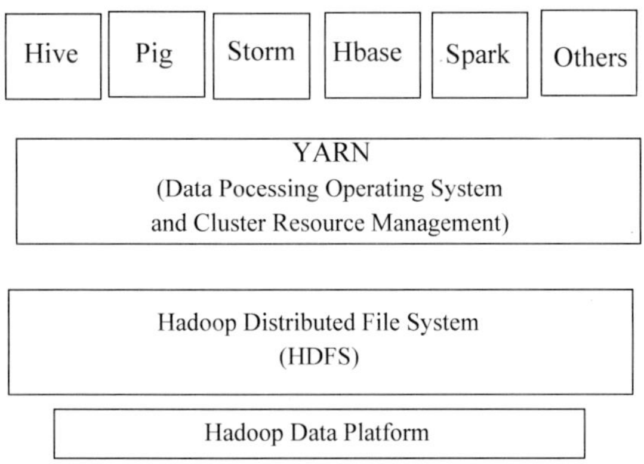

Fig. 10.7: Hadoop Architecture with YARN

The YARN can be divided into two of its main components that are Scheduler and Application Manager. YARN scheduler allocates resources to various requesting applications based on the intangible notion of a resource container. A resource container may include elements such as CPU, storage, memory, network etc. Each machine also consists of a node manager to manage all the containers on that machine, and submits status of resources and containers to the YARN scheduler.

YARN application manager accepts the jobs/works given by applications. YARN in response to the client request first allocates a container with necessary resources to the application and then monitors the status of the execution of the client application. The application manager directly negotiates additional resource containers from the scheduler as needed.

(3) MapReduce

MapReduce is a parallel programming framework for expediting data processing. The MapReduce accepts data input as key-value pair. MapReduce speeds up the process of computation by reading and processing chunks of data by different machines in parallel. The resultant processed chunks after processing also reside on these separate machines and are required to be pooled for a composite result. The results of the outputs from various portions or chunks of data are pooled to summarize the final result with the assistance of another process referred as reducer.

The map process of MapReduce will divide up the input application task into smaller and minor tasks that can be processed on separate machines each using only a small portion of the input data set. The map process will generate an intermediate result. The reduce process will take as input this intermediate result and work to combine these intermittent results to generate final composite result in the form of key-value pair. The programmer shall be required to provide the logic for map and reduce process. In between map and reduce process, the data is also required to be sorted and shuffled for efficient processing and optimized resource utilization. This sorting and shuffling of data is automatically taken care of by the MapReduce framework. A block diagram elaborating the MapReduce process flow is shown in Figure 10.8.

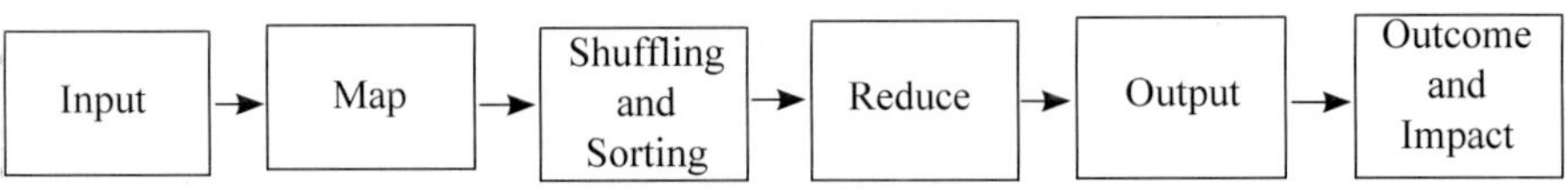

Fig. 10.8: MapReduce Process Flow Diagram

Generally data is stored as one key and one non-key attribute value to manage the varying data structures stored in the HDFS. The intermediate result and final composite result are also required to be in key-value pair. Therefore the main requirement of using the Map Reduce framework is to have input and output data in key-value pair.

10.7.2 NoSQL

The conventional database systems such as relational database are not apt for handling Big Data. Generally NoSQL database systems are required to handle high volume, velocity, variety and veracity of Big Data.

Although there are some NoSQL systems that are completely non-relational, the other NoSQL systems just avoid some selected functionality and constraints of relational database systems. In NoSQL databases, the data is generally not organized as tables unlike SQL databases rather it is organized in key-value pairs. However there is no one single type of NoSQL database catering to all types of data and needs in Big Data, rather there are varying type of NoSQL database systems based on the type of the data to be handled and the application requirement in the Big Data.

Broadly speaking, NoSQL databases for Big Data can be categorized as key-value pair oriented NoSQL database systems, columnar databases, document store oriented databases, graph oriented databases.

(1) Key-Value Pair Databases: These databases are appropriate, where data can be organized in a key – value pair. For example for organizing collection of text messages in a database, it can be organized in a key-value pair, where message identifier can play the role of keys and message contents may play the role of values. Similarly key-value databases may also be apt for storing shopping cart data, user profile information and session information. Some popular NoSQL database framework of key-value pair category includes Amazon DynamoDB, Redis, Memcached, Aerospike, and BerkeleyDB.

(2) Columnar Databases: Columnar databases in NoSQL looks similar to traditional relational DBMS (RDBMS) at first. The columnar databases also have the concepts of rows and columns similar to conventional relational DBMS systems. In columnar databases, we need to define column and column families in the database suggesting that we should have some knowledge about the structure of data before hand. However, columnar databases organize data differently than RDBMS do. Instead of storing data in a row centric order, data is organized in a column centric order for fast operations. This column□ centric view makes columnar databases apt for processing aggregate functions or for querying records that match multiple columns. These types of database systems are useful for organizing and retrieving data for blogging platforms, log aggregations, content management systems, etc. Some popular NoSQL database framework of columnar category includes Apache Hadoop Hbase and Cassandra.

(3) Document Store Databases: These types of databases are similar to key-value pair databases as these databases also have a key and a corresponding value associated with the key. All the keys in the database are required to be unique. However the difference in comparison to key-value database is that in a document database, the value can contains structured or semi-structured data such as JSON or XML documents. Document store NoSQL databases are not appropriate to run complex search queries with aggregate structures or application requires complex transactions requiring multiple operations. The document store databases are apt for blogging platforms, web analytics, ecommerce applications, and real time analytics. Some popular NoSQL database framework of document store category includes MongoDB, Elasticsearch, and Apache CouchDB.

(4) Graph Databases: Graph databases are built upon the entity, attribute and value model. Entities are also referred as nodes in graph databases. Each node may have its own properties. It is a flexible way to describe how data relates to other data. Nodes store data about each entity in the database, relationships describe a relationship between nodes, and a property is simply the node on the opposite end of the relationship. The document store databases are apt for graph based search, social networks, network and IT operations, Fraud detection, etc. Some popular NoSQL database framework of graph database category includes Neo4j, ArangoDB and OrientDB.

10.7.3 Data Ingest

In Big data systems, data comes at tremendous speed from various types of sources. This data is generally of high volume, velocity, and variety and needs to be processed with different target applications. To achieve this, Big Data systems need a data ingest mechanism to receive varying type of data from numerous various type of sources and facilitate the delivery of this data to their target application for processing in such a way that there is no loss of data or speed. This Data ingest system need to be flexible and scalable enough to handle any amount of data, at any speed and from any source to be delivered to their target application without any loss or speed of data. Incoming data are treated as messages and is put into a fast and flexible buffer pool from where target application can fetch this data as per their convenience.

Apache Flume and Kafka are two popular data ingest systems used with Big Data. Flume is an older system and facilitates data ingestion from various data sources and storing them in Hadoop Distributed File System (HDFS).

Kafka is a new data ingest system which works on the methodology of publish and subscribe. Kafka can connect to all types of data sources and target data processing applications. Kafka is a high throughput and low latency data ingest system capable of catering data coming at very high speed such as real time data traffic. Kafka is extensively used in Big Data system as data ingest for catering to the needs of various type of application such as message processing applications, website activity tracking for user's online activity, high speed stream processing application such as application handling real time traffic, log aggregation to gather physical log files from many servers for centralized processing, external commit logs for distributed database systems, etc.

11

Blockchain Technology

11.1 Introduction

With the invention of bitcoin in 2008, the world was exposed to a new technology paradigm called blockchain. Blockchain was conceptualized by an unknown person named as Satoshi Nakamoto in 2008. The identity of Satoshi Nakamoto is still not known. Nakamoto proposed the design of blockchain which uses digital signature and timestamps to enable secure and trusted online transaction without the need of any trusted regulatory or third party.

Blockchain is an evolutionary technology facilitating the development of distributed and decentralized application and data storage and in today's world is being predominantly used as underlying technology for crypto-currencies. The principle trait of this technology is that it facilitate the generation of distributed ledger of transactions, data or events in a distributed computing environment while enabling such distributed ledgers to be tamper resistance, immutable and verifiable with the help of cryptographic techniques. Initially the blockchain technology was developed with view of developing a crypto currency framework for distributed computing environment, where people can do secure and tamper proof transactions among each other without the need of any intermediaries. However, now this technology is also gradually evolving for development of distributed platforms for other applications such as supply chain management, digital ids, digital voting, protection of royalty and copyright, food safety, transfer of movable and immovable property titles, etc.

To summarize the above, blockchain can be defined as distributed digital ledger or database of transactions that are distributed and duplicated throughout the computer network may be over worldwide internet in such a way that ledger remains immutable, secure and safe. Technically speaking blockchain is a cryptographically linked chain of records or blocks in such a way that no one can change or modify any block in the chain that is once a block/record is added in blockchain, it will immutably remain in the blockchain forever. The benefits of using blockchain technology in distributed computing environment includes immutable data, digital decentralization, anonymity and privacy, security, no intermediaries, transparency, low transaction cost and consensus-based (i.e. majority has to agree to finalize a transaction)

To understand the technology behind the blockchain, a good knowledge of computer cryptography and distributed computing is required as prerequisite. Since this is an introductory book for readers who may not have such background, the material presented in this chapter is at the conceptual and application level for easy understanding of every type of readers.

11.2 Blockchain Types

The blockchain can be divided into various categories based on their attributes. Some of the significant types of blockchains are defined in this section.

(i) Public blockchain: These types of blockchain networks are open for anybody and everybody. Anyone on the internet who wishes to join the public blockchain network as a node can do so by following the laid down procedures and can become the part of blockchain decision making process. In other words public blockchains are public owned distributed ledgers on the distributed network or internet which are non-restrictive and permission less. All the users of the public blockchain's permission-less ledger may maintain a copy of the shared ledger on their local nodes and may participate in distributed consensus and proof of work to reach to the final immutable state of the ledger. Public blockchains are generally used for exchanging crypto-currencies. Bitcoin and Litecoin are popular examples of public blockchains.

(ii) Private Blockchain: Private blockchain are private to only a set of individuals or limited to only a organization or consortium of organizations with common interest. Private blockchain work only in closed networks. In private brockchain, the concerned organization decides which nodes or users can be authorized to take part in keeping copies of distributed ledger or can do proof of work or participate in reaching the distributed consensus. Popular examples of private blockchains are hyperledgers such as fabric and sawtooth.

(iii) Hybrid Blockchains: These types of blockchains are combination of public and private blockchains. These blockchains are also referred as consortium blockchain. These blockchains contain both centralized and de-centralized features. In such blockchains the private part of the blockchain is controlled by group of individuals and the public part is open for participation by the general public with constrained authorization. Some popular hybrid blockchains are Energy Web Foundation and R3.

(iv) Sidechains: The sidechains facilitate the running of a parallel chain along with the main chain. Sidechains allows the assets or crypto-currencies to be moved from one chain to another leading to improved efficiency and scalability. One important use of sidechains can be creation of alternate crypto-currency where coins in the old crypto-currency in old blockchain can be moved to the newly formed alternate crypto-currency. An example of popular sidechain is Liquid Network.

11.3 Basics of Blockchain Technology

This section discusses the basic technology concepts and terminologies used in blockchain such as peer-to-peer networks, distributed ledgers, asymmetric key cryptography, hashing, etc.

11.3.1 Peer-to-Peer Network

The peer-to-peer or P2P networks are distributed and decentralized networks without any specific central server as such. In P2P networks, all the computing nodes are assumed to be independent and are connected to other nodes of the networks through routers and switches. In P2P network all peers are assumed to have equal authority, privileges and capabilities in the network unlike client server model where client are connected to a central server and clients send requests to servers to get a job done. A block diagram showing P2P and client-server model is shown in Figure 11.1.

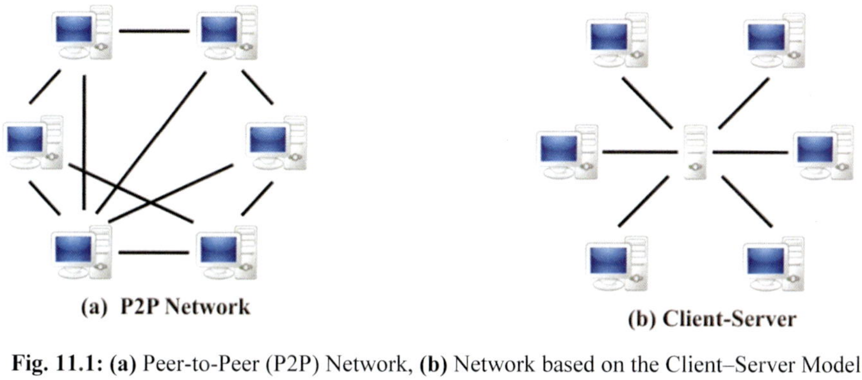

Fig. 11.1: **(a)** Peer-to-Peer (P2P) Network, **(b)** Network based on the Client–Server Model

In blockchain especially public blockchain, P2P underlying network infrastructure is assumed, where any two nodes can successfully transact among each other without knowing or trusting each other. The security in blockchain is so framed that legitimate and authentic transaction can be executed among two nodes in the underlying P2P network without knowing the identities of the sender and the receiver.

11.3.2 Distributed Ledger

This type of ledger is distributed among its participant nodes in the P2P network. In other words, the distributed ledger are not kept with some central authority, rather each participant node in the P2P network will keep an updated copy of the distributed ledger containing latest information about all the transaction that happens on the underlying P2P network. This makes the blockchain network tamper and fraud proof as all the nodes in the network will have a legitimate copy of the ledger. If somebody wants to do a fraud by changing the ledger with illegitimate entries then he will be required to change the copy of the ledger available in all the nodes of the blockchain network, which will be practically impossible due to the enormous requirement of computing resources and time needed to achieve the same.

11.3.3 Key Cryptography

The blockchain network needs to ensure authenticity and integrity of the transaction and validity of participating nodes in the blockchain network. In other words recipient should be able to make sure that the message, it is receiving from the intended sender only and is not tempered in the transit. Similarly, the sender also needs to make sure that the message it is sending should reach the intended receiver without any tempering in the transit. Moreover, these security paradigms for blockchain should work even when the real identities of the participant nodes in the network remain anonymous. For achieving these goals blockchain extensively uses asymmetric key cryptography and hashing. Without going into the greater technical specificities of these security enforcement techniques, this section explains the fundamental concept behind the asymmetric key cryptography and similarly in the next session we will discuss the concept of hashing.

Asymmetric key cryptography also known as public-key cryptography, in which each user is assigned two keys, one key is refereed as private key of the user whereas the other key of the user is referred as the public key. In other words, each user in the network has a pair of private and its corresponding public key. To securely communicate over the network, the sender and receiver uses their public and private key. The private key only remains with the owner/user that is nobody in the blockchain knows about this key except the owner. However public key of the user is known throughout the network that is it is known to everybody.

The relationship between a private key and its corresponding public key is such that, whatever is encrypted by one key can be decrypted by the other. Therefore, if a message is encrypted by say, Mr. A's private key then it can only be decrypted by Mr. A's public key and similarly, if a message is encrypted by

Mr. A's public key then it can only be decrypted by Mr. A's private key. This relationship between the private and its public key is achieved using complex mathematical functions using very large integers which are very hard to factor. The mathematical function is such that it is relatively computationally easy to compute the public key from the private key, but computationally very hard to compute the private key from the public key.

To achieve secure communication in the network, the sender encrypts the message to be sent with the receiver's public key. Remember that public key of a user is known throughout the network. On receiving the message, the receiver decrypts the message with its private key, which is only known to him. The Figure 11.2 explains this secure communication between the sender and receiver with the help of a block diagram.

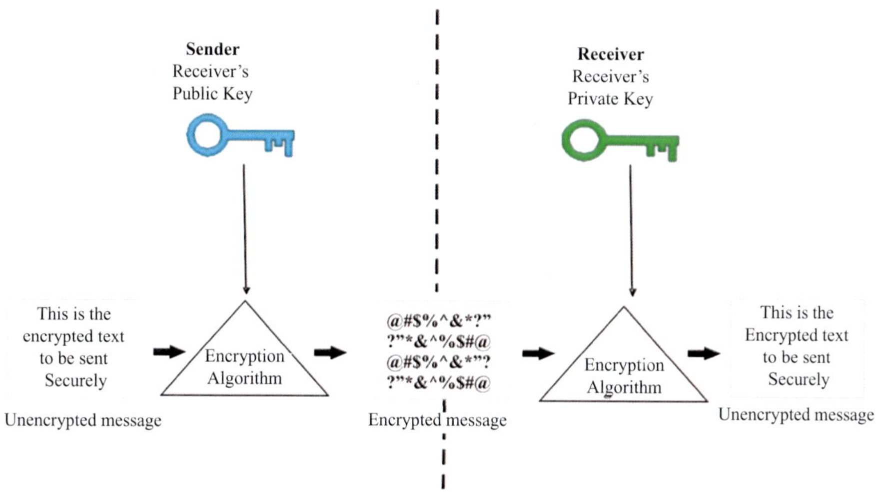

Fig. 11.2: Secure Message Transmission from Sender to Receiver using Asymmetric Key Cryptography

11.3.4 Hashing

Hash function also referred as message digest or digital signature is a complex one way mathematical function to get a fixed length hash value/text from a variable length text. Since hash function is one way, we can never get the original text, given the hash value. In other words, it's a one way encryption which cannot be decrypted. The hash function should satisfy the following characteristics to be used as digital signature in the blockchain network.

1. Given message M, it should be computationally easy to compute Hash of message M (Hash(M)).

2. Given Hash(M), it should be practically impossible to compute message M.
3. Given message M, it should be practically impossible to find another message M', such that Hash(M) = Hash(M')
4. A change to the input of even 1 bit in message M produces a very different Hash(M).

Secure Hash Algorithm 256 (SHA256) is a popular hash function being used as digital signatures in blockchain networks. Hash function or digital signatures are basically used to ensure integrity of messages in the blockchain networks. Figure 11.3 shows the working of hash function.

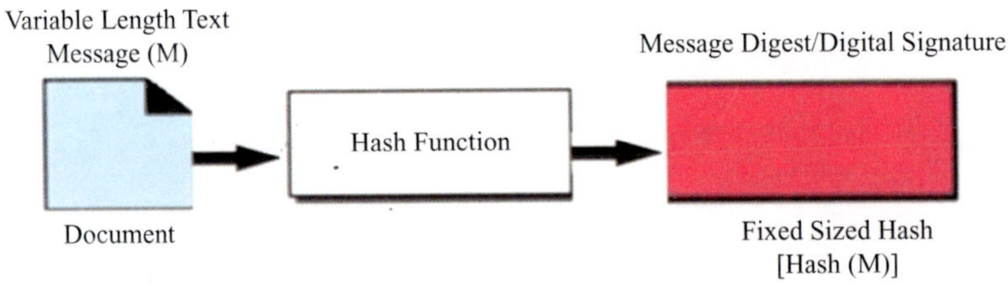

Fig. 11.3: Working of Hash Function or Digital Signature

11.3.5 Blocks and Blockchain

Blockchain is basically chain of blocks as shown in Figure 11.4. Each block is identified by the hash of the block in the blockchain and contains information such as block header, transaction data, transaction counter and block size, where block header of a block contains the metadata of the block such as hash of the previous block, timestamp, etc. Transaction data contains the records pertaining to set of transaction. Transaction counter represents the total number of transaction represented by this block and block size shows the size of this block in number of bytes.

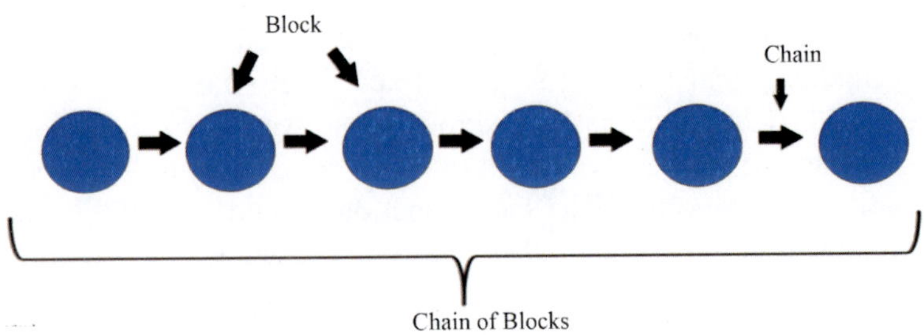

Fig. 11.4: Chain of Blocks in Blockchain

Block Header: The block header plays an important role in creating the tamper resistant chain of blocks in the blockchain and ensuring the integrity of the blocks in the blockchain. The block header of a block contains the information such as block version, previous block hash, markel root, timestamp, nonce, and difficulty target.

Block version in blockheader is generally used to keep track of protocol or software updates. *Previous block hash* is the hash of the preceding block. *Timestamp* is the time of creation of the block. *Nonce* is the number needed for the proof-of-work. Proof of work will be discussed in the later sections. *Difficulty target* is the difficulty level set for the proof-of-work.

Merkle root is the root of merkle tree. We know that a large number of transactions are there in a block and therefore, a technique is required to organize them efficiently in the block and also efficiently and uniquely represent them in the block header. Merkle tree is a popular technique for the same. In merkle tree each transaction is represented by the leaf nodes of the tree. As we move up the tree, hashing and pairing of transaction occurs at each level of the tree as shown in Figure 11.5. After this continued pairing and hashing, as we move towards the root of the tree, finally we will be left with only one hash at the root level. This root hash is referred as merkle root.

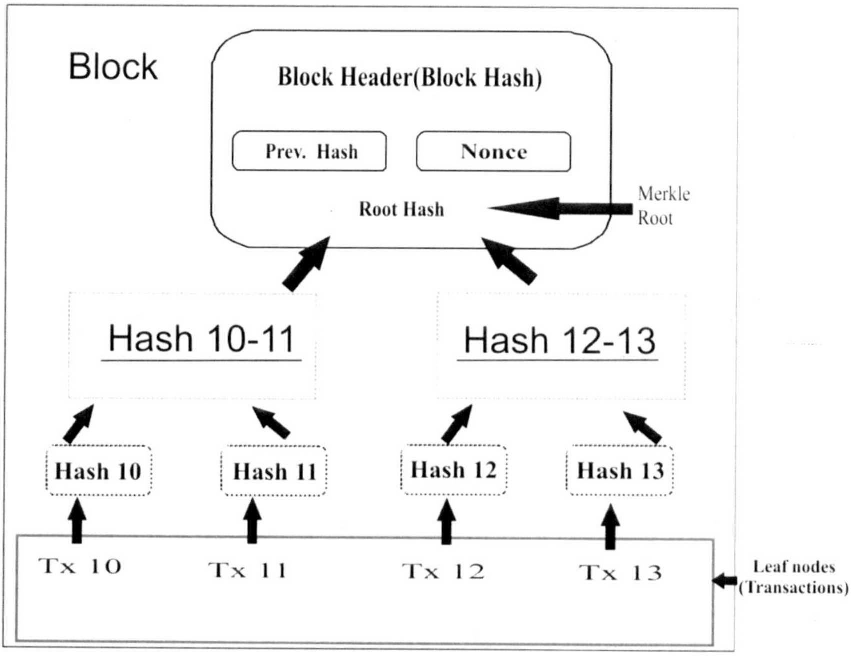

Fig. 11.5: An Example of Merkle Tree and Merkle Root

Block chain structure: Blocks in blockchain are interlinked to form a series or chain of blocks. Each block is identified by its block hash, which is basically the encrypted hash value of the block header. Each block is linked to the previous block through the previous block hash, which is working as the hash identity of the previous block and is also part of block header of the current block. Figure 11.6, shows how blocks in blockchain are interlinked together with the help of hash values of the blocks. The blocks in the blockchain are also indexed by the order in which they have joined the chain. The first block of the blockchain is indexed as block 0. This block is referred as *genesis block*. Genesis block is hard coded and was inserted at the time when blockchain was started. However other blocks are added to blockchain later as time progresses and transactions occur in the system. Each new block can be added to the blockchain only after it successfully completes the proof-of-work (discusses in later sections). The blockchain so formed is tamper resistance and the integrity of the blocks is ensured because if somebody tries to change a block in the blockchain then the block's block hash will change and will not match with the previous block hash value stored in the next block. Therefore to change a block, the intruder has to change all the subsequent blocks in the blockchain with required proof of work for each block, which is computationally impossible as it will require enormous time and computational power and so also the electrical energy to achieve the same.

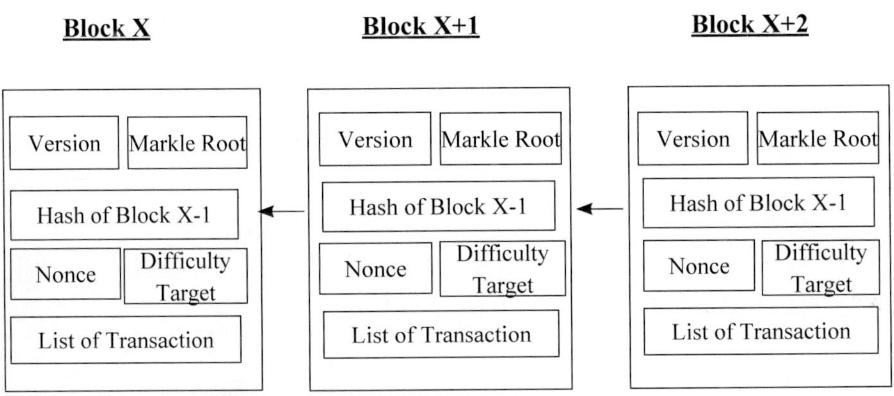

Fig. 11.6: Blockchain as Chain of Blocks Interlinked with Block Hash

11.4 Working of Blockchain

In this section, we will discuss how transactions take place among two nodes in the blockchain network, how the poof-of-work is done for a block before adding it to the blockchain and finally we will summarize in step wise step fashion the working of blockchain.

11.4.1 Transactions in Blockchain

A blockchain network consists of thousands of node in the blockchain network. For the sake of understanding, let us assume that in our blockchain network we have 1000 nodes. Now each of these nodes is capable of doing transaction with any of the remaining 999 nodes in the network. Let us assume that node X in the network want to transact with node Y in the network. Node X will send the message to the node Y regarding the transaction, but the message needs to be sent in such a way, that Y can be sure that this message came from node X and is temper free. Moreover, this is also required to be ensured that none of the remaining 998 nodes should know about the contents of the message. To achieve the above security requirements, Node X encrypts message first with X's private key and then further encrypts it with the public key of Y before sending it on the communication lines of the network. Y on receiving the message will first decrypt the message with the Y's private key and then decrypts it further using the public key of X. Figure 11.7 shows secure communication between 2 nodes in the blockchain network.

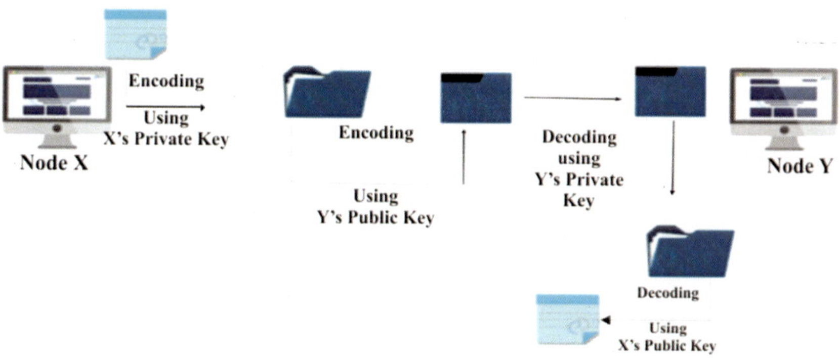

Fig. 11.7: Communication of Transaction Messages between 2 Nodes in Blockchain Network

After the message is completely decrypted by the Y, it sends the transaction verification message to all the remaining 998 nodes in the blockchain network. All the remaining 998 nodes will verify the transaction by checking certain attribute of the transaction such as, does node X have sufficient funds to make this transaction, authenticity of the nodes X and Y, etc. Once the transaction is verified by the majority of nodes in the network, it is added to the new block under creation with other already existing transactions in the block.

11.4.2 Proof-of-Work

Using the technique of proof-of-work, new blocks are added to the blockchain by interlinking with the already existing previous block in the chain with the help of an entry of previous block hash in the header of the new block to be added to the blockchain. The proof-of-work mechanism ensures that only authentic blocks are added to the blockchain and once added will remain tamper proof. To achieve proof-of-work, the system gives a mathematical puzzle to solve to quite a few nodes in the network called miners. The mathematical puzzle is formed using block's hash, nonce and difficulty target available in the block's header. The puzzle is such that it takes significant computational resources, electrical energy and time to solve it by each miner node. The miner nodes try to solve the puzzle (the miners are rewarded in one form or the other to solve the puzzle, like in bitcoin network the miners are rewarded with bitcoin to solve the puzzle). Once a miner node solves the puzzle, it informs the system. When system receives the correct solution of the puzzle from all or majority of miner nodes in the network and hence forming a consensus regarding the authenticity of the block, the block is added in the existing chain of blocks and all the nodes in the blockchain are informed to update their copy of blockchain accordingly.

11.4.3 Step Wise Step Working of Blockchain

This sub-section explains in brief the step by step working of blockchain to gather the broad picture of blockchain working.

1. Let us assume that two nodes say X and Y in a blockchain network desires to make a new transaction.
2. This transaction can be completed successfully, only if all the other participating nodes in the blockchain network verify it as a genuine transaction and so request for verifying this transaction is sent to all the nodes in the network.
3. Each node in the blockchain network will verify the transaction based on factors such as does node X have sufficient funds to make the transaction, authenticity of nodes X and Y, and other constrains prescribed and agreed by blockchain network nodes.
4. If the transaction is verified as the valid transaction by all or significant number of nodes in the blockchain network then this transaction is ready for successful completion and is added to a memory pool.
5. Several such valid and verified transaction are aggregated in the memory pool and are finally combined to form a new block in such a way that the new block will have its own header containing previous block hash,

timestamp, transaction summary etc. Moreover each block is identified by the unique hash (acts like a fingerprint for the block) of its block header.

6. To add the new block in the block chain, the computationally expensive process in terms of time and computational resource referred as proof-of-work as discussed in the earlier sections of the chapter is conducted. Once the proof-of-work is successfully completed by the participating nodes (miner nodes) in the network, the new block is added to the existing chain of block in the blockchain network.
7. Once the block is added, the transaction between X and Y can be deemed to be completed by the system and will remain in the blockchain system as valid transaction forever.

11.5 Pros and Cons of Blockchain

Some of the advantages of blockchain technology are enumerated below.

(i) **Decentralization:** In blockchain technology there is no need of a trusted intermediary to validate a transaction, rather blockchain uses a consensus mechanism to validate a transaction in a distributed and decentralized environment.

(ii) **Transparency and trust:** As anybody and everybody have a copy of the blockchain, everybody can see what is on the blockchain. This provides transparency and trust in the blockchain system.

(iii) **Immutability:** Once a data is written in the blockchain it is immutable. Although it is not truly immutable, but the computational cost and time for changing it is so huge that it can be treated as immutable for all practical purposes.

(iv) **High availability:** As the blockchain system runs on the underlying distributed networked system of thousands and thousands of nodes, with each and every node having a copy of the blockchain data. This makes the system highly available because even if some nodes of the network go down, the system can continue to works with availability of all the data in the system.

(v) **Highly secure:** All the transactions in the blockchain are encrypted using asymmetric key cryptography leading to secure and tamper proof transaction management system.

(vi) **Lower cost:** As there is no intermediary or third party like banks or other financial institution to validate and manage the transaction among two or more users, it eliminates the overhead cost of third party charges leading to reduced cost per transaction.

Although there are quite a few advantages of the blockchain technology as discussed above. However, since the technology is new, there are also quite a few significant challenges (disadvantages) of this technology such as scalability, adaptability and regulatory support by the governments.

(i) Scalability: Blockchain networks consume lot of computational power per node in the system and therefore, if required to be spread throughout the world of internet then the total electric power consumption by all the millions and millions of nodes in the system will be so huge that the world economy will crash, Therefore, at present stage this technology is not scalable to very huge network of distributed systems.

(ii) Adaptability and Personal Responsibility: One of the strongest advantages of blockchain is also its biggest disadvantage. In blockchain, each user is his own bank and controls and protects his digital assets or crypto currency with his private password string. If the user happens to forget or lose it in one way or the other, then there is no way he can get his digital assets or crypto currency back as there is no third party intermediary such as bank who can validate his request for changing the password by checking his credentials and allowing him to continue to operate his account with may be the changed password.

(iii) Regulatory support by the government: Blockchain framework are generally not provided with any regulatory support by government as blockchain is distributed, decentralized and self-sustained system without any geographical and geopolitical boundaries, the governments are not in a position to control or held accountable any person or agency for complained fraud in the blockchain systems.

11.6 Application of Blockchain in Agriculture

Blockchain technology has huge potential in all the domains where one need to conduct financial transaction or exchange records/files over a distributed environment while maintaining the needed security, privacy and transparency without the requirement of any intermediaries. Therefore blockchain technology is quite apt for fields and areas such as crypto currency, healthcare, elections, digital identity management, intellectual property protection, supply chain audits and property management and registry. However, in this section we will be focusing on the application of blockchain technology in the domain of agriculture.

The application of blockchain in agriculture can broadly be categorized into 3 segments:

- Smart Agriculture
- Supply chain
- Agriculture insurance

(i) Smart Agriculture: Smart agriculture or smart farming is the process of availing the advantages of various modern technologies such as IOT, drones, cloud platforms and modern analytics to improve the reliability and efficiency of the agriculture processes. Blockchain technology can help in providing decentralization and data security for the use of amalgamation of these modern technologies for smart agriculture.

The amalgamation of modern technologies such as IOT, drones etc. require centralized data collection and so can become single point of failure due to cyber-attack, distortion or destruction of data due to some technical problems such as power surges, floods or other natural phenomenon or mala fide human/ agency intents. Blockchain technology can help to address this constrain of centralization, while providing security of data. Blockchain can help in generating secured data at every step of the agriculture process while keeping the data transparent, tamper proof and available for all the stake holders. However, one disadvantage can be that data generated over time will become enormous as blockchain technology does not allow data deletion or removal leading to increased requirement of computational resources over time.

(ii) Supply Chain: Blockchain technology can have great potential in bringing transparency in supply chains of agriculture. It can facilitate in providing immutable and secure records from provenance to the product's retail store. This can not only help reward the farmer for cultivating good quality produce by employing apt agricultural practices, but will also help the consumer in building trust in the product. Gradually this can lead to sustainable farming and responsible consumption.

Starting from cultivation, treatment, harvesting, transportation, storage, quality control to retail outlet and consumer, all the steps can be tracked in an authentic, non compromisable, immutable and secure manner with the help of blockchain technology leading to efficient use of resources in the supply chain, ensuring food safety, reducing food supply chain frauds and delivering quality product to the end consumers.

(iii) Agriculture Insurance: In developing nations like India, low cost insurance schemes are effective tool for providing social security to large number of small farmers affected by droughts, floods and other natural calamities to help them bear the burden of their loss because of such natural events. However adaption of such low cost insurance scheme is still relatively low in low income group farmers. The primary reason of low adaptability of such insurance scheme may be that the mechanisms and procedures that are generally required to validate such claims and subsequent payouts are time consuming and are also dependent on the integrity and efficiency of the validator. Therefore these days governments are focusing on index based insurances for the farming community.

Index insurance is an innovative approach especially for farmers. Such index insurance pays out benefits on the basis of predetermined indices such as rainfall, temperature, wind speed, earthquake magnitude, crop yield or livestock mortality rates, etc to cater to the catastrophic events. Since index insurance does not necessarily require the traditional services of the claims assessors or validator, it can help the finalization of settlement claims to be more objective and quick. Index insurance for farmers can be implemented in a secure and authentic manner using blockchain technology, where automatic reliable data feeds from various sources such as sensors, weather stations, etc from time to time can be provided to blockchain insurance network for assessment. Such process can remove the necessity of a surveyor or validator, making the process less time consuming, incorruptible and authentic. The farmer and blockchain insurer may sign a smart contract on the block chain, which may trigger the payout, when the necessary conditions regarding the natural parameter such as rainfall, temperature, etc are met. Smart contract in blockchain are simply programs stored on a blockchain that gets executed when some predetermined conditions are fulfilled. Smart contracts in blockchain are typically used to automate the execution of an agreement without the need of any intermediaries.

In addition to the above, the blockchin technology can also be useful in the domain of *land registration*, fisheries and forestry. Blockchain based land registration can provide immutable and incorruptible ledger of agriculture land records. Each time property exchange hands through sale of property over time can be captured in blockchain leading to transparent real time traceability of the state of the property. In *fisheries sector*, blockchain technology can be used to check and deter unregulated and illegal fishing. This can be done using blockchain technology to track the fishing supply chain from vessel to the supermarket. Similarly in *forestry*, blockchain technology can be used to manage the supply chain of wood supply from forest to the market to check and deter illegal logging.

Bibliography

A Cambridge Assessment publication. http://www.cambridgeassessment.org.uk/research-matters5

Adisa, O. M., Botai, J. O., Hassen, A., Darkey, D., Adeola, A. M., Tesfamariam, E., and Adisa, A. T. "Variability of satellite derived phenological parameters across maize producing areas of South Africa". Sustainability, 10(9), pp. 2018, 3033.

Ahmad, L., and Mahdi, S.S. "Recent Advances in Precision Agriculture". Satellite Farming, 2018, pp. 129-138.

Allurwar, N. "Basic architecture of Internet of Things, IoT dunia", 11 june 2020.

Ana De Pablo Escolá. "Development of a Wireless Sensor Network with 6LoWPAN Support". Doctoral dissertation, 2009.

Ansari, S., Hasnain, S. F., and Ansari, A. "Introduction and Overview of Wireless Sensor Networks". In Wireless Sensor Networks and Energy Efficiency: Protocols, Routing and Management, IGI Global,2012, pp. 1-13.

Bagchi, A. "Artificial Intelligence in Agriculture". Millennium Development Goal, UN Summit, 2000.

Baranowski, P., Jedryczka, M., Mazurek, W., Babula-Skowronska, D., Siedliska, A., and Kaczmarek, J. "Hyperspectral and thermal imaging of oilseed rape (Brassica napus) response to fungal species of the genus Alternaria". PloS one, 10(3), 2015, e0122913.

Barbedo, J. G. A. "Detecting and Classifying Pests in Crops Using Proximal Images and Machine Learning: A Review". AI, 1(2), 2020, pp. 312-328.

Barcode and barcode scanner: honeywell spec HH660 datasheet, Safety and Productivity Solutions.

Barramou, F., and Addou, M. "An agent based approach for simulating complex systems with spatial dynamics application in the land use planning". IJACSA Journal, 3(11), 2012.

Bashir, I. "Mastering blockchain". Packt Publishing Ltd., 2017.

Basic communication system : ICEET ,EEE technology, by Engr. Mizan in july 28,2019.

Belal, M. A. "Optimum Route Selection For Linear Man-Made Features, Using GIS Techniques". Doctoral dissertation, UOFK, 2015.

Big Data and Agriculture. A Complete Guide: https://www.talend.com/resources/big-data-agriculture/7

Bisdikian, C. "An overview of the Bluetooth wireless technology". IEEE Communications magazine, 39(12), 2001, pp. 86-94.

Bishop, R. H. "The Mechatronics handbook-2 volume set". CRC press, 2002.

Bomber, M., and Portelli, R. "Multi-scale analysis of jack pine saplings after fire across burn severities". The International Archives of Photogrammetry, Remote Sensing and Spatial Information Sciences, 43, 2020, pp. 671-675.

Bravo, J., Fuentes, L. and de Ipina, D.L. "Theme issue:"Ubiquitous computing and ambient intelligence", 2011.

Cameroni, F. D., and Fort, H. Towards scientifically based management of extensive livestock farming in terms of ecological predator-prey modeling. Agricultural Systems, 153, 2017, pp. 127-137..

Chebbi, I., Boulila, W., and Farah, I. R. "Big data: Concepts, challenges and applications". In Computational collective intelligence Springer, Cham. 2015, pp. 638-647.

Corrigan, F. "Drone with Multispectral Sensor for Soil Health Monitoring: Multispectral Imaging Camera Drones In Farming Yield Big Benefits". February 10, 2020.

Coulouris, G., Dollimore, J., Kindberg, T., and Blair, G. "Distributed Systems Concepts and Design". International Computer Science Series, 2012.

Curry, E. The big data value chain: definitions, concepts, and theoretical approaches. In New horizons for a data-driven economy , Springer, Cham , 2015, pp. 29-37.

Das, H., Barik, R. K., Dubey, H., and Roy, D. S. "Cloud computing for geospatial big data analytics". In Intelligent Edge, Fog and Mist Computing, Springer, 2019.

Data Flair Big Data Tutorial Library. https://data-flair.training/blogs/big-data-tutorials-home/3

Deepa, R., Moorthy, V., Venkataraman, R., and Kundu, S. S. "Smart Farming Implementation using Phase based IOT System". In International Conference on Communication and Signal Processing (ICCSP), 2020 July, pp. 0930-0934. IEEE.

Dharmaraj, V., and Vijayanand, C. (2018). "Artificial intelligence (AI) in agriculture". International Journal of Current Microbiology and Applied Sciences, 7(12), 2018, pp. 2122-2128.

Dreyfus, S. E. (1990). Artificial neural networks, back propagation, and the Kelley-Bryson gradient procedure. Journal of guidance, control, and dynamics, 13(5), 926-928.

E-Agriculture in action: Blockchain for agriculture –opportunities and challenges, Food and Agriculture organization of the united nation and the International Telecommunication Union, Bankok, 2019

El-Bendary, M.A. (2015). "Developing security tools of WSN and WBAN networks applications". Springer Japan, 2015.

El-Jarn, H., and Southern, G. "Can co-creation in extended reality technologies facilitate the design process?". Journal of Work-Applied Management, 2020.

G. Sylvester, Blockchain in Agriculture: How crypto is disrupting farming. https://stories.pinduoduo-global.com/agritech-hub/blockchain-in-agriculture

Geroimenko, V. "Augmented Reality in Tourism, Museums and Heritage: A New Technology to Inform and Entertain". Springer Nature, 2021.

Guru 99 Big Data Hadoop Tutorial. https://www.guru99.com/bigdata-tutorials.html2

Hammami, M., Jarraya, S. K., and Ben-Abdallah, H. "A comparative study of proposed moving object detection methods". Journal of Next Generation Information Technology, 2(2), 2011.

Haque, T. "Resource use efficiency in Indian agriculture". Indian Journal of Agricultural Economics, 61, 2006, pp. 902-2016-66798.

Hassan, M. B., Ali, E. S., Nurelmadina, N., and Saeed, R. A. "Artificial intelligence in IoT and its applications". Intelligent Wireless Communications. IET Book Publisher, 2020.

Haveson, S., Lau, A., and Wong, V. "Protecting farmers in emerging markets with blockchain". Cornell Tech, 2017.

Heath, Stephan. "Systems, computer media, and methods for using electromagnetic frequency (EMF) identification (ID) devices for monitoring, collection, analysis, use and tracking of personal, medical, transaction, and location data for one or more individuals." U.S. Patent Application No. 14/998,746.

Hockett, P., and Ingleby, T. "Augmented reality with HoloLens: Experiential architectures embedded in the real world", 2016.

Howard, A. M., Nibbelink, N., Bernardes, S., Fragaszy, D. M., and Madden, M. M. "Remote sensing and habitat mapping for bearded capuchin monkeys (Sapajus libidinosus): landscapes for the use of stone tools". Journal of Applied Remote Sensing, 9(1), 2015, pp. 096020.

Hung, J. C., Yen, N. Y., and Li, K. C. (Eds.). "Frontier computing: theory, technologies and applications". Springer, Vol. 375, 2016.

IoT enabled Soil Health Monitoring System, MPUAT, Udaipur.

Jain, V. K. "Big Data and Hadoop". Khanna Publishing, 2017.

Jenkins, M. W., Krofcheck, D. J., Teasdale, R., Houpis, J., and Pushnik, J. "Exploring the edge of a natural disaster". Open Journal of Ecology, 2(4), 2012, pp. 222.

Jokela, T., Ojala, J., and Väänänen, K. (2019, November). How people use 360-degree cameras. In Proceedings of the 18th International Conference on Mobile and Ubiquitous Multimedia (pp. 1-10).

Jokela, T., Ojala, J., and Väänänen, K. "How people use 360-degree cameras". In Proceedings of the 18th International Conference on Mobile and Ubiquitous Multimedia, November 2019, pp. 1-10.

Jones, E. C., Rathore, A., and Muthukumar, S. "Investigation, Testing and Development of an RFID System for Effective Maintenance of the Existing National Transportation Infrastructure", 2020.

Karygiannis, T., Eydt, B., Barber, G., Bunn, L., and Phillips, T. "Guidelines for securing radio frequency identification (RFID) systems". NIST Special publication, 80, 2007, pp. 1-154.

Katsaros, A., Keramopoulos, E., and Salampasis, M. "A prototype Application for cultivation optimization using augmented reality". In Proceedings of the 8th International Conference on Information and Communication Technologies in Agriculture, 2017 September, pp. 805-811.

Koblick, D., and Shankar, P. "Evaluation of the modified picard-chebyshev method for high-precision orbit propagation". Journal of Aerospace Engineering, 28(5), 2015, pp. 04014125.

Kocal, B. "Unifying remote sensing and web GIS infrastructure design and implementation of weighted overlay analysis on vegetation indices". Doctoral dissertation, Bilişim Enstitüsü, 2017.

Kondali, R. K. "IoT enabled Soil Health Monitoring System". Research gate, National Institute of Technology, Warangal, December 2016.

Kumar, A. R., Divya, T. M., Jayasudha, B. S. K., and Sudha, P. N. "Precision agriculture: A review on its techniques and technologies". Int. Res. J. Mod. Eng. Technol. Sci., 2, 2020, pp. 1326-32.

Kumar, A., Bharti, V., Kumar, V. K. U., and Meena, P. D. "Hyperspectral imaging: A potential tool for monitoring crop infestation, crop yield and macronutrient analysis, with special emphasis to Oilseed Brassica". Journal of Oilseed Brassica, 7(2), 2016, pp. 113-125.

Kumar, N. M., and Mallick, P. K. "The Internet of Things: Insights into the building blocks, component interactions, and architecture layers". Procedia computer science, 132, 2018, pp. 109-117.

Kumar, P. "Sensor data on AR enabled display". Augmented Reality-based sensor data display, Chennai, India , October 1, 2020.

Kumar, P., and Ashok, G. "Design and fabrication of smart seed sowing robot". Materials Today: Proceedings, 39, 2021, pp. 354-358.

Kumar, T. V., and Sud, K. "AI and Robotics in Disaster Studies". Springer Singapore, 2020.

Kusiak, A. "Convolutional and generative adversarial neural networks in manufacturing". International Journal of Production Research, 58(5), 2020, pp. 1594-1604.

Lang, B., and Batallé, J. "An introduction to positional tracking and degrees of freedom (DOF)". Road to Virtual Reality, 2018.

Laurence, T. "Introduction to blockchain technology". Van Haren, 2019.

Lloret, J., Garcia, M., Bri, D., and Sendra, S. (2009). A wireless sensor network deployment for rural and forest fire detection and verification. sensors, 9(11), 8722-8747.

Location based AR : "Augmented Reality (AR)". augmentedrealityon.com. Archived from the original on 5 April 2012. Retrieved 18 June 2019.

Lomte, S.S. and Ponde, M.S.S. "A survey of energy efficient approaches of wireless sensor network for precision agriculture". INTERNATIONAL JOURNAL, 2(7), 2017.

Lu, Z., Chen, X., Li, Q., Zhang, X., and Zhou, P. "A hand gesture recognition framework and wearable gesture-based interaction prototype for mobile devices". IEEE transactions on human-machine systems, 44(2), 2014, pp. 293-299.

Madakam, S., Lake, V., Lake, V., and Lake, V. "Internet of Things (IoT): A literature review". Journal of Computer and Communications, 3(05), 2015, pp. 164.

Maheshwari, A. "Big Data". McGraw-Hill Education, 2019. .

Margaret, R. "Relationship between Internet of Things and Wireless Sensor Network", "internet of things (IoT)". IOT Agenda, 14 August 2019.

Message digest. https://www.sciencedirect.com/topics/computer-science/message-digest.

Meulenberg, A., Suresh, R., and Ramanathan, S. (2010). LEO-based optical/microwave terrestrial communications. arXiv preprint arXiv:1009.5506..

Meyers, R. A. "Handbook of petrochemicals production processes". McGraw-Hill Education, 2019.

Mittal, M., and Bhadoria, R. S. (2017). "Aspect of ESB with Wireless Sensor Network". In: Exploring Enterprise Service Bus in the Service-Oriented Architecture Paradigm, IGI Global,2017, pp. 142-155.

Murphy, K. P. (2012). Machine learning: a probabilistic perspective. MIT press.

Murugan, A., and Vijayalakshmi, J. "Detecting Multi-Block Double Spent Transaction Based On B-Tree Indexing", 1979.

Muthumari, M. "Design and realization of radio communication using LoRa and XBee module for an e-Bike". In 2018 IEEE International Conference on Computational Intelligence and Computing Research (ICCIC),2018 December, pp. 1-4. IEEE.

Niku, S. B. "Introduction to robotics: analysis, control, applications". John Wiley and Sons, 2020.

O'Connor, B., and Secades, C. "Review of the use of remotely-sensed data for monitoring biodiversity change and tracking progress towards the Aichi Biodiversity Targets", 2013.

Onishi, Y., Yoshida, T., Kurita, H., Fukao, T., Arihara, H., and Iwai, A. "An automated fruit harvesting robot by using deep learning". Robomech Journal, 6(1), 2019, pp. 1-8.

Oseghale, P. O., and Chukwuchekwa, N. "Development of an Android Based SCADA System for Induction Motor Application". European Journal of Electrical Engineering and Computer Science, 3(4), 2019.

Panchal, F. S., and Panchal, M. "Review on methods of selecting number of hidden nodes in artificial neural network". International Journal of Computer Science and Mobile Computing, 3(11), 2014, pp. 455-464.

Panda, S. S., Ames, D. P., and Panigrahi, S. "Application of vegetation indices for agricultural crop yield prediction using neural network techniques". Remote Sensing, 2(3), 2010, pp. 673-696.

Panwar, N. L. "Design and performance evaluation of energy efficient biomass gasifier based cookstove on multi fuels". Mitigation and Adaptation Strategies for Global Change, 14(7), 2009, pp. 627-633.

Patidar, P., and Joshi, S. "A Cloud based Soil health Digitalization and Monitoring Technique for Optimum Resource Utilization in Smart Farming". In 2019 2nd International Conference on Intelligent Communication and Computational Techniques (ICCT), 2019 September, pp. 157-160. IEEE.

Pattnaik, P. K., Kumar, R., and Pal, S. (Eds.). "Internet of Things and Analytics for Agriculture". Springer Singapore, Volume 2, 2020.

Peddie, J. "Augmented reality: Where we will all live". Springer, 2017.

Pedersen, S. M., and Lind, K. M. (Eds.). (2017). "Precision Agriculture: Technology and Economic Perspectives". Springer International Publishing, 2017, pp. 52-53.

Penmatsa, P. L., and Reddy, D. R. K. "Smart detection and transmission of abnormalities in ECG via Bluetooth". In IEEE International Conference on Smart Cloud (SmartCloud),2016 November, pp. 41-44. IEEE.

Popescu, F. "From the iot to the iobt. The path to superior situational understanding". Revista Academiei Fortelor Terestre, 24(4), 2019.

Prasad, A., and Chawda, P. Power management factors and techniques for IoT design devices. In: 2018 19th International Symposium on Quality Electronic Design (ISQED), March 2018, pp. 364-369. IEEE.

Prasada, G. S. L. H. V., Rao, V. U. M., and Rao, G. G. S. N. "Climate change and agriculture over India". PHI Learning Pvt. Ltd., 2010.

Prashar, N., and Sangal, A. L. Plant Disease Detection Using Deep Learning (Convolutional Neural Networks). In International Conference on Image Processing and Capsule Networks Springer, Cham. May 2021, pp. 635-649).

Prieto Emhart, M. "Exploring Machine Learning Models for Wind Speed Prediction". Master's thesis, Universitat PolitÃ© cnica de Catalunya, 2018.

Psotka, J. "Immersive training systems: Virtual reality and education and training". Instructional science, 23(5-6), 1995, pp. 405-431.

Public key cryptography. https://docs.huihoo.com/globus/gt4-tutorial.

Rachel, E. "Drone for Crop yield monitoring using multispectral imaging: Eyes in the sky: 5 ways drones will change agriculture". Knowable Magazine. doi:10.1146/knowable-101118-3, 2018.

Rajaduraimanickam, K., Shanmugam, J., and Anitha, G. "ADDR-GPS data fusion using Kalman filter algorithm". In 24th Digital Avionics Systems Conference, Vol. 2, 2015, pp. 7. IEEE.

Reflective type IR Sensor: datasheet ,Vishay Semiconductors, Rev. 1.9, 10-Apr-2019, Document Number: 82458.

RoopendraVishwakarma. The Different Types of NoSQL Databases. https://www.opensourceforu.com/9

Ruiz-Garcia, L., and Lunadei, L. The role of RFID in agriculture: Applications, limitations and challenges. Computers and Electronics in Agriculture, 79(1), 2011, pp. 42-50.

Sarkar, L. "IoT in Precision Farming". IoT EDU, Apr 18,2020.

Satapathy, S. C., Bhateja, V., and Das, S. "Smart computing and informatics". In: Proceedings of the First International Conference on SCI , Vol. 1, 2016.

Satellite landset-8 : [[File:Baku, Azerbaijan, satellite image, LandSat-8, 06-OCT-2015.jpg|thumb|Baku, Azerbaijan, satellite image, LandSat-8, 06-OCT-2015]]

Schowengerdt, R. A. "Remote sensing: models and methods for image processing". Elsevier, 2006.

Sennaar, K. "AI in agriculture–Present applications and impact". Available at: emerj. com/ai-sector-overviews/ai-agriculture-present-applications-impact.1 August 2019.

Senouci, M. R., and Mellouk, A. "Deploying wireless sensor networks: theory and practice". Elsevier, 2016.

Sensor Node:CENS: Center for Embedded Networked Sensing, Archived 2009-04-07, at the Library of Congress Web Archives.

Sethi, P., and Sarangi, S. R. "Internet of things: architectures, protocols, and applications". Journal of Electrical and Computer Engineering, 2017.

Shafi, U., Mumtaz, R., García-Nieto, J., Hassan, S.A., Zaidi, S.A.R., and Iqbal, N. (2019). "Precision agriculture techniques and practices: From considerations to applications". Sensors, 19(17), 2019, pp. 3796.

Sharma, B., and Sharma, R. AGRICULTURE and FOOD: e-Newsletter.

Shaw, K. K., and Vimalkumar, R. "Design and development of a drone for spraying pesticides, fertilizers and disinfectants". Engineering Research and Technology (IJERT), 2020.

Singh, P. K., Bhargava, B. K., Paprzycki, M., Kaushal, N. C., and Hong, W. C. (Eds.). "Handbook of Wireless Sensor Networks: Issues and Challenges in Current Scenario's", 2020.

Singh, S. K., Singh, R. S., and Chaudhary, A. "IoT-Based Data Analytics for the Healthcare Industry". Academic Press, 2020, November.

Singh, V., and Verma, N. K. "Intelligent Condition Based Monitoring Techniques for Bearing Fault Diagnosis". IEEE Sensors Journal, 2020.

Siregar, I. M., and Salvator, R. Barcode Scanner using Android Platform. IT for Society, 1(1), 2016.

Swan, M. "Blockchain: Blueprint for a new economy". O'Reilly Media, Inc., 2015.

Tasatanattakool, P., and Techapanupreeda, C. "Blockchain: Challenges and applications". In International Conference on Information Networking (ICOIN) January 2018, pp. 473-475. IEEE.

Tavakoli Dehkordi, A. "Optimisation and algorithms in wireless networks for mission critical applications". Doctoral dissertation, University of Greenwich, 2015.

Tekchandani, P. and Trivedi, A. "Clock Drift Management Using Nature Inspired Algorithms". Journal of Information Technology Research (JITR), 5(4), 2012, pp. 48-62.

Texas instruments Datasheet: Inductive proximity Sensor, SNOSCS3B –SEPTEMBER 2013–REVISED MARCH 2014.

Texas instruments Datasheet: LM35 Temperature Sensor, SNIS159H-August1999- Revised December2017.

The Apache Hadoop. https://hadoop.apache.org/docs/current/hadoop-project-dist/hadoop-hdfs/HdfsDesign.html8

The MR is interactions between computers, humans, and environments, IoT zone, David AyzaEnero, 26 jan 2018.

Tomar, P., and Kaur, G. (Eds.). "Artificial Intelligence and IoT-based Technologies for Sustainable Farming and Smart Agriculture". IGI Global, 2021.

Traditional Programming versus Machine Learning, Researchgate , Sidharthmehra, cork institute of technology , in May 2020, DOI:10.13140/RG.2.2.23097.80485.

Tramontana, G., Jung, M., Schwalm, C. R., Ichii, K., Camps-Valls, G., Ráduly, B., and Papale, D. "Predicting carbon dioxide and energy fluxes across global FLUXNET sites with regression algorithms". Biogeosciences, 13(14), 2016, pp. 4291-4313.

Tyagi, S. S., and Bhatia, S. (Eds.). "Blockchain for Business: How it Works and Creates Value". John Wiley and Sons, 2021.

Ultrasonic sensor : P.marian , HC-SR04 electroschematics : SEN13959.

Vidal, C. (2019). Pulsar positioning system: a quest for evidence of extraterrestrial engineering. International Journal of Astrobiology, 18(3), 213-234.

Vila, H., Hugalde, I., and Di Filippo, M. (2011). Estimation of leaf water potential by thermographic and spectral measurements in grapevine. RIA: Revista de Investigaciones Agropecuarias.

Wang, L., and Alexander, C. A. "Big data in design and manufacturing engineering". American Journal of Engineering and Applied Sciences, 8(2), 2015, pp. 223.

Williams, R. J. (1986). Reinforcement learning in connectionist networks: A mathematical analysis. University of California, San Diego.

Wu, H. K., Lee, S. W. Y., Chang, H. Y., and Liang, J. C. (2013). Current status, opportunities and challenges of augmented reality in education. Computers and education, 62, 41-49..

Wu, H. K., Lee, S. W. Y., Chang, H. Y., and Liang, J. C. "Current status, opportunities and challenges of augmented reality in education". Computers and education, 62, 2013, pp. 41-49.

Yasin, A. S. M., Haque, M. M., Adnan, M. N., Rahnuma, S., Hossain, A., Naha, K., and Serratosa, F. "Localization of Autonomous Robot in an Urban Area Based on SURF Feature Extraction of Images". International Journal of Technology Diffusion (IJTD), 11(4), 2020, pp. 84-111.

Ylioja, J. "Wireless Mains Sensor for Monitoring Domestic Energy Consumption", 2014.

You, I., Kwon, S., Choudhary, G., Sharma, V., and Seo, J. T. "An enhanced LoRa WAN security protocol for privacy preservation in IoT with a case study on a smart factory-enabled parking system". Sensors, 18(6), 2018, pp. 1888.

Zhai, C., Landers, A., and Zhang, B. "An RFID-based solution for monitoring sprayer movement in an orchard/vineyard". Precision Agriculture, 19(3), 2018, pp. 477-496.

Zhang, X., Cao, Z., and Dong, W. "Overview of Edge Computing in the Agricultural Internet of Things: Key Technologies, Applications, Challenges". IEEE Access, 8, 2020, pp. 141748-141761.

Zhao, W., Lin, S., Han, J., Xu, R., and Hou, L. "Design and implementation of smart irrigation system based on LoRa". In 2017 IEEE Globecom Workshops (GC Wkshps), December 2017, pp. 1-6. IEEE.